Natural Language Processing

Artificial Intelligence Texts

Consulting Editors

T. ADDIS BSc, PhD

Department of Computer Science
University of Reading

B. DuBOULAY BSc, PhD, PCE

Centre for Cognitive Studies
University of Sussex
Brighton

A. TATE BA, PhD

Director
Artificial Intelligence Applications Institute
University of Edinburgh

Artificial Intelligence Texts

NATURAL LANGUAGE PROCESSING

H. M. Noble

BLACKWELL SCIENTIFIC PUBLICATIONS

OXFORD LONDON EDINBURGH

BOSTON PALO ALTO MELBOURNE

© 1988 by
Blackwell Scientific Publications
Editorial offices:
Osney Mead, Oxford OX2 0EL
  (*Orders*: Tel. 0865 240201)
8 John Street, London WC1N 2ES
23 Ainslie Place, Edinburgh EH3 6AJ
Three Cambridge Center, Suite 208,
  Cambridge, MA 02142, USA
667 Lytton Avenue, Palo Alto
  California 94301, USA
107 Barry Street, Carlton
  Victoria 3053, Australia

First published 1988

Set by DP Photosetting, Aylesbury, Bucks
Printed and bound in Great Britain by
Mackays of Chatham, Kent

DISTRIBUTORS
USA and Canada
  Blackwell Scientific Publications Inc
  PO Box 50009, Palo Alto
  California 94303
  (*Orders*: Tel. (415) 965-4081)

Australia
  Blackwell Scientific Publications
  (Australia) Pty Ltd
  107 Barry Street,
  Carlton, Victoria 3053,
  (*Orders*: Tel. (03) 347 0300)

British Library
Cataloguing in Publication Data
Noble, Hugh
  Natural language processing.—(Artificial
  intelligence texts).
  1. Linguistics—Data processing 2. Man-
  machine systems
  I. Title   II. Series
  006.3'5   P98

  ISBN 0–632–01738–4
  ISBN 0–632–01502–0 Pbk

Library of Congress
Cataloging-in-Publication Data
Noble, Hugh.
  Natural language processing / Hugh Noble.
  —(Artificial intelligence texts)
  Includes index.
  ISBN 0–632–01738–4 : £25.00
  ISBN 0–632–01502–0 (pbk.) : £12.00
  1. Linguistics—Data processing.
  I. Title.   II. Series.
  P98.N57 1988   87–27887
  410'.28'5—dc19   CIP

Contents

Acknowledgements, vii
Introduction, ix

Part 1, 1

 1 An Initial Problem, 3
 2 Ambiguity, Pronominal Reference and Concepts, 23
 3 Reference to Objects Undergoing Transformation, 31
 4 The Representation of Time, 39
 5 Word Structure and Verb Endings, 46
 6 The Tense of Verbs, 49
 7 Nouns and Noun Phrases, 56
 8 Pattern Matching, 66
 9 A Grammar of English, 85
10 From Syntax to Semantics, 99

Part 2, 103

11 Case Grammar, 105
12 Frame-Based Systems, 115
13 Scripts and Plans, 122
14 Conceptual Dependencies, 126
15 Conceptual Dependencies and Scripts, 139

Part 3, 141

16 Outstanding Problems, 143
17 The Meaning of Meaning, 150
18 Meaning and Communication, 158
19 Causation, 165
20 The Representation of States, 172
21 Modelling Motivation, 176
22 The Representation of Truth and Knowledge, 184
23 Representing Objects, 187
24 Representing Events, 196
25 Conjunction, Disjunction and Negation, 200

26 Quantification, 205
27 Metaphor, 210
28 Combining Representations, 213

Conclusion, 217
Bibliography, 219
Appendix: An Introduction to POP11/POPLOG, 222
Index, 235

Acknowledgements

To Ben who got me started and kept me going, and to Frances who put up with things not done, which should have been done, while this was done.

Introduction

The construction of a computer system which understands natural language is an important enterprise for two reasons:

(a) such a system would enable people to converse easily with a computer system and extract useful work from it without the restrictions imposed by the use of an artificial programming language, and

(b) the techniques involved would provide valuable insights into the mechanism of the human mind.

Both of these claims are contentious. A solution to the problem of natural language processing would not only make it easier for every user to converse with a computer system, but would make it easier for the unscrupulous person (or organisation or government) to invade the privacy of others by automating the task of mass surveillance, which at present is prohibitively labour intensive. It is appropriate, therefore, that we pursue our goal in the public domain so that the social implications can be debated openly and in an informed way. The proper way to prevent abuses of technology is through enlightened political policies and not through an inhibition of technological development.

Many people would object to the suggestion, implicit in our statement of reason (b) above, that a computer system which appears to understand natural language will of necessity do this in a way which is similar to the way humans understand natural language. There are, after all, numerous examples of 'clever' computer systems which carry out their task in a way which has very little similarity to the way humans do the same task. Automatic landing systems for aeroplanes make use of radar beams and the recognition by a robot of machine parts will often make use of sensors placed under the delivery tray to sense the weight of the objects. These use mechanisms which have little similarity to human skills.

We can, however, specify the criteria for the successful landing for an aeroplane in a way that does not involve human judgement. There is a clear goal in relation to which the success or otherwise of an automated landing system can be judged, and any system which achieves the specified goal can be described as successful no matter how it achieves it. We would argue, however, that the task of understanding natural language is somewhat different. Natural language is a product of the human mind as well as its servant. We cannot specify the successful processing of language in a way which does not involve what the human mind does to that language, and so there can be no definition of 'meaning' or of 'understanding' which does not involve the subjective judgement of humans. When humans judge a natural language processing system as 'successful' we submit that what they are saying is 'The observable behaviour of the system is such that it is reasonable to assume that it is doing internally the same things that we do when we understand language. It has formed internally the same or nearly the same functional/logical structures which we form. It is able to make the same deductions and will note the same implications.' That seems to be the assumption which we make about a fellow human being when we say that another person 'understands' something we have said. We have no direct evidence that the minds of other people function as our own do, but alternative explanations for the behaviour of other people seem very far fetched indeed.

Therefore while it may be possible to build a computer system which processes natural language, and responds to it in some interesting way, what it does cannot be described as 'understanding' unless what it does is in some way logically equivalent to what humans do. We speak only of the functional or logical mechanism, however. The actual physical mechanism can be quite different. When we use a data structure to represent some element of meaning in a computer we do not wish to imply that humans will necessarily construct an actual data structure of the same kind, with pointers in the same places and so on. What we do think is that the human mind may have its logical equivalent. That is, it will associate elements of information in the same way using some storage technology of its own and use it for the same purpose.

But the goal of developing a fully functional natural language processing system is an extremely elusive one. Some progress has been made. One can purchase a natural language front-end to a database system, or conduct a helpful conversation with a computerised 'medical consultant'. Computer systems can scan press reports and produce standardised summaries, and crude systems are available which translate from one natural language into another. Full natural language processing which is comparable to human performance has not been attained, however, and is unlikely to be attained in the near future.

We should not be too disheartened or surprised by this. The only surprising thing is that anyone should be surprised by the failure. A typical child learns to speak and understand language gradually over many years, and has at his or her disposal (24 hours a day), the brain, a computer immensely more complex and powerful than any artificial computer built to date. No one knows how many millions of years the 'program' which executes this process took to be developed. The human mind also has at its disposal perceptual apparatus which provides it with 'experiences' in terms of which its representations can be couched. In a computer system we will need to construct these for ourselves.

In this book we shall try to explain the nature of the difficulties rather than provide a solution to them, but we also hope to provide limited solutions to specific application-oriented problems. We shall begin with the simplest of systems and add complications gradually, so that we can see the limits for particular techniques and why it is necessary to abandon them for new and better techniques. The 'solutions' provided in the early parts of the book will be seen to be inadequate later in the book.

A few years ago most of the literature on natural language processing by computer was contained in technical journals, monographs and research papers which were not always accessible to people who were not members of staff in one of the academic centres for such research. Fortunately this position is changing and a wealth of new books on the topic are now appearing. They still tend, however, to be oriented towards research reports, and reprint these without much analysis or comparison. In this book we have tried to describe different approaches as a coherent progression, characterised by increasing complexity and richness of semantic description, and have not, for the most part, identified particular techniques with particular researchers or systems. To maintain the continuity we have occasionally ignored certain aspects of a particular published system. Since the book is intended for undergraduates the bibliography is confined to the most accessible sources.

The book is in three parts.

In Part 1 we begin with a very simple system, but one which has a very practical function – a user front-end to a microcomputer-based graphics facility. With this as our basic example we illustrate certain general principles – the need for a formally defined grammar, the need for a formal internal representation, the need for pattern matching, the notion of 'focus', the use of transition networks, and the need for the creation of 'side-effects' and for recursive mechanisms to deal with failure and backtracking. Finally we try to generalise this work by providing a general strategy for writing an ATN parser and a grammar of English.

In Part 2 we study various approaches which have been tried for dealing with the semantics rather than the syntax of language. We have organised these approaches in sequence of increasing semantic content. We begin with case grammar and end with Schank's Conceptual Dependencies and the use of scripts which, at least in some implementations, almost completely abandon any kind of formal grammatical analysis.

In Part 3 we discuss some of the philosophical issues which we avoided earlier in the book. To prevent this discussion becoming entirely esoteric and unrelated to practical matters, we have also provided a formalism for the representation of meaning. It is incomplete and cannot be considered a solution to the NLP problem, but it allows us to discuss some of the issues in a concrete way within a common representational framework. Our concern here is to provide the reader with an exposition of the problems to be faced and to help him or her avoid the overconfident naivety which has afflicted research workers in this field in the past.

Research in this area is usually justified, in public, in terms of practical applications, and these are real enough. But the true motivation is that this is a fascinating problem, the solution for which seems tantalisingly near and yet just beyond our grasp.

Note

POP11 was chosen as the main programming language for illustrating various algorithms because its syntax is similar to that of Pascal and C, which is not true of either LISP or Prolog, the other two languages which have all of the features required for this type of programming.

A brief introduction to POP11 is provided in an appendix.

Part 1

CHAPTER 1

An Initial Problem

1.1 The Micro-graphics 'World'

A small personal microcomputer is equipped with a simple graphics facility and an appropriately simple graphics language. We wish to construct a user-friendly interface which will accept a user's commands in natural English and translate these commands into the equivalent statements in the graphics language. The natural language allowed will be restricted, so that the interface will not be too difficult to construct, but it will be sufficient to illustrate a number of points and lead us towards more complex examples.

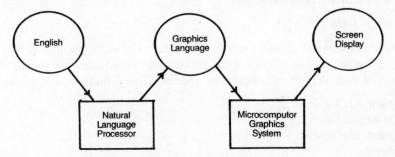

Fig. 1.1. The outline structure of the micro-graphics system.

The problem is therefore characterised as follows. The input text is a very limited subset of English, constrained to conform to a strict and limited grammar and the 'meaning' of the input text statements is represented in the form of statements in an internal language (the internal text).The internal text is the graphics language supplied with the machine. There is therefore no complication about what we mean by the 'meaning' of an input statement. If a statement cannot be translated into a statement in the graphics language then it must be considered to have no meaning at all. That is why we refer to the system as a 'world'. It has a definite boundary beyond which it cannot see and beyond which (so far as the system is concerned) nothing else exists. The problem is illustrative of a number of interesting and successful natural language processing systems which have been constructed for limited worlds such as this.

The problem for our system is to convert English into graphics language. But recognising that the text which is input cannot be unrestricted English, and that the output need not only be graphics commands, we can generalise the requirement to that of achieving the conversion: *input text -> internal text*

1.2 The Internal Text

Points on the screen (or pixels) are defined by X,Y coordinates (1000 × 1000). The user may provide names for specific points thus:

point fred 123 456

which attaches the user-defined name *fred* to the point 123, 456. Such a statement is always preceded by the keyword *point*.

Lines may be defined by the user thus:

line fred tom

which defines a straight line drawn from the point with name *fred* to the point with name *tom. Fred* and *tom* must be predefined. Alternatively the user may refer directly to coordinates thus:

line 123 456 678 901

which defines a line drawn from the point 123, 456 to the point 678, 901. A typical program in this limited graphics language would therefore consist of a series of point definitions followed by a series of line definitions. For example:

point p 123 456
point q 678 901
point r 543 654
line p q
line q r
line r p

which would draw a triangle. This or any similar program is an example of the *internal text*.

1.3 The Input Text

Suppose now that a user typed the following:

'*Let p be the point 234 456 and q be the point 678 901. Draw a line from p to q and then draw a line from q to r which is the point 543 654. Join p to r.*'

Clearly there are very many ways in which a user could express the same meaning. For the purposes of this exercise we wish to limit the variety of forms which the input text could take, and we deal with this by defining:

(a) an allowed vocabulary of lexical items (or words) and

(b) a grammer, which is a set of rules indicating the allowed patterns in which the words may appear.

The reader should beware of using the word 'word' carelessly in the presence of linguists. We need to distinguish between the 'lexical item' (or string of characters) and the 'sense' of a word (or its meaning). Even the term 'meaning' is fraught with difficulties and misunderstandings because linguists like to distinguish between 'intentions' and 'implications' and 'sense'. Consider for example:

'John means well'
'You did not bring a pen so that means that I will have to lend you mine.'
'"To cry" means "to produce tears".'

We do not intend to be pedantic about this and when we use the term 'word' or the term 'meaning' it will usually be obvious from the context which interpretation is required. If not, we shall qualify the term.

It will be seen that the *internal text* consists of two kinds of statement: *definitions*, or *assignment statements*, which associate names or labels with actual coordinate points; and *action statements* which cause some graphic images to appear on the screen, usually drawing lines between the points which have been defined. We shall consider these two kinds of statement separately.

1.4 Assignment Statement Analysis

Consider first the statement which the user might type in order to define point p. We shall call this an 'assignment statement' because it assigns coordinates to a label (p).The assignment statement might take the form:

    let p be x y
or *let x y be p*
or *let the point p have coordinates x y*

where p is a user-defined name or label for a point and x and y are numeric values. To cover such possibilities we classify words and phrases so that our description of the allowed statement structure can be more general. Let us use the classification *determiner* to stand for the set of words *a, an, the*. Therefore when we want to save space we simply write *<determiner>* and the reader should understand that the expression (including the angle brackets) should be replaced by any of the words in the set. In any such definition there is a danger of ambiguity between the use of words (such as 'a', 'an' and 'the') within the definition and the use of words (such as 'means', 'or', 'the set') as a part of the definition (the 'meta-words'). To avoid such confusion we shall adopt Backus-Naur Form notation (BNF), so that the definition of the classification 'determiner' becomes:

    determiner := a/an/the

The symbol := is taken to mean 'is defined as' and the slash '/' means 'or'. Any word which appears as itself on the right-hand side of such an expression is taken to be the literal version of itself. On the left-hand side of each expression there should be only one term, the entity being defined. In our grammar defined below the expression:

assignment := let<pt_defn> / <pt_defn>

means that the expression 'assignment' is defined as consisting of either the word 'let' followed by a 'pt_defn' expression, or it is just a 'pt_defn' on its own.

A 'pt_defn' (or 'point definition') expression is defined thus:

pt_defn := <ptname><verb><coorddefn> /
       <coorddefn><verb><ptname>

That is, it has two possible patterns:

ptname	verb	coorddefn
p	(let) be	123, 456
point p	(let) be	the point 123, 456
the point p	(let) have	coordinates 123, 456
p	is	123, 456
point p	has	coordinates 123, 456

coorddefn	verb	ptname
123, 456	(let) be	p
123, 456	(let) be called	p
point 123, 456	(let) be	p
the point 123, 456	is called	p

The verb is in some cases prefixed by (let). This indicates that the verb which follows (the infinitive form) is acceptable only if the whole statement is prefixed by the word 'let'. In the other cases the verb is acceptable only if the word 'let' does not appear. It is still necessary to define ptname, verb and coorddefn. This definition will fail if the user employs names such as 'a' as the name of a point because 'a' is also a word in the English language. We shall return to this point later. In the meantime we shall assume that the user avoids these ambiguities.

Without further ado we can write down the remainder of the complete grammar of the assignment expression in Backus-Naur form:

(a) *assignment:= let <point-defn> / <point-defn>*
(b) *point-defn:= <pt-name> <verb> <coord-defn> / <coord-defn>*
       <verb><pt-name>
(c) *verb:= is / has / is called / (let) <infinitive>*

(d) *infinitive:= be / have / be called*
(e) *coord-defn:= <coord-pair> / <classifier><coord-pair>*
         / <determiner><classifier><coord-pair>
(f) *coord-pair:= number number / number , number*
(g) *classifier:= coordinates / line / point*
(h) *determiner:= the / a*
(i) *pt-name:= <user-defined-name> / <classifier><user-defined-name>*
         / <determiner><classifier><user-defined-name>
(j) *user-defined-name:= any lexical item with an undefined value.*

It is not necessary in BNF to number or label the clauses. We have done so here (a,b,c,...j) to make it easier to refer to individual clauses.

1.5 The Function 'ptname'

We now have a grammar for our input text assignment statement and the next requirement is to analyse this in terms which are easily converted into a program. A good strategy is to subdivide the problem into smaller problems, and so we shall consider first the *ptname* and develop an analysis and a program for that. (We shall assume the existence of a function *isname(w)* which takes as its argument a single 'word' (in POP11 terminology, or a textual *atom* in a list) and yields *true* or *false* depending upon whether or not it is a user-defined name.

We assume that the input text is presented to this system in the form of a list of atoms (words and numbers) e.g.:

[the point fred has coordinates 123, 456]

The program will scan the input text from left to right and test for the existence of a ptname at the start of the list. If a ptname is found the program (a POP11 function) must return three results:

(1) *true* or *false*
(2) The internal text sub-list, e.g. *[point fred]* (i.e. a sub-part of the graphics language statement) (or *nil* if *false*)
(3) The remainder of the input text.

The performance of the required function is as shown below.

input-text = [the point fred has coordinates 123, 456]
result =   *true,*
                 [point fred],
                 [has coordinates 123, 456]
input-text = [to be or not to be]
result =   *false*
                 nil
                 [to be or not to be]

In this way the required function can test the input text. If it is successful it will extract the part of the input text it has processed, prepare a sub-part of the final internal text that is appropriate, and hand on the remainder of the input text for further processing. If it is unsuccessful in finding a ptname phrase it will report failure, deliver up a NIL list instead of the sub-part of the output text, and hand back the complete input text for an alternative form of processing.

If the function is successful and the sub-list *[point fred]* has been formed, the processing of the remainder of the input text may construct the second half of the internal text list *[123 456]*. This will be concatenated with the first part giving the correct internal text form: *[point fred 123 456]*

Now consider the finite state diagram (FSD) shown below.

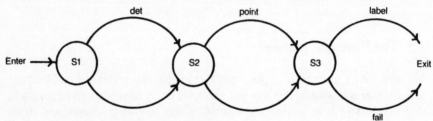

Fig. 1.2. The finite state diagram for 'ptname'.

This illustrates a system with three states (S1, S2 and S3). Each represents a 'state of expectancy' of the system. The system is, of course, our required function, which is processing the input text for a ptname phrase. Initially it is 'expecting' the determiner *the*. If it gets it it switches to state S2 and expects the classifier *point*. If this is found it switches to state S3, in which it expects a user-defined name. If this is found it exits, leaving the results indicated above.

If, on the other hand, the input text omits the determiner *the*, or both the determiner and the classifier *point*, then the system still switches to states S2 and S3 but takes different action as it does so. If the expected item is encountered, the system removes that item from the input text and goes on to test the next item in the list. If the expected item is not encountered, the input text is left unchanged and the system goes on to the next state to make a different test on the same first item as before.

Switching to a new state without making any alteration to the input text or taking any other action is shown in the FSD by the un-named arcs. These are often called 'jumps', and the introduction of jumps augments the FSD to become a new type of system.

It is very easy to turn a finite state diagram of this kind into a short program or function.

```
define isname(w);
ismemb(w,[a b c p q r tom dick harry]);
enddefine;
```

```
define ismemb(x,l);
if l.null then false;
elseif x=l.hd then true;
else ismemb(x,l.tl);
endif;
enddefine;

vars dets;
[the an a]->dets;

define ptname(intext);
vars savetext;
intext->savetext;              ;;;  for safe keeping
s1: if hd(intext)="the" then
        tl(intext)->intext;    ;;;  chop off the head of intext
        goto s2;
    else
        goto s2;               ;;;  otherwise jump straight to s2
    endif;
s2: if hd(intext)="point" then
        tl(intext)->intext;
        goto s3;
    else
        goto s3;
    endif;
s3: if isname(hd(intext)) then
        true;                  ;;;  success!
        [point]<>[%hd(intext)%]; ;;;  assemble the list from "point"
                                 ;;;  and whatever is the head of intext
        tl(intext);
    else
        false;                 ;;;  failure!
        nil;                   ;;;  nothing to report
        savetext;              ;;;  the original intext
    endif;
enddefine;
```

Prog. 1.1. The POP11 program for 'ptname'.

The reader will recognise that there is a small amount of redundancy in this program. This is deliberate in the interests of clarity. GOTOs have been used in spite of the tenets of structured programming to emphasise the parallelism with the finite state diagram. In this particular program definition, all the GOTO statements can be omitted because the normal linear sequencing of the code will take control to the correct point. This is somewhat fortuitous, however, and it would not in general be possible to omit the GOTOs without a considerable redesign of the function. We shall leave the consideration of a better program structure until later (Chapter 8) and concentrate for the time being on the structure of the grammar.

1.6 Word Classes and Determiners

We have 'cheated' slightly in writing this program in that we have tested directly for the words *'the'* rather than for the classes of words. The program would therefore succeed if the user typed *'let the point fred have coord...'* but would fail if *'let a point fred have coord...'* was typed. To correct this and allow the program to accept any determiner, we construct a list of all determiners, thus:

[the a] -> dets;

This in effect places the words *a* and *the* in the same grammatical category 'determiners'. Now instead of writing *'if hd(intext)= "the" then...'*, we can write *'if ismemb(hd(intext),dets) then ...'* which is equivalent to saying *'if the head of intext is a member of the set dets then'*. Although this is valid and will suffice for our simple problem, it ignores the fact that the meanings of these determiners ('the' and 'a') are subtly different. Later we shall need to take cognizance of this difference.

The whole idea of placing words in categories is fundamental to the notion of syntax. We cannot define a language by writing down every possible sentence, because the number of possible sentences is infinite. The fact that the number of sentences is infinite can be seen from a simple example. Consider the sentence: *John is very tired.* The sentence is grammatical and remains grammatical even if we repeat the word 'very' several times: *John is very very very tired.* In fact there is no limit to the number of 'very's which we can insert without the sentence becoming ungrammatical. Therefore this simple example is actually an infinite set all on its own. Consider also: *John is very tired (after his run).* We can add to this a qualifying clause – *(which was arranged by the sports committee), (which was formed in 1984), (which is the year mentioned in George Orwell's novel)* and so on and on.

Even if we ignore the possibility of infinitely long sentences and place an arbitrary limit on the length of a sentence (say 100 words), we are still confronted by an astronomically large set of possible sentences. To define the allowed structures we must therefore classify and generalise so that one pattern can represent a whole class of sentences.

The traditional grammatical categories are in fact curiously cyclic in their definition. When children begin to learn grammar they are usually taught that verbs are 'doing' words and nouns are 'naming words for things or sets of things'. These notions serve to establish the categories in our minds but there are obvious exceptions to these rules, for example 'The shouting was very loud'. Here the word 'shouting' is being used as a noun, and yet it describes an action and the word is usually described as a verb. (The term 'gerund' is sometimes used to describe a verb used in this way as a noun.) Consider also the sentence 'His embarrassment was acute'. What kind of thing is 'embarrassment'? It is a state of mind, a feeling with all kinds of social implications. The initial concrete notion of a 'thing' needs to be modified. What kind of doing is 'was'? Again it indicates a state of affairs. The naive notions given to a child are clearly over-simplifications.

It seems that having established a category, we note that it usually occurs in sentences in a particular positional relationship to other word categories. We label that position as the location associated with the category. The category has now become a label for a position within a pattern. Any word which is now found in that position acquires the label. But the position would not have been recognisable without the notion of the word categories for the other words in the pattern. Thus category defines position and position defines category. Fortunately there are a few words which are not ambiguous in this respect and these can serve as markers for the remainder of the sentence. The determiners ('a', 'an' and 'the') are such words.

We can write down the list of all words in a language (because the list is not infinite) and label them as nouns, adjectives, verbs etc. Even so we have problems about ambiguous words which can have more than one category. This is an example of the context-dependent nature of natural language. In constructing a formal grammar for our input text we are to some extent destroying this property, and for that reason we cannot consider the input text as a genuinely 'natural language'.

1.7 The Coordinate Definition Phrase

Now we consider the development of a program for processing coordinate definition phrases <coorddefn>. Again we represent this first as a finite state diagram.

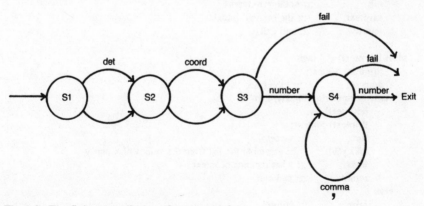

Fig. 1.3. The finite state diagram for 'coorddefn'.

Note the loop arc in the diagram which corresponds to the possible presence of a 'comma'. In this form, without some form of counting mechanism, the FSD would pass as correct an infinite number of commas. A counting mechanism is easily introduced by allowing the traversal of this arc to check and update a register storing the number of times this arc has been traversed. Alternatively a new state can be introduced to which the FS-automaton would advance from S4 and from which state the occurrence of another comma would be the selector for a 'failure' arc.

The equivalent POP11 function is as follows:

```
define coorddefn(intext);
vars savetext x y;
intext->savetext;
s1: if ismemb(hd(intext),dets) then    ;;; dets =list of determiners
        tl(intext)->intext;
        goto s2;
    else
        goto s2;
    endif;
s2: if (hd(intext)="coordinates")or(hd(intext)="point") then
        tl(intext)->intext;
        goto s3;
    else;
        goto s3;
    endif;
s3: if isnumber(hd(intext)) then
        hd(intext)->x;
        tl(intext)->intext;
        goto s4;
    elseif hd(intext)="with" then
        tl(intext)->intext;
        goto s1;
    else
        false;          ;;; failure!
        nil;            ;;; nothing to report
        savetext;       ;;; the original intext
        return;         ;;; and exit
    endif;
s4: if hd(intext)="," then
        tl(intext)->intext;
        goto s4;           ;;; loop back
    elseif isnumber(hd(intext)) then
        hd(intext)->y;
        tl(intext)->intext;
        true;           ;;; success!
        [%x,y%];        ;;; assemble the list from the values of x and y
        intext;         ;;; what remains of intext
        return;         ;;; and exit
    else
        false;          ;;; failure!
        nil;            ;;; nothing to report
        savetext;       ;;; the original intext
        return;         ;;; and exit
    endif;
enddefine;
```

Prog. 1.2. The POP11 program for 'coorddefn'.

1.8 Verb Phrase Analysis

Consider now the verb phrase analysis. We are prepared to allow two forms of verb:

(1) *let ... be*
    let ... be called
    let ... have ...

(2) *... is ...*
    ... is called ...
    ... has ...

We shall call (1) the 'infinitive' form and (2) the 'present tense' form. In the case of the infinitive form the verb is split up. The program analysing a phrase in the infinitive form will encounter *let* and must 'remember' to expect the infinitive form *be* or *have* at a later time. To cope with this we allow 'side-effects' to be created by the processing function as it traces an arc in the finite state diagram. That is, it updates a global register. We denote this side-effect by (*let*).

The FSD for the verb analysis is shown below:

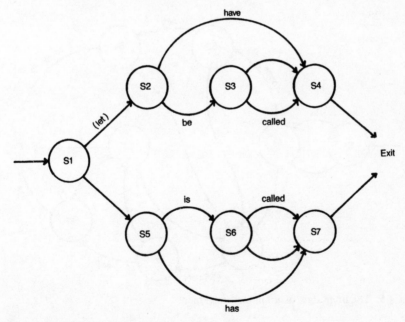

Fig. 1.4. The finite state diagram for 'verb'.

From S1 the system goes straight to S2 or S5 depending upon whether the (*let*) side-effect is true. A global switch can be used to indicate (*let*) say letsw=1. We leave to the reader the exercise of turning this FSD into a POP11 program.

1.9 The Full Assignment Statement

We are now in a position to consider the full assignment statement

<assignment>:=let<pt_name><infverb><coord—defn>/
      let<coord_defn><infverb><pt_name>/
      <pt_name><presverb><coord_defn>/
      <coord_defn><presverb><pt_name>
<infverb>:= be / be called / have
<presverb>:= is / is called / has
<pt_name>:= <user_defn_name> / <classifier><user_defn_name> /
      <determiner><classifier><user_defn_name>
coord_defn>:= <coord_pair> / <classifier><coord_pair> /
      <determiner><classifier><coord_pair>
<coord_pair>:= <number><number> / <number> , <number>
<classifier>:= coordinates / line / point
<determiner>:= the / a / an
<user_defined_name>:= any lexical item with an undefined value

The FSD is shown below.

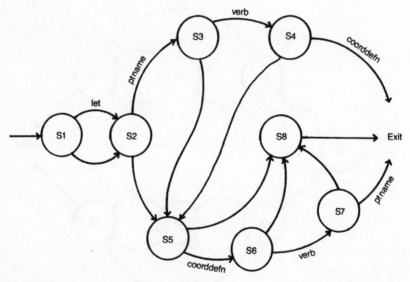

Fig. 1.5. The finite state diagram for 'assignment'.

The POP11 program for this is as follows:

```
vars letsw; false->letsw;

define assignment(intext);
```

```
vars savetext remainder success out1 out2 out3;
intext->savetext;
s1: if hd(intext)="let" then
      true->letsw; tl(intext)->intext;
    else
      false->letsw;
    endif;
    goto s2;          ;;; to be the same as the fsd
s2: ptname(intext)->remainder->out1->success;
    if success then
      remainder->intext; goto s3;
    else
      goto s5;
    endif;
s3: verb_phrase(intext)->remainder->out2->success;
    if success then
      remainder->intext; goto s4;
    else
      goto s5;
    endif;
s4: coorddefn(intext)->remainder->out3->success;
    if success then
      true; out1<>out3; remainder; return;
    else
      goto s5;
    endif;
s5: coorddefn(intext)->remainder->out3->success;
    if success then
      remainder->intext; goto s6;
    else
      false; nil; savetext; return;
    endif;
s6: verb_phrase(intext)->remainder->out2->success;
    if success then
      remainder->intext; goto s7;
    else
      false; nil; savetext; return;
    endif;
s7: ptname(intext)->remainder->out1->success;
    if success then
      true; out1<>out3; remainder; return;
    else
      false; nil: savetext;
    endif;
enddefine;
```
Prog. 1.3. The POP 11 program for 'assignment'.

At S1 we detect the *let* and set the global switch letsw. The switch can be detected by the verb function.

At S2 the program tries a possible analysis with ptname(intext) and if this fails it tries the alternative analysis with coorddefn(intext).Only if this fails does the function exit with a failed result.

In this section we have been concentrating upon the problem of backing out of an unsuccessful attempt to match ptname or coorddefn. At the same time we have done some violence to the structure of the FSD by introducing new types of arc. These changes are the subject of the next section.

1.10 Transition Networks

We introduced the idea of the finite state network or diagram (FSD) in section 1.5 without much formality. The idea is simple but powerful, and the reader may already be familiar with the use of FSDs from the study of formal languages or finite state automata. For those unfamiliar with the basic ideas and the capabilities of the various types of transition network we will provide some clarification here.

Each node in a transition network represents a 'state of expectancy' of a system, and each arc leading from a node represents the transition of the system from one state to another after the occurrence of an expected event. A loop which returns to the node from which it started represents an event which does not change the state of the system. Such a loop can therefore be used to represent the (possible) multiple occurrence of some event (e.g. the 'comma' arc in Fig 1.3).

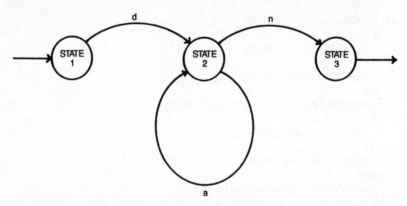

Fig. 1.6. The finite state diagram for the expression 'd(a)n'.

Finite State Machines (FSM). When we use an FSM diagram to represent a grammar we can think of each arc as being the occurrence of a particular type of word in the input text as it is being processed. We can denote each class of word by a single character (a,b,c,d,...) and place in brackets each category which may be repeated an indefinite number of times. For example if 'n' denotes a noun, 'a' denotes an adjective and 'd' denotes a determiner, we might write down the pattern corresponding to a noun phrase as d(a)n, to indicate that it consists of one determiner, possibly several adjectives and a noun. With this notation, and not bothering about what word categories the letters stand for, we can illustrate the various patterns which an FSD can process correctly.

The limitations of FSM. With the formalism of the FSM we can represent simple sequences, optional items, repeated items and repeated sequences. We have difficulty, however, in representing a pattern in which an optional item (if it does occur) may occur just once (or a fixed number of times), and we cannot represent palindromic sequences such as abcd-dcba, where the sequence of the second half is determined by the sequence (reversed) of the first half. Palindromes are not of any particular importance in natural language but they do occur frequently in formal languages such as programming languages (e.g. brackets are always palindromic because the close brackets ')' must match the open-brackets '(').

Recursive Transition Networks (RTN). The mechanism which makes recognition of a palindrome possible is very powerful and has other uses.

A palindrome P which is made up of the characters a,b,c, has the structure *aPa, bPb* or *cPc,* where *P* stands for another palindrome with exactly the same structure (hence recursive). At some stage the sequence must stop, and so we need to provide for any of the palindromes to have a value which does not involve any other palindromes within it:

P :- a / b / c / aa / bb / cc / aPa / bPb / cPc

This can be represented by a modified FSM,

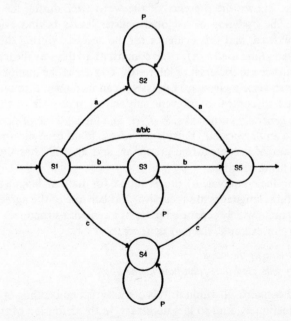

Fig. 1.7. The recursive transition network for the palindromic expression 'P'.

where the middle arc is labelled not by a simple word category but by a complete network label. In this case the the middle arc is labelled by the name of the network we are actually defining. Such a structure is called a 'Recursive Transition Network' (RTN).

It is conventional also to include within the definition of an RTN the possibility of a null or 'jump' arc. A jump arc is one which does not process any words in the input text but merely advances the system to a new state so that the input text can be subjected to a new batch of tests. The jump arc can be regarded as an 'else' condition, an arc which is traversed after all other possibilities have been tried and found wanting.

The limitations of FSMs and RTNs. The simple FSM has no 'memory'. If the system is currently at state S it has no way of 'knowing' that it has been in that state before, nor does it know by what pathway it reached its current state. The RTN does have a memory, but only the (recursive) memory of arcs started but not completed (which are then completed in a 'last started, first finished' sequence). An RTN cannot therefore be used to represent the circumstances in which the tracing of a particular arc at an early stage can influence the choice of arc at a later stage (except for recursion). Neither can it be used to represent a pattern containing an element which is repeated a fixed number of times (greater than one) without having an explicit arc for each occurrence.

Augmented Transition Networks (ATN). A network can be provided with a memory in the form of registers and counters which are updated while an arc is being traversed. We used these mechanisms to count the number of commas, and to make known the presence of the word LET during the verb-phrases processing. The updating of a global register leaves behind evidence of the pathway followed, and this evidence can be accessed during the traversal of subsequent arcs (and used as a further condition). In this way the traversal of one arc can influence the traversal of later arcs. To restrict the number of times the system may traverse a given arc the system can increment a counter which can then be used to control or prevent subsequent traversals of that arc. Such features are generally known as *side effects* and the addition of side effects turns an RTN into an *Augmented Transition Network*. It has been shown that an RTN has the power of a context-free grammar, and an ATN has the power of a Universal Turing Machine.

ATNs (or their equivalent) are required for natural language processing because natural languages are recursive, and because of the agreements which hold across quite widely separated parts of a sentence structure.

Consider, for example, the two sentences :

S1: 'John bought the book'
S2: 'Mary was glad that John bought the book'.

Sentence S2 contains S1 within it. It is obvious that embedding of this kind can continue indefinitely, and so it is necessary, in the definition of the syntactical pattern of a sentence, to include the possibility of it containing a sentence. If we denote a sentence by 'S', then one possible pattern for S is given by

    $S := nvT$
where *n is a proper noun*
      v is a verb
      T is a 'that' clause.
and $T := $ *'that' followed by S.*

S is therefore embedded recursively in the definition of S.
    Consider also the sentence:

    *'I gave a bat and a ball * to Tom and Bill respectively'.*

Here the two items *bat* and *ball* must agree exactly in number with the two recipients *Tom* and *Bill*, and the two parts of the sentence which must agree could be widely separated by qualifying phrases inserted at the point marked '*'.

1.11 Action (or Line) Definitions

The statements of the graphics language are of two types: assignments (e.g. *Let fred be the point 123, 345)* and action definitions (e.g. *Draw the line fred joe).* We have dealt with the former and given POP11 programs which handle these. Rather than repeat the process for the action definitions we leave that problem to the reader, and show instead how the problem of action definitions might be handled in Prolog. The Prolog programs hide their mechanism to some extent, but it will be found that the underlying mechanism is very similar to that employed in the POP11 programs.

    First we note the variety of statement which might be accepted as valid input text.

    draw p q
    draw a line from p to q
    join p to q
    join p q
    draw a line to q from p

where p and q have been defined. In each case the output text is to be

    line p q

We note that the input text can be analysed into the following sub-statements:

a source

    from p
    from the point p
    p
    the point p

That is, a ptname, optionally preceded by *from*.

a destination

> *to q*
> *to the point q*
> *q*
> *the point q*

That is, a ptname optionally preceded by *to*.

a line segment

> *from p to q*
> *to q from p*
> *<source><destination>*
> *<destination><source>*

an object

> *line*
> *a line*
> *the line*
> *<obj>*
> *<determiner><obj>*

where <obj> is a member of the set *[line, ...]* We may add other objects to this list later.

an act

> *draw*
> *join*
> *sketch*
> *draw a line*
> *<verb>*
> *<verb><object>*

an action definition

> *<act><line-segment>*

These definitions translate directly into Prolog. Before giving the program we wish first to explain the structure of the Prolog program using the definition of a determiner as an example.

> *det([W\R],R):-ismemb(W,[a,the]).*

The predicate 'det' takes two arguments — [W|R] and R. The first of these represents the input text and the second represents the remainder of the text left behind for further processing. The notion is exactly the same as used before in the POP11 functions. Each sub-part of the program will nibble off a part of the input text and spit out the remainder for further processing. If the part nibbled off is not as expected then the sub-part (predicate) will fail and the Prolog will automatically backtrack to try another form of analysis. The program is therefore simpler than the equivalent POP11 program because the backtracking and the detection of failure is automatic. For this reason the program is also harder to understand.

The test of success or failure is shown on the right-hand side of the expression above.

ismemb(W,[a,the]).

this succeeds if W, the first element in the input text [W|R]is a member of the set [a,the].

R is the tail of the input text [W|R]. Put colloquially, then, if the first element in the input text is a member of the set [a,the] the predicate 'det' bites it off and returns the remainder of the input text for further processing.

Now we provide the remainder of the Prolog program:

```
det([W|R],R):-ismemb(W,[a,an,the]).
% det leaves a remainder "R", which is the tail of the list. %
% det(L,R) is true if the head of L is one of the set (a,an,the)%

ismemb(X,[X|_]).
ismemb(X,[Y|L]):-ismemb(X,L).

obj([W|R],R):-ismemb(W,[line]).
obj(T,R):-det(T,R1),obj(R1,R).

% obj(L) is true if the head of L is the word "line".     %
% obj leaves a remainder which is the tail of L.          %

% The input text is "T".                                  %
% If T is processed by det leaving R1 as remainder, then obj %
% is applied to that remainder and leaves "R" as remainder"  %


isname(W):-ismemb(W,[p,q,r,tom,dick,harry]).

% We restrict the list of names for demonstration purposes  %

pt_name_1([W|R],[W],R):-isname(W).
%   The remainder "R"= the tail of the input list           %
%   The middle parameter "W" is the internal text produced   %

pt_name_1([point|T],P,R):-pt_name_1(T,P,R).

% Alternatively if a name is preceded by the word "point"    %
% Throw away the word and process the remainder of the list  %
```

% leaving whatever result it leaves, and its remainder.   %

pt_name_1(T,P,R):-det(T,R1),pt_name_1(R1,P,R).

% If preceded by a determiner, strip it off and process what %
% remains.   %

source(T,P,R):-pt_name_1(T,P,R).
source([from|T],P,R):-pt_name_1(T,P,R).

dest(T,P,R):-pt_name_1(T,P,R).
dest([to|T],P,R):-pt_name_1(T,P,R).

ln_seg(T,P,R):-source(T,P1,R1),
          dest(R1,P2,R),
          concat(P1,P2,P).

ln_seg(T,P,R):-dest(T,P1,R1),
          source(R1,P2,R),
          concat(P2,P1,P).

concat([],[],[]).
concat(X,[],X).
concat([],Y,Y).
concat([X|Y],Z,[X|L]):-concat(Y,Z,L).

act([W|R],[line],R):-ismemb(W,[draw,sketch,join]).
act(T,P,R):-act(T,P,R1),obj(R1,R).

action_defn(T,P,R):-act(T,P1,R1),
             ln_seg(R1,P2,R),
             concat(P1,P2,P).

action_defn(T,P,R):-ln_seg(T,P1,R1),
             act(R1,P2,R),
             concat(P2,P1,P).

action_defn(T,P,R):-source(T,P1,R1),
             act(R1,P2,R1),
             dest(R2,P3,R),
             concat(P2,P1,P4),
             concat(P4,P3,P).

action_defn(T,P,R):-dest(T,P1,R1),
             act(R1,P2,R2),
             source(R2,P3,R),
             concat(P2,P3,P4),
             concat(P4,P1,P).

Prog. 1.4. The Prolog program for 'action_defn'.

The reader should now try writing the line definition processor in Prolog.

CHAPTER 2

Ambiguity, Pronominal Reference
and Concepts

2.1 The Ambiguous 'A'

If the user of our natural language system does not avoid the use of the symbol
'a' as a label for a point, we may have to deal with the two sentences:
   (a) *a point fred has coordinates 259, 563.*
   (b) *a has coordinates 259, 563*
the system cannot 'know' which of the two sentence forms it is processing after
it has read just one word 'a'. It could therefore take the wrong arc. If the user has
input sentence (b) and the system has taken the arc S1 -> S2 the error will be
discovered when it fails to find the word *point* which would enable it to take the
arc S2 -> S3. What is required is a mechanism to allow the system to backtrack
to S1 and reinstate the input text to its original condition. Our original ATN for
this was shown in Figure 1.2. The ATN would advance to S2 and S3 if the 'det'
arc and the 'point' arc failed. Unfortunately the 'det' arc will not fail because 'a'
will be accepted as a determiner and the system will advance to S2. At this point
the system will advance to S3. Instead of advancing to S3 it should fail and
restore 'intext'. We do have a general solution for this problem. Note first that
every function produces the results shown below:

success	failure
true	false
output-text	nil
remainder	intext

In the failure condition the intext is restored. One method of solution is therefore
to make each of the alternative parsings a separate function or sub-function of
ptname. Let these be called *ptname1* and *ptname2*. Ptname1 will assume that 'a'
is a determiner and will then fail if the word *point* is not found. It will exit and
restore intext which will allow ptname2 to try by assuming that 'a' is a label for
a point.

(i) ptname-1

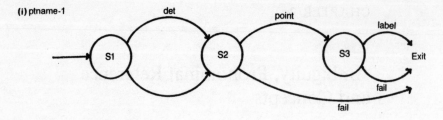

(ii) ptname-2

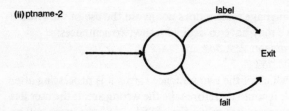

(iii) ptname

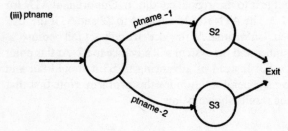

Fig. 2.1. The finite stage diagram for 'ptname' dealing with an ambiguous 'a'.

The program in POP11 for 'ptname' utilising these two sub-functions would be:

```
define ptname_1(intext);
vars savetext;
intext->savetext;              ;;; for safe keeping
s1: if ismemb(hd(intext),[a an the]) then
        tl(intext)->intext;    ;;; chop off the head of intext
        goto s2;
    else
        goto s2;               ;;; otherwise jump straight to s2
    endif;
s2: if hd(intext)="point" then
        tl(intext)->intext;
        goto s3;
    else
        goto s3;
```

```
      endif;
s3: if isname(hd(intext)) then
      true;                    ;;; success!
      [point]<>[%hd(intext)%]; ;;; assemble the list from "point" and whatever is the head of intext
      tl(intext);
   else
      false;                   ;;; failure!
      nil;                     ;;; nothing to report
      savetext;                ;;; the original intext
   endif;
enddefine;

define ptname_2(intext);
vars savetext;
intext->savetext;              ;;; for safe keeping
s3: if isname(hd(intext)) then
      true;                    ;;; success!
      [point]<>[%hd(intext)%]; ;;; assemble the list from "point" and whatever is the head of intext
      tl(intext);
   else
      false;                   ;;; failure!
      nil;                     ;;; nothing to report
      savetext;                ;;; the original intext
   endif;
enddefine;

define ptname_both(intext);
vars remainder txt success;
ptname_1(intext)->remainder->txt->success;      ;;; try ptname_1
if success then
   true; txt; remainder;                        ;;; success!
else
   ptname_2(intext)->remainder->txt->success;  ;;; failure! then try ptname_2 on the original intext
   if not(success) then false; nil; intext;
   else true; txt; remainder;
   endif;
endif;
enddefine;
```

Prog. 2.1. The POP11 program for 'ptname' dealing with an ambiguous 'a'.

2.2 The Prolog Equivalent

Earlier, in program 1.4, we suggested that 'isname' could be defined:

isname(W):-ismemb(W,[p,q,r,tom,dick,harry]).

This needs to be extended so that the list of items for which 'isname' yields 'true' includes 'a'.

The definition of ptname shown in program 2.2 will assume it should test for the pattern *'a point <label>.....'* failing which it will test for the pattern *'point<label>.....'* and only if this fails will it test for the pattern *'<label>.....'*

```
ismemb(W,[W|_]).
ismemb(W,[Q|R]):-ismemb(W,R).

isname(W):-      ismemb(W,[a,b,c,p,q,r,tom,dick,harry]).

det([W|R],R):-   ismemb(W,[a,an,the]).

label([W|R],R):-    isname(W).

ptname(T,R):-    det(T,R1), ptname(R1,R).
ptname([point|T],R):-ptname(T,R).
ptname(T,R):-label(T,R).
```

Prog. 2.2. The Prolog program for 'ptname' dealing with an ambiguous 'a'.

Automatic backtracking is one of the most powerful features of Prolog and allows such programs to be written very succinctly.

2.3 Pronominal Reference and the Use of 'it'

The use of the word 'it' to refer to some entity previously mentioned is a common and useful device in natural language. This device does introduce complications, however. Clearly the meaning of 'it' varies dynamically with the context of the discourse and so the use of 'it' can never be allowed in context-free languages. It would be natural, however, for the users of our graphics system to write a statement such as:

x has the coordinates 123, 456 and y is the point with coordinates 567, 789. Join it to x.

Here there is not much doubt that 'it' refers to the point y, that being the last mentioned entity. Such a straightforward case can be dealt with by introducing a global variable called 'focus' which has assigned to it the output text:

[y] -> focus;

This assignment is made as that piece of internal text is created. The value of *focus* will therefore change dynamically as processing continues, and at any time *focus* will contain the definition of the most recently mentioned *point*. During processing 'it' should be replaced by the value of *focus*. The input text would then read:

let x have coordinates 123, 456.
y is the point with coordinates 567, 789.
join y to x.

This simple strategy works well for some examples but goes wrong in many interesting ways. Suppose our user had written:

let x have coordinates 123, 456.
y is the point with coordinates 567, 789.
join y to it.

Here the word 'it' refers to 'x', because 'y' has already been referenced explicitly and we all know that it would be inappropriate to ask for y to be joined to itself. Nevertheless 'y' is the last point mentioned in the previous sentences and so the simple strategy which we outlined above would interpret 'it' as 'y'.

The difference between the two examples appears to be small but is in fact profound. In the first example the referent for 'it' can be found by the application of a simple rule. In the second example the true referent for 'it' is determined not by a simple rule but by appealing to common sense. 'We all know that it is inappropriate to ask for 'y' to be joined to itself'. Common sense of this kind could be represented by a formal rule:

if [line p q] is a statement in the output text p and q must be distinct.

It would not be difficult to write a POP11 function which tested each internal text statement and returned false if this rule was violated. Next we must allow *focus* to have more than one possible meaning, and so instead of assigning the last mentioned point to *focus* we add that point to the top of a push-down stack. The interpretation of 'it' will therefore be found on that stack, with the most likely candidate (the last mentioned) on the top. If substituting that value for 'it' produces a false condition as tested by the rule above, the system must back-track and try the next possible value on the stack.

This argument illustrates clearly a general idea which will crop up many times. Often there is no clear-cut rule which can be applied to determine the interpretation of a statement in natural language. Instead we have rules which represent common sense about the world, and various interpretations must then be tried until one is found that is compatible with these common sense rules.

Our way of dealing with pronominal reference will undergo further changes as we progress and find that even our modified way of handling the *focus* is inadequate. The basic idea of a *focus of attention* is, however, fundamental.

2.4 Triangles and Concepts

Let us extend the vocabulary and grammar of the input text so that we allow the user to type *'Draw the triangle p q r'*. The word 'triangle' has not been used before, and so we must provide a definition of it, so that the system 'understands' what we are talking about. That is, the system must be able to translate the word 'triangle' into the corresponding set of elements of the internal text. Somewhere we must store the correspondence:

$$triangle\ p\ q\ r\ =$$
$$line\ p\ q$$
$$line\ q\ r$$
$$line\ r\ p$$

We might achieve this by defining a function called *triangle*, e.g.:

```
define triangle(X,Y,Z);
    [%"line",X,Y%];
    [%"line",Y,Z%];
    [%"line",Z,X%];
enddefine;
```

The parameters X, Y, Z are formal parameters which can be replaced by specific values (say p, q, r).

When the function *triangle* is called, with the parameters X, Y and Z given values, it will leave behind as its result three *line* statements which are valid statements in the internal text. This function can be used to generate the internal text for any triangle (which could be drawn by the system) and for that reason we call it a 'generic structure'.

There are two ways of looking at such a structure. The function definition can be regarded as a representation of the *concept* 'triangle', or as a way of representing the *set of all* triangles. These are not the same thing, and for reasons which will become apparent later we prefer to regard function definitions with formal parameters as representations of the concepts.

A concept, then, is a generalised idea which acts as a skeleton (generic structure) which can be fleshed out with specific information to form the representation of a specific entity.

The vocabulary of our NL-system could be greatly enriched by the addition of many such words which act as the labels for similar concepts (e.g. *square, rectangle, ...*). These could be added to the list of objects defined by <obj> in section 1.11.

2.5 Introducing Colours

The repertoire of the graphics language could also be extended to permit colours to be used. Let the internal text contain such statements as:

line n x y

where n = colours as follows:

0	white
1	red
2	green
3	blue
4	black

Now our user could write *'draw the green line p q'* and we could handle this because our output text would have a specific parameter which would be modified to correspond to the colour specified.

An appropriate set of ATNs would be:

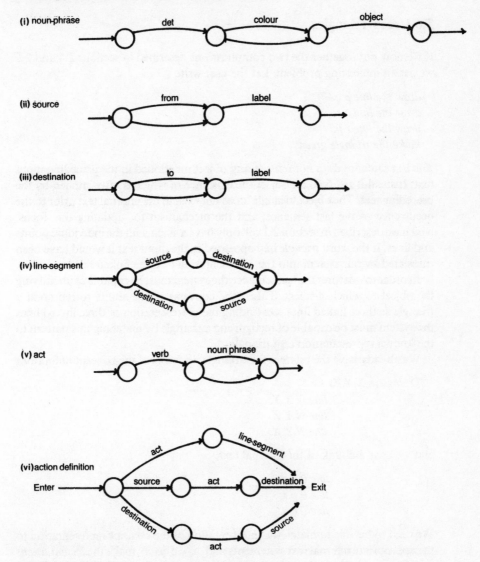

Fig. 2.2. An ATN for the 'action-defn' involving colours.

The conclusion to be drawn from this is that extensions to the vocabulary of the input text must be matched by extensions to the range of things which can be represented in the internal text. Understanding language means being able to identify the appropriate representation. Furthermore, the representation must be such that it can be acted upon. In this example the microcomputer is able to respond to the representation by drawing lines of the desired colour.

2.6 Green Triangles

If we now put together the two complications described in sections 2.4 and 2.5 we get an interesting problem. Let the user write

draw the line p q.
draw the line q r.
draw the line r p.
make the triangle green.

The last sentence does not refer to any object mentioned in the preceding input text. Instead it refers to an object the existence of which is only implied by the preceding text. The object 'triangle' does not exist in the internal text prior to the occurrence of the last sentence, and the mechanism for updating the 'focus' which we described in section 2.3 will only have a stack with the individual points and lines. If the word *triangle* had appeared in the input text it would have been translated by our system into the representation of three linked lines.

In order to interpret the last sentence the system must be capable of identifying the object to which it refers. This is the converse of the ability to represent a triangle as three linked lines. On finding the representation of three linked lines the system must be capable of recognising a triangle by matching this pattern to the known representation of a triangle.

We already have the referent for 'triangle' in terms of the concept definition:

Triangle(n,X,Y,Z) ->
              line N X Y.
              line N Y Z.
              line N Z X.

and we have a chunk of the internal text:

              line 0 p q.
              line 0 p r.
              line 0 r p.

We need to be able to match the interpretation of the concept representation to the appropriate internal text statements and, as we do so, make the *instantiations* (see Chapter 8) X=p, Y=q, Z=r, n=0. Note however that the object referred to may be distributed over several parts of the output text. That is, the three line representations may not be together and may not even be in the right sequence. We will discuss mechanisms for carrying out such a matching operation in Chapter 8. In the mean time we note the nature of the problem.

CHAPTER 3

Reference to Objects Undergoing Transformation

3.1 Movement

The graphics language would be greatly improved if it had the facilities for representing the movement of an object about the screen. Normally this is done by redrawing the object in background colour to delete it and then redrawing it yet again in a new position. It can be done with the final coordinate positions to produce the effect of instantaneous displacement, or it can be done for successive intermediate positions to produce the effect of gradual translation to its new position. Let us assume that the latter is preferred.

One complication involved in implementing this as a single *move* command is that the segment of code (for example a group of three line-drawing expressions) will vary, and must be supplied as a parameter to the *move* command. That is, *move* will refer to and must be matched with a segment of internal text which has already been defined, and will call and re-call that segment several times while varying the parameter values (P,Q,R). There would also need to be a default value for step size.

Let the required statement in the internal representation take the form:
Form 1

> *move* *<internal code segment>*
> *from* *<starting parameter values>*
> *to* *<final parameter values>*
> *step* *<step size>*

For example:

> *move (line 0 P Q; line 0 Q R; line 0 R P)*
> *from (P=x1,y1; Q=x2,y2; R=x3,y3)*
> *to (P=x4,y4; Q=x5,y5; R=x6,y6)*
> *step s*

To make the system more flexible it would also be desirable to allow the *move* statement to use a relative displacement vector rather than starting and final parameter values. Such a statement might have the form:
Form 2

> *move* *<internal code segment>*
> *from* *<starting parameter values>*

by   <displacement vector>
step   <size>

Even this is not entirely convenient for users, who cannot be expected to remember the exact parameter values at all times. A more convenient form for the natural language interface would be

Form 3
move <object identification>
*   <direction>*
by   <distance>
*   <speed indication>*

e.g.: *'move the triangle upwards by 10 units quickly.'*

In Form 3 the <object identification> is some statement or set of statements which will identify the appropriate segment of code with the existing (or starting) parameter values. In Form 2 the first parameter was an exact representation (or copy) of the statements to be found. In Form 3, however, the first parameter should be some simple identifier for the set of statements as a single unit. The first parameter of Form 3 therefore provides the information for the first two parameters of Form 2, the direction and distance parameters of Form 3 correspond to the vector parameter of Form 2, and the speed parameter of Form 3 corresponds to the step parameter of Form 2. Either Form 2 or Form 3 will therefore be adequate for our purposes. Form 2 is closer to the facilities often provided in programming languages, while Form 3 is closer to the structure of the natural language statements we might expect from our users.

Once we know what is required of the graphics language implementation we can assume it has been provided by some assiduous systems programmer and concentrate our attention on the implications for the natural language interpretation.

3.2 Reference Associated with 'Move'

The fact that *move* must refer to a segment of internal text which has already been defined means that we require some method of collecting a group of lines of code in the internal text into a single unit and giving it a single name or identity. This in turn means that while a concept such as 'triangle' can be translated into the equivalent set of three line drawing statements, it must not be allowed to lose its identity as a triangle. There must at least be the means of redefining the group of isolated lines as a group. This requirement was identified in section 2.6 where we used the example:

draw the line p q.
draw the line q r.

draw the line r p.
make the triangle green.

To this we can now add the statement *'Move it upwards 10 units.'*.

The 'it' in this case is the group of three line drawing statements which were identified as corresponding to the concept 'triangle'. It is not sufficient simply to identify the three lines as we did in section 2.6. We must, in effect, place a 'box' round them and give them a collective identifier. This identifier becomes the value of the first parameter of *move* (Form 3). Remember that the set of lines may not actually occur sequentially in the internal text. They could be distributed throughout a much larger segment of code with many other lines of code occurring between them.

To allow for ease of reference every entity (line or point or triangle) could be given an identifying number (id). It would then be possible to construct a kind of symbol table for these entities showing their sub-entities. A value table showing the coordinate positions of points would also be helpful. e.g.:

---

statements

---

draw the line p q.
draw the line q r.
draw the line r p.
make the triangle green.
move it upwards 10 units.

Symbol table

---

id	type	descrip	parts
1	point	p	
2	point	q	
3	line	(p,q)	(1,2)
4	point	r	
5	line	(q,r)	(2,4)
6	line	(r,p)	(4,1)
7	triangle	(p,q)(q,r)(r,p)	(3,5,6)

Value table

---

id	name	coordinates	
		x	y
1	p	123	456
2	q	234	567
4	r	345	678

(i) move phrase

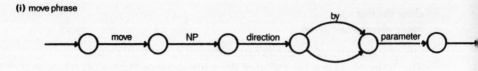

(ii) NP

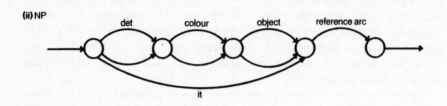

(iii) direction

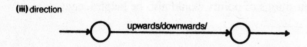

(iv) parameter

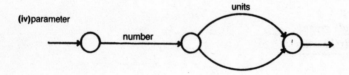

(v) object

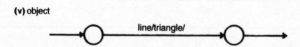

Fig. 3.1. An ATN for the 'move phrase'.

The *move* statement will call and re-call the appropriate group of statements (e.g. 'move it' in our example, would refer to entity 7) and the subordinate parts (lines 3,5 and 6) would be called several times while varying the coordinate values of p, q and r (points 1,2 and 4). The behaviour of the *move* statement is rather like that of the *for* statement which is provided by most programming languages, but in the case of the *move* statement, the values of all parameters are modified together as a group at each iteration and not as a series of nested loops in which one parameter is modified at a time.

The hard question, and one which we do not intend to answer at this point, is what happens to the value table? Do we modify the value of the coordinates in the table, or do we merely use the table to find the starting values and leave it unmodified during the *move* operation?

An ATN for processing the *move* statement is shown in Figure 3.1. We have introduced in this ATN the notion of a 'noun phrase'. A noun phrase has the general pattern:

?*<det>* ?**<adj>* *<noun>*
Where *<det>* *is a determiner (e.g. 'the')*
    <adj> *is an adjective (e.g. 'green')*
    <noun> *is an entity (e.g. 'triangle')*

Here we have prefixed *<det>* by a question mark (?) to show that it is optional, and *<adj>* is prefixed by both a question mark and an asterisk (?*) to show that it is optional and may occur several times. In this ATN and the associated notation we are anticipating the notation we will use in Chapter 9.

Note that the ATN contains arcs which are themselves full ATNs ('noun-phrase' (NP) and 'parameters') and also an arc labelled 'reference_arc'. The latter corresponds to a condition of the noun phrase which is set 'true' when the noun phrase contains 'the' or consists simply of the word 'it'. Tracing that arc consists of searching backwards to find a match for the referent, (see Chapter 8) and the result is a pointer to that referent. Failure to find a referent results in failure to trace the arc.

3.3 The Multiplicity of a Reference Object

Suppose that we have processed the following statements:

draw a triangle p q r.
move the triangle upwards by 10 units.

What are we to make of the statement '*now make it blue*'? We remarked in section 3.1 that the segment of code corresponding to the reference object would be called and recalled to produce the effect of movement on the screen. If, however, we change the colour parameter of the appropriate line drawing statements we will change the colour for the whole of the process. The statement above, however, makes it clear that what is required is for the triangle to be moved (while retaining its original colour) and then changed to blue. 'It' in the last statement refers only to the triangle as it exists at the end of the moving process.

The problem is related to the one noted in the previous section: what happens to the coordinates in the value table when an entity is moved? Briefly we have a requirement to distinguish between the various 'incarnations' of the triangle — at the beginning of the move process, at the end, and at all of the intermediate stages. It would appear, however, that the 'calling and recalling' idea will make this impossible. A more appropriate method would therefore be to convert the various calls of the reference drawing code, into macro-expansions so that each separate incarnation of the triangle will correspond to a separate set of segments of code laid down in the internal text, which can then be separately referenced. The symbol table must also go through several incarnations, each corresponding to a different incarnation of the object in question. We have therefore not one, but many objects which are all separate manifestations or incarnations of a single object at different moments in time.

We shall refer to this phenomenon as 'the multiplicity of a reference object'.

3.4 The Persistence of a Reference Object

Providing a separate segment of code to represent each incarnation of a reference object solves the problem of multiplicity, but introduces a new problem. There are times when we want to refer to the entire set of incarnations and not just to one of them. If we had said 'make it blue' instead of 'now make it blue', then although the statement is ambiguous it might have been interpreted (reasonably) as meaning 'make it blue throughout the moving process'. There is a sense, therefore, in which the entity 'triangle' in this example can be said to transcend all its incarnations. That is, the identity of the triangle persists in spite of a change to the values of the coordinates of its vertices. The identity of 'it' can be (ambiguously) one of the incarnations or all the incarnations (collectively). This phenomenon — the notion that the identity of an object remains (or persists) even when the values of its parameters change — we shall call 'the persistence of a reference object'.

The difficulty in knowing whether a reference is to the general entity or merely to one of its instances (or incarnations) is a difficulty shared by humans and not peculiar to computerised natural language systems. It is one aspect of a problem called *referential opacity* (or the lack of clarity of a reference). A classic example of referential opacity, much discussed by philosophers, concerns the way we should interpret the two phrases 'the evening star' and 'the morning star' It is an astronomical fact that both of these objects are the planet Venus, but can it be said that both statements refer 'to the same thing'? One approach to the problem is to regard the two statements as referring to different incarnations of the same object.

To change the example, if I refer to 'the British Prime Minister', do I refer to the person who at the moment is the British Prime Minister (Margaret Thatcher at the time of writing), or do I refer to the collective idea or office of 'British Prime Minister' which has been in existence for centuries? If I say 'The British Prime Minister lives at 10 Downing Street' then I probably refer to the general notion, the office of Prime Minister and therefore by implication also to the present incumbent.

When the reference matching routine does its work, it must be able to return as its result a segment of internal code which it has found to be a match, and also a reference to the collection of occurrences of which this is one. Such a reference could be a list of identifiers to all occurrences. This list is then the general referent itself.

We shall return to the topic of referential opacity later. One thing is clear, however. If an NL-system is to capture the subtleties of natural language it must be capable of identifying a reference both ways.

3.5 Transformation of Shape

The persistence of a reference object occurs even in cases where the shape of the object is changed so that it is no longer in the same shape classification. Consider, for example, the following statements.

draw the square p q r s.
make it blue.
move it by 10, 10.
delete r s.
join r p.
make it green.
move it back to its original position.
make it red.

In this sequence of commands, the entity to which 'it' refers undergoes extensive changes. By the sixth statement 'it' could refer to the line r-p, or it could refer to an instance of the general object which started as a square and has been transformed into a right-angled triangle as a result of the fourth and fifth statements. The seventh statement suggests that the latter interpretation is correct, because the line r-p had no previous position whereas the general object (a previous instance) did have. The last statement seems to refer to the final instance of this general object.

These considerations suggest that the identity of reference-objects should not be dependent upon their properties at any given instant, although these may be used as an aid to identification in the pattern-matching process. An alternative view, which has often found expression in many 'knowledge representation languages' equates the identity of an entity with the possession of a set of properties which in turn confers set membership on the entity. This form of representation seems to overlook the possibilities of properties changing with time to the extent that the object has, for at least a period of time, *none* of the properties it had in its first incarnation. As an example, and one not too divorced from our micro-graphic world example, consider the modifications of shape, size and other properties which that object we refer to as 'Tom' undergoes during a *Tom and Jerry* animated cartoon — and all without losing the identity 'Tom'.

The classification of an object does depend to a degree upon its properties. It is important to bear in mind, however, that it is not necessary for an object to possess all of the anticipated (or default value) properties, or even to possess some of them all of the time. It is sufficient for an object to have possessed a characteristic sub-set of 'standard' properties at some time in its career for it to be given a particular classification.

We will return to these ideas many times.

CHAPTER 4

The Representation of Time

4.1 Time-stamps

In the previous section (3.5) we considered an example which included the statement *'move it back to its original position'*. To deal with such a statement, and with its use of the word *'original'*, we require our NL system to have some sense of time — of the chronological sequence of events. Fortunately the means to deal with this is to hand, although a full treatment is fraught with difficulties.

If we printed the internal text and laid it out for inspection, we would see a sequence of lines of code, each of which was created at a different moment in time. If our computer had a system clock we could have appended a 'time-stamp' to each line of code to identify the instant at which it was created. And herein lies a clue as to how we might deal with the representation of time.

We should note that there are at least two kinds of clock. Some clocks begin counting from zero when the computer is switched on. We might describe that as 'relative time', since it is relative to the start of each session. Others, which have a built-in battery, record 'Greenwich Mean Time' or some similar standard time, and so we might describe that as 'standard time'. There is of course no such thing as truly 'absolute time' since all time values are relative to some arbitrary standard, but there is one absolute point in time which corresponds to the time at this very instant, which we shall call 'now'.

There is also one invariant property of time. Given two times T1 and T2 such that these are not equal, if $T1 < T2$ in some measure of time, the same relationship will hold no matter what measure of time we use. There are some peculiar circumstances which arise in high energy particle physics but these lie outside the scope of our discussion. Another point to note is that if a line of code is such that it refers to some moment in time, then we actually have two times to consider. To explain this it is best to leave the micro-graphics world for a moment and consider a database of birth records. For each record there is the time (date of birth) to which it refers, and there is the time at which the record was inserted into the database. These are not necessarily the same and usually will not be. When we wish to make this distinction, the time at which the record was created will be called the 'physical time'.

With these ideas established let us now consider the sequence of events laid out for inspection in our listing of the internal text.

4.2 Origins

Returning now to our micro-graphics world, if we inspect a listing of the internal text we would be able to recognise that some of the lines of code (not necessarily adjacent) might be considered as forming a group which defines an entity. Three lines of code might specify a triangle, for example. Another entity (a point, for example) might be defined by a single line of code. At any instant in the chronological sequence of coded lines, an entity will have a particular set of parameter values (e.g. a colour, or values for its coordinates). These values will be provided by our value table (as described in section 3.2). The implication is that the rows of the value table will need to be time-stamped. The values will remain fixed until they are changed by some other line of code.

Consider now the example shown below. In this example most of the lines of code are of no interest and we will represent them by dotted lines (.....).

....	*t0*
....	*t1*
line 0 p q	*t2*
....	*t3*
line 0 q r	*t4*
....	*t5*
line 0 r p	*t6*
....	*t7*
....	*t8*
....	*t9*
line 1 p q	*t10*
....	*t11*
....	*t12*

We have denoted the time-stamps by t0, t1, t2, t3, ... The lines timed at t2, t4 and t6 define a triangle. The question which now arises is this. At what time did the triangle pqr come into existence? We submit that the correct answer is 't6', because that is the time-stamp value of the line r-p, and until that line was drawn the triangle did not exist (although two sides of the triangle did exist before that time). From t6 until t10 the parameter values of the triangle pqr remained unchanged. At t10 one of the lines (pq) was redrawn in a different colour (0=white, 1=red). The original incarnation of the triangle therefore had an existence which extended over the period (t6-t10). An argument could be developed along the lines that an object need not have an origin which is an identifiable moment in time, but it is sufficient to note here that the issue is not entirely clear-cut. If that seems rather vague the reader should be warned — worse is to come.

4.3 Object Histories

By examining the internal text like this, we could identify the history of an object or entity, leading from its origin through a series of states, each with a particular set of parameter values and its own time-period. But to talk about this we need some terminology.

A 'state' is a condition which lasts for a period of time and during which the properties of a specific entity or collection of entities remain unchanged. A state therefore has two logical time-stamps corresponding to its starting time and its ending time. However the ending time is not shown: it must be discovered by examining the other states and finding the time-stamp of the next state which is different.

An 'event' occurs when there is some change of the properties of an entity or set of entities. An event is therefore a change of state.

The time-period associated with each state indicates its place in the chronological sequence. Other statements and entities in the internal text could be labelled in the same way to produce multiple traces showing the entire history of events leading from the start of the dialogue to the logoff message.

We can recognise that an entity may have persisted over an extended period of time, through several incarnations, and we could define a 'life-time' or 'object history' for the entity, starting at the origin when it was first defined and terminating when it was deleted by redrawing it in background colour. But if the identification of the start of an object history was difficult, the identification of the termination of an object history is doubly so. Redrawing in background colour occurs many times during a *move* process, and so a difficult problem now arises concerning the point at which we can definitely consider the entity as having been 'killed off'. We might try, for example, to define a maximum period of extinction. Less than this period we may consider to be 'momentary' and a longer period will be considered to be a definite 'death'. When we consider how human beings perceive motion in a rapid sequence of still photographs (e.g. a cine film), we see that our notion of the 'momentary' extinction, which can be ignored, has some basis in fact. The visual mechanism appears to retain the image of an object and fuse it with another which appears within a short period of time. There is, however, another form of retention which lasts much longer, and that is the focus of attention.

If an entity is extinguished from the screen we can wait for quite a long period of time and then make the request *'redraw the triangle.'* This is possible because the memory of the triangle remains. It may have disappeared from the screen, but it has not disappeared from that 'inner eye' of the mind. The focus of attention remains on the object recently extinguished. This is only the case if nothing of any significance has happened in the mean time which could have changed the focus of attention.

Now — if the triangle is redrawn, has the life-time of the original triangle been extended or are we talking about the start of a new life-time for a new triangle?

The problem is actually 'undecidable'. The point we wish to make is that the life-time of an entity depends upon the perceptions of the viewer (or the perceiver) and their focus of attention. It is not a simple matter of time periods and physical extinctions. The question above can be answered correctly in either way, provided one assumes a suitable context.

4.4 Before and After

Now suppose that our user requests the system to draw a red triangle, move that triangle about and then change its colour to green, move it about again and then change its colour once more to yellow. The sequence is:

red(t0)-move(t1)-green(t2)-move(t3)-yellow(t4).

Here the triangle was red from t0 to t1, it was moved during the period t1 to t2, and so on. The 'present' time is represented by the system clock and the most recent time-stamp is t4. We shall represent the current value of the system clock by 'now'. Our user might then make the statement *'Before making the triangle green move it upwards 10 units.'* The user is inserting an additional command retrospectively (physical time = 'now', logical time = before(t2)) and we have introduced by implication the idea of the 'action replay', that is, that the internal text can be re-run to produce the graphic images once more at a later time. This will require the regeneration of the text as for a 'macro-expansion' as we described in section 3.3.

The word 'before' refers not to a time period before the present time ('now'), but to a time before t2, which was the time at which the triangle was made green (in each of the incarnations of that internal text). The time-stamp t2 is relative to the other time-stamps in the sequence. In terms of standard time it could be in the actual past (before 'now') or it could be in the actual future (during a future action replay). The time-stamp 't2' therefore has multiple occurrences (in each incarnation of an action). Each time-stamp within an incarnation therefore has a 'standard' component (different for all versions of t2) and a 'relative' component (the same for all versions of t2).

Notice that the focus of attention has been switched to t2, which now becomes a kind of 'pseudo-present' time. That is, 'before' and 'after' refer to before(t2) and after(t2). The pseudo-present status of t2 can be seen in the fact that the user can change the tense of the verbs to present tense while still referring to t2. For example *'As it is becoming green it should flash rapidly.'* Note that *'As it is becoming ...'* is in the present tense even although the user is referring to t2, which in its original incarnation was in the past (relative to 'now').

If there are two green triangles on the screen the user may refer to *'... the green triangle which will become yellow...'*. Here we see even the future tense *'.. will become ..'* can be used to refer to an event which is in the standard past, but is in the future relative to the time associated with the focus of attention (t2).

To interpret the statement *'Before making the triangle red move it upwards 10 units'* the NL-system should:

(a) create a representational pattern corresponding to the making of the triangle green (code-segment).

(b) initiate a search back through the internal text to achieve a match with the pattern. (Note that the pattern matching technique will be needed — see Chapter 8).

(c) copy the relevant segment of internal text to create a new incarnation of that segment

(d) insert a new line (or lines) of code which moves the triangle upwards 10 units.

(e) re-run text at absolute time 'now'.

By inserting the lines of code for a change of position we leave behind in the internal text a reference object for such statements as *'and after making the movement make the triangle flash'*.

The new incarnation is essentially timeless in standard time until it is re-run on the screen, but the (relative) relationships between t0, t1, t2, ... etc remain constant (t0 occurs before t1 which occurs before t2, and so on). It therefore seems that although we need to represent both standard and relative time components, there is no necessity for more than one parameter. We can assign identifying labels to the time-stamps (e.g.: t0, t1, t2, ...). We can then declare certain properties which we wish these to have (e.g.: $t0 < t1 < t2 < ...$). We can also relate any of these to a standard time scale (e.g.: $t2 = now$). Once t2 is known to be equal to 'now' we can make certain deductions about the other time-stamp parameters (e.g.: $t1 < now$). This seems a flexible and economical way to represent time. When a segment of code is copied to produce a new incarnation of it, the relative time relationships must be copied as well. The whole sequence of events can be located in standard time later by relating the standard value 'now' to one of the time-stamp parameters. This relationship to 'now' is a property of the incarnation, not of the individual states within that incarnation. If a sequence of events takes place in three steps at t0, t1 and t2 we can place the whole action in the past by declaring '$t2 < now$'. The whole action can be declared to be in the future by the statement '$t0 > now$' and the action can be declared to be actually happening in the present by the statement '$t1 = now$'.

The idea of multiple incarnations of a sequence of events, each of which can be separately located in standard time, has its counterpart in storytelling. We might say 'Hamlet will kill the king' (future tense) although the actions have been portrayed innumerable times in the past (in previous incarnations or performances).

4.5 Tense

These ideas fit rather nicely with the way time is expressed through the tense of verbs. The present continuous (e.g.: 'it is moving') is equivalent to 't1=now'. Past tense (e.g.: 'it moved') is equivalent to 't2 < now', and future tense (e.g.: 'it will move') is equivalent to 't0 > now'.

The more complex tenses are expressed by more complex verb structures (e.g.: 'it has been moving'). In the example above we used t1 to indicate the time at which the action is in 'mid-process'. The tense of the verb above indicates that that point in the action is in the past 't1 < now'.

To deal with 'it will have been moving' we must introduce another time-stamp parameter (t3). The tense of the verb indicates that t3 is in the future ('t3 > now') and that the state of mid-action (t1) occurred before that ('t1 < t3'). From this we cannot deduce the relationship between t1 and absolute 'now'. All we know is that some time in the future the action will have been in the past (relative to the new future 'now').

Finally the infinite tense (e.g.: 'it moves') corresponds (except in special (real-time) storytelling techniques) to the situation in which there is no relationship to absolute 'now'. It is essentially timeless.

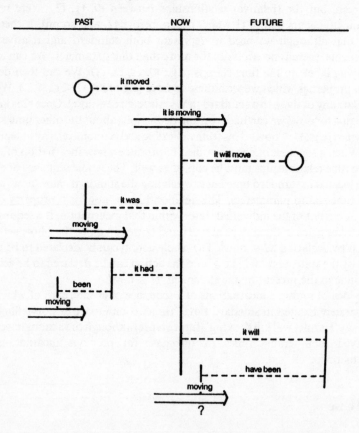

Fig. 4.1. The relationship between the tense of expressions, events and 'now'.

4.6 Simultaneous Actions

The use of the words 'while' and 'during' in the input text suggests the idea of parallel execution in the relative time of the graphics display. Present-day computers have some difficulty with parallel execution, but future machines may not have this difficulty. In the mean time it is often possible to achieve pseudo-parallelism with a swapping mechanism which executes two or more sequences of instructions by swapping from one to the other, one instruction at a time.

A possible solution might therefore be the introduction of a *swap* macro-generator, in the same way as we used the *move* macro-generator.

We need not concern ourselves with the actual mechanism by which parallelism is to be achieved, but we note that the internal representation must be able to assign identical relative time-stamps to segments of the internal text. It follows that we cannot rely upon the linear sequence of lines of code in the internal text to indicate relative time. There must be some explicit representation of the relative time component of each time-stamp (as well as the standard component).

The suggestion is, therefore, that each line of code in the expanded internal text is provided with a time-stamp parameter (t0,t1,t2,t3,...) and that in addition we have a database of 'facts' about the values of these parameters. These facts may be global or local (being tagged on to some incarnation). The chronological sequence of the lines of code can be discovered only by reference to this database.

4.7 Summary

In Chapter 4 we have sought to make the following points.

(a) The chronological sequence of events can be represented as a series of discrete states each with a time-stamp, together with a database of facts indicating the relative positions of each time-stamp parameter.

(b) Objects have object-histories but the starting and ending points of such histories are defined ambiguously.

(c) Time-stamps have absolute, standard and relative components. These can be represented by arbitrary time-stamp labels to which are attached relationship information. When the relationship is relative to 'now' the time-stamp has been located relative to the present time.

(d) When the focus of attention is directed at a particular event or state the time-stamp (relative component) acquires a pseudo-present status.

We shall return to these issues when we deal with verbs in Chapter 6. First we must digress (in Chapter 5) to study how the important verb endings and structures (which indicate tense) can be recognised.

CHAPTER 5

Word Structure and Verb Endings

5.1 Word Stem and Verb Endings

In processing the input text it would be helpful to be able to recognise word stems within different versions of the same word. For example it would be helpful to be able to recognise *move*, *moved*, *moving* and *moves* as different versions of the same word stem (*move*). This would avoid needing to store explicit interpretations of all versions. In addition it would be helpful to be able to recognise the various endings which are tacked on to the word stem so that we can take account of the extra information provided by these word endings.

Irregular verbs are harder to deal with, but it would greatly reduce the volume of work if we could deal with regular verbs in a consistent way.

5.2 POP11 Programs for Processing Stems

POP11 provides us with facilities for dealing with these problems.

```
destword("fred");
```

will place on the stack the individual characters of the word "fred", and in addition an integer giving the length of the word. Thus after execution of destword("fred") the status of the stack will be as shown on the illustration below:

```
4
d
e
r
f
..........
```

The command destword("fred")->n; will remove the integer 4 and assign it to n. Knowing the number of items on the stack we can then remove and test them in turn to detect the presence of the various word endings. What remains on the stack will be the word stem.

The function 'consword' reverses the operation of 'destword' to create a word of given length from the individual characters stored on the stack. For example, if we have just completed the procedure:

```
destword("fred")->n;
```

so that the stack contains the characters 'f','r','e','d' (reading from the bottom upwards) then the call:

```
consword(3)->w;
```

will assign to w the word "red", leaving behind the character 'f'. The requirements which are additional to these facilities consist of three functions. The function 'top_of_stack(n)' is similar to consword(n) except that it restores the stack to the condition it was in before the call by replacing the characters used from the stack. The function 'stem(n)' is also similar to consword(n) except that it discards the character 'e' if that is the top character on the stack. The function 'stem_end(w)', where w is a word, leaves two results on the stack. These are the word stem and the word ending (both formed into words). It works only if w is more than 3 characters long. It recognises only the word endings 's', 'ed' and 'ing'. It always removes a final 'e' from the word stem it creates. If the word w has no recognisable ending then the function creates for it the dummy ending 'none', and it still strips the final 'e' off the word itself.

```
/* A POP11 program to handle word endings */

define stem_end(w);
vars n stem x y z;
destword(w)->n;
if n>1 then ->x;
  if x=115 then consword(n-1); "s";
  elseif n>2 then ->y;
    if ((x=100) and (y=101)) then consword(n-2); "ed";
    elseif n>3 then ->z;
      if (((x=103) and (y=110)) and (z=105)) then consword(n-3); "ing";
      else consword(n); "none";
      endif;
    else consword(n); "none";
    endif;
  else consword(n); "none";
  endif;
else consword(n); "none";
endif;
enddefine;
```

Prog. 5.1. The POP11 program to handle verb endings.

The reader is invited to implement this function and to try it out on a number of verbs. The result left on the stack should be the verb stem with the verb ending above it, e.g.:

stem_end("hearing")=>	hear, ing
stem_end("walked")=>	walk, ed
stem_end("moves")=>	mov, s

stem_end("moved")=>	mov, ed
stem_end("move")=>	mov, none
stem_end("fred")=>	fred, none
stem_end("have")=>	hav, none

The (move,moved,moving) example illustrates a problem with this simple-minded approach. The endings are not simply tacked on to the end of verb stem but take into account the termination of the verb stem. One solution is to strip off the final 'e' on any verb stem and use this reduced version as the true stem. In this case the verb stem of "move" would be "mov" in all cases. If we did not strip off the final 'e' we would find that the stem of "move" = "move", while the stem of "moving" = "mov". The function stem_end is obviously fairly crude, and the reader is invited to develop more sophisticated functions to deal with more alternatives.

5.3 Irregular Verbs

The 'stem_end' function will, of course, only operate successfully on regular verbs. Irregular verbs could be dealt with by listing the stems and endings explicitly. In the table below we provide the 'regular' verb endings for the irregular verbs, and in this way force them into conformity with the regular verbs. Thus when the verb "ran" is used, our stem_end function will yield the result stem = "run", ending = "ed". This means that any function which makes use of the stem_end function will not need to make special provision for irregular verbs.

verb form	stem	ending
taken	tak	ed
taking	tak	ing
took	tak	ed
takes	tak	s
take	tak	
run	run	
ran	run	ed
running	run	ing
go	go	
gone	go	ed
going	go	ing
went	go	
goes	go	s
... and so on.		

CHAPTER 6

The Tense of Verbs

6.1 Verb Structure

The forms of verbs in which we are interested are:

it moves
it moved
it is moving
it was moving
it has been moving
it will move
it will be moving
it will have been moved
it has moved
... etc.

The verb 'to move' has been chosen for illustration because it is relevant to our discussion of screen displays and because it is a regular verb. Each of these verb forms contains a main verb (a form of the verb 'to move') and possibly several auxiliary verbs (forms of the verbs 'to be' and 'to have'). Each describes a similar action (movement) but different forms carry different implications with respect to the following factors:

(a) *Time* (or tense) — whether the action is in the present, past, future or neutral with respect to some reference point in relative time, which is the current focus of attention. A neutral tense mark leaves the tense undefined.

(b) *Continuing* — whether the action continues or continued over a period of time.

(c) *Finished* — whether or not the action has been completed.

(d) *Active/Passive* (or voice) — whether the reference-object is playing an active or passive role. In the case of an inanimate object such as a triangle, the active form 'it is moving' merely leaves unstated who or what is responsible for the movement, but in the case of an animate object, the active form declares it to be the cause of the movement.

An ATN for the structure of the verb group is shown in Figure 9.7 and a grammar is provided in section 9.4.

6.2 Marking

In linguistics it is said that the various verb and word forms are 'marked' with these semantic factors. Taking the set of factors, or marks, listed in the previous section we can characterise every verb form by means of a four-term symbol:

(a) The time-stamp is denoted (Now/Past/Future) or (N/P/F)

(b) The Continuing/not-continuing is denoted by (C/-)

(c) The Finished action/not finished action is denoted (F/-)

(d) The Active/Passive factor is denoted (A/P)

We can then write down all possible permutations of these factors to obtain the following table:

NCFA	it has been moving
NCFP	it has been being moved (?)
NC-A	it is moving
NC-P	it is being moved
N-FA	it has moved
N-FP	it has been moved
N--A	it moves
N--	it is moved
PCFA	it had been moving
PCFP	it had been being moved (?)
PC-A	it was moving
PC-P	it was being moved
P-FA	it had moved
P-FP	it had been moved
P--A	it moved
P--P	it was moved
FCFA	it will have been moving
FCFP	it will have been being moved (?)
FC-A	it will be moving
FC-P	it will be being moved
F-FA	it will have moved
F-FP	it will have been moved
F--A	it will move
F--P	it will be moved

Some of these (with a question mark) are distinctly clumsy, and it is questionable if they would be accepted as grammatical English. Nevertheless they represent intelligible English. The pattern of these forms is clear.

Main verb endings:

'...ing' denotes the continuing factor.

'...ed' denotes the past and the finished factors unless the verb is immediately preceded by a form of the verb 'to be', in which case it denotes the passive and the finished factors.

'...s' denotes present tense (or it is neutral with respect to time indicating that the object is capable of being moved and does so from time to time). Note that there are forms (e.g.: I move) in which the verb has no ending, but which should be interpreted as though it had an 's' ending (e.g.: it moves). The function 'stem_end' might be modified accordingly.

The auxiliary verbs 'to be' and 'to have' also have time, continuing and finished marked forms:

BE = neutral time displacement
IS = present
BEING = neutral, continuing
BEEN = past, finished
WILL = future

HAVE = neutral time displacement
HAS = present
HAD = past

In an ideal information communication system designed for maximum flexibility and no ambiguity, any flags or mark indicators such as word endings would be *orthogonal*. That is, they would each be associated with a single type of mark and could be used freely without it being necessary to take into account the other flags which may occur in the same segment of text. This is not the case in English because, for example, the word ending '...ed' can be used both to indicate 'past tense' and 'action finished'. It is also used to indicate 'passive voice' (in association with the verb 'to be'). This double use of a flag means that additional flags must be inserted when both the marks associated with '...ed' are required.

For example, if we require both passive voice and the 'continuing' mark we cannot use both the endings '...ed' and '...ing' on the main verb. We therefore use the '...ed' ending to denote passive voice and add the '...ing' ending on to the auxiliary verb to give 'being moved.'

The fact that some of the verb forms shown above are grammatically suspect reflects the fact that they describe a relatively rare state of affairs which is difficult for humans to envisage. Careful thought will, however, show that they do have an intelligible meaning.

In the case of verbs in which the difference between active and passive forms is crucial (e.g. 'takes') the active/passive form may be distinct from the past-tense form.

For example:

it moves	it takes
it is moved	it is taken
it moved	it took
it was moved	it was taken
	(not it was took)

The verb form 'taken' normally carries a mark for passive voice, and if it is used to carry the past-tense mark for the verb as a whole, the passive voice mark must be cancelled by preceding it with a form of the verb 'to have'. For example, 'he has taken' is not identical to 'he took'. In the case of 'he has taken' the focus of attention is still 'now', (i.e. we are discussing an historical event relative to the current focus of interest). In the case of 'he took' we are discussing an historical event only. In most cases the distinction is too subtle to prevent the two forms being substituted for each other, but the distinction can be seen in the examples below:

'He took the book and he read it.'
'He has taken the book and it cannot be found.'
'He has taken the book and he read it.'
'He took the book and it cannot be found.'

All four of these sentences are grammatical and understandable, but the second two are slightly odd in that they appear to switch emphasis from the present to the past or vice-versa, whereas the first two focus on a single time reference. The fourth sentence is quite acceptable, however, because the switch is made from a past event to a present consequence of that event.

6.3 Time Displacement

The notion of a time displacement noted against 'be' and 'have' reflects the fact mentioned above, that all these notions of past, present and future are expressed as being relative to some relative-time reference point (or pseudo-present — see Chapter 4). There can be more than one reference point within the verb form. For example the verb form 'will have been moving' has more than one reference point. The auxiliary verb 'will' generates a new reference point (say T1) which is in the future with reference to 'now' ('now' is the relative time associated with the focus of interest). 'Have' being neutral, preserves T1. 'Been' generates a new reference point (say T2) in the past relative to T1. 'Moving' adds the continuing factor and adopts the reference point T2 as the time-stamp of the action. The verb as a whole indicates that at some time in the future T1 (relative to 'now') 'it' will be in a state in which it 'has been moving' (at time T2). There is no indication whether or not T2 is before or after 'now'. All we know is that at T1 the object of reference ('it') will have the movement (at T2) as part of its history.

Figure 9.7 illustrates the ATN which analyses the structure of a verb. Figure 6.1 is a simplified version of this. The reader is invited to develop a POP11 or Prolog program which will correspond to the diagrams in Figure 6.1.

The program should accept a verb in any of the forms illustrated above and should yield as its result the three items:

true
[<word-stem>]
[<remainder or input text>]

The program should also create a side-effect which updates a data structure of
four elements:

T,C,F,AP

corresponding to the four factors Time, Continuing, Finished, Active/Passive

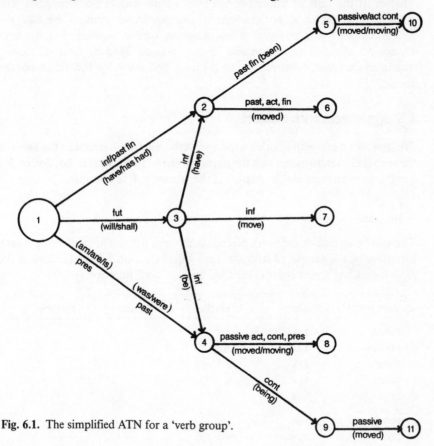

Fig. 6.1. The simplified ATN for a 'verb group'.

6.4 Using the Verb Factor Analysis to aid a Search

We have discussed in previous chapters the interpretation of the pronominal
reference 'it' and the verb 'move'. Consider the interpretation of a statement
which begins 'Before moving it ...'. The statement requires a referent for 'it', and
the only clue is that it is something which has been moved. It will be necessary

therefore to search back in the internal text for something which was moved. The verb 'moving' will be associated with a structural pattern, which can be used as a template for a pattern matching search to find a reference-object for 'it'.

The verb factors will provide further aids for the search. In the case of 'before moving it...', we do not know whether or not the action is in the past or the future. If the statement had begun 'Before it was moved...' we would know it had taken place in the past, and the search would be directed backwards. It will also indicate whether the action is spread over a period of time (continuing) and whether at the time of interest it has been terminated or not (finished). The active/passive factor is not relevant to our particular example because the reference-object (e.g. triangle) is not animate, and in normal circumstances cannot be regarded as responsible for any actions. Had we been discussing animated cartoons, however, we might have had a use for the active/passive factor.

6.5 Agreement with Subject

We have not dealt with another aspect of verb structure — the way the form of the verb is chosen to agree with the nature of the subject (person: 1st, 2nd or 3rd person; number: singular or plural) of the sentence. For example:

I go
He goes

This can be an additional mark placed on the verb form. The reader might now turn back to the sample of irregular verb forms (section 5.3) and complete the table by adding a new column labelled 'person' and 'number'.

verb form	stem	ending	person	number
taken	tak	ed		
taking	tak	ing		
took	tak	ed		
takes	tak	s		
take	tak			
run	run			
ran	run	ed		
running	run	ing		
go	go			
gone	go	ed		
going	go	ing		
went	go	ed		
goes	go	s		

The programs written for the 'stem_end' function should also be modified so that they update a global register with the information concerning person and number. Not all verb forms provide information of this kind, and so it will be necessary to provide a mark indicating that several types of 'person' are allowed. One way to achieve this is to use an octal numbering system so that each bit of the octal number corresponds to a person classification, so that:

$1 = 001 = $ 1st person
$2 = 010 = $ 2nd person
$3 = 011 = $ 1st or 2nd
$4 = 100 = $ 3rd person
$5 = 101 = $ 1st or 3rd
$6 = 110 = $ 2nd or 3rd
$7 = 111 = $ 1st, 2nd or 3rd

A similar arrangement can be used for the 'number' mark.

CHAPTER 7

Nouns and Noun Phrases

7.1 Why Noun Phrases?

In Chapter 1 the grammars developed for dealing with assignment statements and line definitions were ad hoc and peculiar to the application under consideration. By extending the facilities of the micro-graphics world to deal with events in the past and the future, we have been required to introduce the idea of 'tense', and in consequence we were required to describe a grammar for conventional verb phrases. These can be found in any natural language sentence and are not peculiar to our application. Having discussed verb phrases it is appropriate, therefore, to go on and discuss the noun phrase, as it occurs in all natural language sentences, although we shall still refer back to our micro-graphics application for illustration. The verb phrase and the noun phrase are the main structural units of a natural language sentence.

If we draw an analogy between a sentence and a play (on the stage) then noun phrases are concerned with the parts to be played, and the verb phrase is concerned with the action of the play. The overall structure of the sentence indicates which role is associated with which part. Other bits of a sentence are often concerned with scene setting and with stage directions.

7.2 Entities and Concepts

In section 2.4 we introduced the term 'concept' to describe the structural unit which is in effect the definition of a word such as 'triangle'.

---

triangle(X,Y,X)

    [line X Y]
    [line Y Z]
    [line Z X]

We described this structure as 'generic' because it could be used to generate specific examples of the concept triangle by assigning specific coordinate values to the points X, Y and Z, and then constructing what is in effect a macro-expansion of the definition.

We need to distinguish between the generic structure and the examples which can be derived from it. We call the generic structure a *concept*, and each example we shall call an *entity* or *object*. In the micro-graphics world an entity is always a concrete thing like a triangle or a square, but in natural language in general an entity can be abstract, like 'an idea' or 'an embarrassment'. An entity is usually identified by a noun phrase. For example:

The big horse won the race.
He had *a good idea*.
We want to go to *the pictures*.
She arrived on *a bicycle*.

A concept is usually identified by a single noun. For example:

Horse, idea, pictures, bicycle, man

A noun is the most important constituent of a noun phrase. It tells us what generic concept or class of entity our specific example of an entity belongs to. That tells us what properties we can expect it to have.

Other words in the noun phrase may provide us with additional information, and perhaps modify the properties identified by the noun (if they are unusual or non-default). For example, the noun 'canary' tells us that the entity under consideration is a bird, has wings, is yellow, and so on. The words '..green canary' tell us that although the entity concerned has most of the expected properties of a canary, it is unusual with respect to its colour.

Our discussions in sections 3.3 and 3.4 have shown that an entity can live through several 'incarnations' and that we need some method of 'throwing a lasso' round the lines of code which represent these incarnations so that we can refer to the entity as a whole.

7.3 Proper Nouns

A proper noun (e.g. John, Fred) is a name label or identifier for one particular entity, that is, one for which the parameters have been assigned particular values. In the micro-graphics world a proper noun is represented by a label such as 'P' or 'Q' or 'triangle ABC'. We already have the facilities for dealing with this in our symbol table.

Because a proper noun is the name of an entity, it can form a noun phrase on its own. In general a proper noun must be defined before we can associate it with a particular entity. There are some proper nouns, however, which have certain prior expectations associated with them. The proper noun 'fred' for example, suggests (without definition) that the entity referred to is human and male. The proper noun 'fido' suggests a dog, and so on. There is no reason why these default associations cannot be overridden, but it is interesting to note that in some cases we should be prepared to associate some proper nouns with concepts as though they were normal nouns. For example we might describe someone as 'a Hitler'.

7.4 The Indefinite Article 'a'

The phrase 'a triangle' identifies a single example of the concept triangle. Where there is no reason to suppose that the triangle has any particular parameter values we may assign arbitrary values to the parameters. It may be wise, however, not to give such a triangle values which make it a special case. We can think of the triangle as being a random selection from the set of all triangles, but the selection is not entirely random since what is selected will be a 'typical' triangle. What 'typical' means will vary from individual to individual (and from computer system to computer system), but normally it will not be isosceles or right-angled or zero-angled, and normally it will be located roughly in the centre of the screen or the blank area of the screen in such a way that if the available area was subdivided as shown in the diagram below the triangle would more or less fill the centre square.

The avoidance of special cases means that if the user makes the statement 'draw a triangle', the system will not draw a triangle which is too small to be seen, or which occludes other figures on the screen, or for which one of the sides coincides with the side of the screen, and so on.

This notion of 'typical' case is inherent in natural language. If we speak of 'a man', we imagine a 'typical' man. We do not normally imagine a one-legged man, or a blind man, or a giant, or a man with any abnormal characteristic. Indeed, if we are asked afterwards what was the colour of hair of the man we imagined on hearing the statement 'a man', it is doubtful if we could give a simple answer. The probability is that our imagination did not supply that level of detail. It was simply 'a normal or standard man'.

If we wish to draw attention to some characteristic we speak of 'a tall man' or 'a fat child', 'a large mouse' and 'a small elephant'. The terms 'tall', 'fat', 'large' and 'small' do not correspond to absolute dimensions but are related to the typical dimensions of objects of these various classes. A small elephant is still

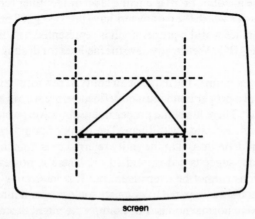

screen

Fig. 7.1. The location of an arbitrary triangle.

much larger than a large mouse. Being 'near to' a mountain does not imply a distance of separation of the same scale as being 'near to' another person. Our sense of 'normal' is strongly related to the properties of the object being discussed, and that means influenced by the concept labelled by the noun in the relevant noun phrase.

To represent the entity referred to by the phrase 'a triangle', therefore, we need two things:

(a) A representation using formal parameters which can be given absolute values to reproduce any required triangle.

(b) A set of 'typical' parameter values which can be used as default values if no clue is given to the actual parameter values. They also serve as a standard of comparison for the interpretation of adjectives such as 'small' and 'large'.

We use the generic representation of a concept to generate an entity and assign to it the parameter values we find there. These are the 'typical' or 'default' values of the concept. In the case of our micro-graphics world, these default values may be relative to the free space which is currently available on the screen.

One way to look at the processing of the phrase 'a triangle' is to think of the NL process picking out of its memory a generic concept structure identified by its label 'triangle'. This defines an infinite set of all possible triangles, because the parameters have no values. In the micro-graphics world the set may not actually be infinite because it is bounded by a finite screen, but it is as good as infinite for practical purposes.

The meaning of the determiner 'a' is represented by a function call which performs a selection process upon that infinite set to pick one typical example. This is the first time we have introduced the idea of the meaning of a word being represented by a function which operates upon the representations associated with other words, but it is a useful idea which we shall utilise frequently.

In terms of the ATN processing of a noun phrase, we can think in terms of side-effects. As the system traces the arc corresponding to the word 'a', it must place a function identifier in a global register. When the next arc corresponding to 'triangle' is traversed, the side-effect must be the placing of the appropriate concept definition in another 'argument slot' of the global register. When the 'exit' arc of the ATN is being traced, the side-effect must be the application of the function to its arguments yielding the internal text required.

This is a much more complicated procedure than the one we described earlier, in which we recognised but otherwise ignored the presence of the determiner 'a'.

7.5 The Definite Article

The phrase 'the triangle' will be processed in very much the same way as the phrase 'a triangle', but the use of 'the' instead of 'a' introduces a reference to some previously mentioned triangle, and will therefore initiate a search backwards to discover the referent.

The processing is identical for the two phrases up to the point where the internal text has been generated. The search associated with 'the', then begins and uses this internal text as a template for the matching process. The interpretation of 'the' therefore involves the use of two functions, one to select the entity example from the infinite set of possible examples, and the other to carry out the search. The adjective 'red' in 'the red triangle' adds information to help make the search more precise and resolve any ambiguity.

The use of the definite article 'the' also refers to and determines the focus of attention. This explains the special effects which can be obtained by the use of 'the'. For example:

'The tall man was approaching steadily, and as he did so he glanced towards Julia.'

If this was the first sentence in a story where there is no previously mentioned 'tall man' to which this can refer, then the writer is using 'the' to establish the 'man' in question as the focus of attention.

7.6 Standard Parameter Values

The colour adjectives in our graphics language example are absolute (e.g.: 'red' is always a standard red). But in other contexts this cannot be assumed. The 'red' of 'red hair' is not the same red as the 'red' of 'red sun'. Each is interpreted as:

RED X = 'redder than the standard colour for objects of type X'.

There will not only be a standard colour for each object type but a standard range of variation. This allows us to interpret the phrase 'a very red sun'.

One approach which might be adopted for the representation of these standard values uses the same type of mechanism which we used in the representation of time (Chapter 4). We might provide each standard parameter value with an arbitrary unique label, and then provide information about how these are related to each other. Thus we can have STD-RED-1 and STD-RED-2, and a relationship which tells us that STD-RED-1 > STD-RED-2 (with respect to redness). The same method will serve for measures of 'nearness'. Each object will be associated with a normal or standard distance of separation. Each can be assigned a unique label STD-DIST-1, STD-DIST-2 and so on. To describe an object as 'near' we assign to the distance of separation a new unique label (DIST-3) and then note that DIST-3 < STD-DIST-1.

Such a technique might suffice for a very limited micro-world in which there are only a few standard values to be considered, but for the world in general it is inadequate. The prior assignment of a specific standard size and a standard distance of separation to every object would be a mammoth task. Every parameter value must have its standard value, and so this idea of prior assignment would overload our system with unique values which may never be required. It would be preferable to have some way of generating only those values we actually need, as the need arises.

A possible solution lies in the idea of having a function which takes an object label and the property concerned as arguments, and yields a unique standard value as a result. We can then refer to the unique standard value by means of the function name and its arguments, instead of referring to it by the unique label which it would generate. In effect the activation of the function (or its application to its arguments) is held in suspense, and the function call itself is used as the label for its result. If we wish to represent a value 'red' of some object X of concept Y which is redder than standard red for some such objects, we first give the object X a colour parameter value = R, and then write R > STD-RED(Y).

This does not solve the problem completely. It removes the need to assign unique labels to every possible standard value, but it leaves us with the problem of indicating what the symbol '>' means. For simple numeric values its meaning is obvious, but in other cases it could mean 'redder' or 'greener' or 'darker' or 'lighter' or 'bigger', or 'farther' and so on. Its interpretation is in fact related to the parameter values we are considering.

One possibility is to replace '>' by a specific parameter-related predicate:

redder(R,STD-RED(Y))

Another possibility is to associate each parameter with an 'axis of discrimination' (in this example — degree of redness). We will discuss a way of implementing this idea later (Chapter 21 onwards).

Functions which replace a possible infinity of parameter values are known as 'Skolem Functions'.

7.7 Adjectives

Loosely speaking an adjective is a 'describing' word. More strictly, and in terms of the representational approach we have been describing, the meaning of an adjective is a modification carried out on the parameter values of a concept representation.

Consider the processing of the words '...red triangle'. The traversal of the ATN arc corresponding to 'red' will create as a side-effect a representation of a concept (say X) which has only one known property — it has the colour red. The tracing of the next arc corresponding to the word 'triangle' generates as a side-effect the generic structure for the concept 'triangle'. The next process is to try to unify these two structures, and the simplest way to do that is to unify the unspecified concept (X) with the concept 'triangle'. The result is a new concept (red triangle). Note that it is the representation of a concept, not an entity. The word 'a' or 'the' is required to process the concept representation and turn it into an entity.

The virtue of this two-step mechanism is that it deals with situations in which there is no concept to which (X) can be unified. Consider the sentence 'The red is very bright'. Here there is no concept specified, which is being described as 'red'. But there is a concept of something. It is after all impossible to imagine the colour red without also imagining something which is that colour. (Even an unbroken field of colour is still a 'something'.)

There is not really a great deal of difference between an adjective and a noun. The difference lies in the roles which they normally play within a noun phrase, and depends on which is the dominant role. Consider, for example, the two phrases 'the red pillar-box' and 'the pillar-box red'. In the latter case the result of interpretation will be an unspecified entity with the parameter value equal to a particular kind of red (the standard colour of pillar-boxes). The focus of attention is on the colour, not the entity.

Since nouns identify concepts, and concepts have default parameter values, a noun can be used as an adjective to apply that default value to some other concept which does not have that particular value as its default value.

7.8 Gerunds

A gerund is a verb which is being used in the role of a noun. We might refer, for example, to 'the moving of the triangle'. Here the noun phrase 'the moving' has no noun, but has instead the present participle of the verb 'to move'. In these circumstances the noun phrase is referring not to an object, but to a segment of internal text which describes an action carried out on an object. The prepositional phrase 'of the triangle' is appended to, and is part of, the noun phrase, it provides additional information (to allow identification of the reference entity or segment of code).

As in the case of the adjective, we see that the important aspect, from the point of view of the interpretation, is the role that the gerund plays within the noun phrase. The word 'moving' describes the process to be carried out on some entity. If this entity is unspecified (e.g.: 'The moving was completed') we must, as for the adjective, create a representation of some dummy construct representing a movement of some kind. Its properties are provided by the prepositional phrase 'of the triangle'.

A classic case of ambiguity occurs in the case where it is not clear which aspect of a concept is being described by the gerund. This ambiguity is illustrated by the example 'The shooting of the hunters'. Here it is not clear whether the shooting is being carried out *by* the hunters or being carried out *on* the hunters. This problem is generated by the fact that the hunters are entities which can both shoot and be shot, and so we do not know how to unify the structures for the two concepts. There is no similar ambiguity with the phrases 'The shooting of the rifles' or 'The shooting of the targets'.

These examples illustrate the importance of semantic analysis and the impossibility in some cases of determining the correct syntactical analysis in the absence of semantic considerations.

7.9 The Syntax of a Noun Phrase

Once we understand what we are trying to do to a noun phrase (np) let us see if we can establish its word pattern (or grammatical structure). In its simplest form we have phrases such as:

'A triangle'
'The triangle'
'A red triangle'
'The red triangle'

i.e.:

np :- <determiner><noun>
np :- <determiner><adjective><noun>

To save ourselves the bother of writing out many alternative structures we shall use the notation:

np :- <determiner><?adjective><noun>

where the '?' symbol indicates that the adjective may or may not be present. Of course the adjective can also be repeated, e.g. 'the large red triangle', and so we shall use the '*' symbol to indicate that a term may be repeated several times.

np :- <determiner><?*adjective><noun>

Next we notice that the adjectives often occur in pairs: 'the fast moving triangle'. Here the word 'moving', which is not normally thought of as an adjective, is being used as part of a word group 'fast moving', and that word pair forms an adjectival group. There are many more such adjectival groups, e.g. 'right angled', 'ham fisted', 'double talking', 'barrel chested', 'clear thinking', 'man eating', 'fly bitten', and so on. Note that in each group the second word is a verb and the first word is either an adjective or a noun.

Consider first the noun-verb pairs. These fall into two categories — those with the present participle (e.g.: 'talking') and those with the past participle (e.g.: 'chested'). In the case of the present participle the noun of the noun phrase pair is the entity carrying out the action, and the noun of the noun-verb adjectival group is the recipient of the action. In the past participle form the noun of the noun phrase is the recipient of the action described by the verb. For example, 'a man eating tiger' and 'a man eaten tiger' are two very different things. In some cases the verb of the adjectival group does not normally have an agent (e.g.: 'fisted' (with exceptions)). In these cases the noun of the noun-verb adjectival group is being used as an adjective. The first word of the adjectival group word-pair can be an adjective or an adverb (e.g. 'clear' in 'clear thinking').

These are complex problems which we shall discuss in more detail later. For the moment we are interested in establishing a usable syntactical structure. In view of the possibility of the adjectival group, our grammatical structure ought

(i) adj-GRP

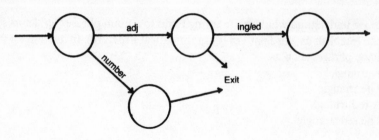

(ii) NP

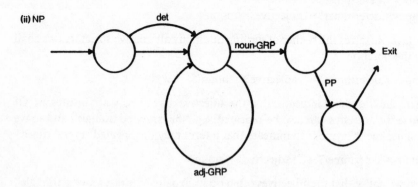

(iii) PP

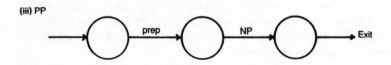

Fig. 7.2. The ATN for a 'noun phrase'.

to replace the simple adjective with an adjectival-group component (adj-group):

    np :- <determiner><?*adj-group><noun>

Next we note that the determiner is not present if the noun phrase refers to more than one entity — 'triangles have three sides', or 'men were breaking down the door'.

    Therefore we have:

    np :- <?determiner><?*adj-group><noun>

Lastly we replace the simple 'noun' with the 'noun-group' which includes the possibility of it being a gerund.

np :- <?det><?*adj-group><noun-group>

To these we can add prepositional phrases, e.g. 'the triangle above the square'.

np :- <?det><?*adj-group><noun-group><?pp>

where 'pp' is a prepositional phrase with structure given by:

pp :- <prep><np>

This grammar is also represented by the ATN shown in Figure 7.2

One of the difficulties associated with a grammar such as this is that it is not easy to show the agreements which must exist between the various options. For example, the fact that a determiner may be present or not present <?det> may be shown clearly, but what is not shown is that the determiner is not present when the noun phrase is plural. Likewise the adjectival group used must agree for number with the noun, and so on.

One way to cope with this is to subdivide the classifications noun, adjective, determiner etc. into sub-classifications, and refer to these in the grammar. Thus we can have:

s-n (singular nouns)
pl-n (plural nouns)
m-n (mass nouns)

and we can also have

m-quant (mass quantifier, e.g. 'much')
quant (quantifier, e.g. 'many', 'some')

and so on. With these sub-classifications we can be more precise about what is grammatical and what is ungrammatical. It is possible to take this strategy to ridiculous lengths, and it is our belief that many grammarians have done exactly that. The end-point of this process will be reached when every word is in a classification of its own, at which point syntax will (virtually) have become semantics.

In Chapter 9 we have provided a reasonably detailed grammar of English which uses many more sub-classifications than we have described here, but it is certainly not complete. Much of the latter part of this book represents an attempt to abandon the classical approach to NL processing, which is based on syntactical analysis, and to develop a purely semantic approach.

In Chapter 8 we discuss the problem of pattern matching which emerged clearly in this section as a requirement. We also consider better ways to implement a grammar.

CHAPTER 8

Pattern Matching

8.1 Pattern Matching in General

Pattern matching is a process with applications in many fields including natural language processing. One particular need is to identify the patterns of word types in order to recognise the grammatical structure of a sentence. Another is concerned with the matching of structures to identify the target of some reference. These needs have emerged from the discussion in Chapters 1 to 7 in this book, and it is now time to take stock and establish some techniques which can be used to satisfy these needs.

The need for pattern matching is important, and is so general in artificial intelligence work that considerable effort has been expended to create special facilities for the process. Indeed, Prolog might be described as a language specifically designed for pattern matching. Some languages, such as POP11, have powerful pattern matching facilities. What we intend to do here is to examine some primitive facilities which illustrate the basic principles, and to develop a suitable set of algorithms for processing and matching patterns in a perspicuous way. It is not intended that these facilities should supplant the much more efficient facilities already available.

We shall first discuss the problem of testing items for simple equality, and then for a more general and arbitrary 'correspondence'. The reader will be invited to code these functions and to use them as the basis for the development of a family of functions able to test items, or 'terms', and check if they have particular properties, or if two such terms 'agree' with respect to particular properties.

Having established such a family of functions we can then consider how we might re-implement the algorithm for an ATN parser in a way that will not offend structured programming enthusiasts and yet will retain a close affinity with the original ATN diagrams. The ATN algorithm will depend upon our family of property testing functions, and will in addition be able to introduce 'agreement testing'. That is, we shall be able to introduce tests which ensure that adjective and noun agree with respect to number and countability, that subject and verb agree with respect to number and person, and so on.

We shall then consider the mechanisms underlying the use of 'formal parameters' as a pattern matching facility. This will allow us to assert a temporary (or trial) correspondence between items during an attempt to match two arbitrary data structures, a process often called 'unification'. It is important that such trial correspondences can be undone automatically when a match fails, so that alternative trial correspondences can be examined. The provision of such facilities is one of the main attractions of the language Prolog. Such facilities will allow us to examine the internal representation and find there examples of particular structures by matching them with generic structures which are defined by means of formal parameters.

8.2 Equality, Correspondence and Agreement

Equality

The basic function used in a pattern matching procedure is that which determines equality between two entities. We can say that two variables are 'equal' because they have the same value assigned to them. We could (alternatively) say that they are 'equal' because they are of the same type, or because they have the same relationship to some other variable (e.g. members of the same list) and any one of a host of other possibilities. The point is that we must define what we mean by 'equality', and it is open to us to define it in any way we wish. It is always possible to write a function equal(X,Y) which will return the result 'true' under any conditions we choose.

At the simplest level we can have a POP11 function defined thus:

```
define equal(x,y);
    x=y;
enddefine;
```

but this is appropriate only for simple numerical variables or (if x and y are pointer variables) they will be found to be equal if and only if they 'point' to the same address. This is a useful but limited test. We could improve it by writing a function which would follow all address pointers until it reached the final reference addresses for both x and y, and then compared these. This process is known as 'de-referencing', but such a function, although useful, does no more than test for a basic kind of equality.

Correspondence

A more powerful test is one which tests the correspondence of two entities in an arbitrary list of pairs. Consider a list with the structure:

[[a b] [c d] [e f] ... [y z]] -> corresp_list;

We can then define a POP11 function which will test any two items, say 'p' and 'q', to see if the pair [p q] appears anywhere in corresp_list. Let us call this function 'corresp' to distinguish it from the simpler equality testing function above. The reader is invited to write and test this function.

The function is particularly powerful because we can then establish a correspondence between any two entities in an arbitrary way to suit our own purposes. It is also possible to establish that (for example) 'x' corresponds to both 'y' and 'z' without 'y' and 'z' corresponding to each other. It is also the case that if 'x' corresponds to 'y' and 'y' corresponds to 'z' we cannot assume that 'x' will correspond to 'z'. Furthermore 'x' does not necessarily correspond to 'x', and if 'x' corresponds to 'y' we cannot assume that 'y' corresponds to 'x'. That is, 'corresp' defined this way does not automatically have the properties of reflexivity, transitivity, associativity and symmetry unless we take the trouble to build these properties into the definition.

In Prolog we can at any time assert that two entities are equal, or that they correspond, and later retrieve that information as a fact. Again the properties of transitivity etc. must be defined explicitly if they are desired.

Has_Properties

An even more general function makes use of a list structure which we shall call a 'dictionary'. The dictionary has the structure:

```
[
  [term property property property ..]
  [term property property property ..]
  [term property property property ..]
  ........
  ........
]
```

Here 'term' is used to indicate a 'word' or 'lexical item', and 'property' is used to indicate a short list structure with the form:

[property_name property_value]

For example one entry in our dictionary might be for the term "man":

```
[man
    [gram noun]
    [ntype count]
    [num sing]
    [entity physobj]
    [anim animate] ]
```

The list of properties associated with it tells us that it has the grammatical property 'noun', that it is of ntype (noun type) 'countable', that it has the number 'singular', that it is a 'physobj' (physical object) entity, and that it is 'animate'.

Now we can define a function has_prop(t,v,p) which tests to see if the term 't' has the property_value 'v' associated with the property_name 'p'. For example, we might enquire:

has_prop("man","noun","gram")=>

which asks 'is the word "man" classified grammatically as a noun?' Again the reader is invited to write and test such a function.

Such a function has great power, and can be used as the basis for a whole family of functions designed to test various aspects of the properties associated with various terms. For example we can now define a grammatical classification testing function:

has_prop(%"gram"%) -> is_gram;

The function is then identical to the function has_prop with its third argument 'frozen' at the value 'gram'. It can be used in the form:

is_gram("man","noun");

which is identical to: has_prop("man","noun","gram"); We can also freeze the last two arguments thus:

has_prop(%"noun","gram"%)->is_noun;

which is then used in the form is_noun("man").

Agreement

We can also use the function has_prop as the basis for testing two terms for agreement. The reader is invited to write and test a function agree_prop(t1,t2,p) which will yield 'true' if and only if the terms 't1' and 't2' have the same property_value with respect to the property_name 'p'. For example

agree_prop("man","dog","gram");

meaning 'do the words "man" and "dog" have the same grammatical classification'? Such a function can then be used to create a family of functions which test for grammatical agreement, or number agreement, or ntype agreement (e.g. both countable or both mass). In this way we can ensure that expressions such as 'few air' or 'less cows' do not pass unnoticed.

Multiple Property Agreements

A still more powerful version of this function, agree_all(t1,t2,pl); will test two terms 't1' and 't2' for agreement with respect to a whole list of property names (pl). For example:

agree_all("man","dogs",[gram num anim]);

would yield the result 'false', because although the words 'man' and 'dogs' are both nouns and are both animate, 'man' is singular while 'dogs' is plural. That is, they agree with respect to two of the properties on the list but not with respect to all of the properties. It is arguable that that this is too harsh a test, and that the terms should be given the benefit of the doubt if one or both of the terms has (or have) no value for a given property name. This relaxation of the strict rule would allow us to omit a property from a property list if that particular term could have any of the values normally associated with a given property. For example, some adjectives are suitable for use with both countable and mass nouns. Another variation would compare values for the property 'person' where these values were given as an octal digit, as described in section 6.5.

Best Fit Agreement

An even greater relaxation of the agreement rule might allow some non-agreement between words. In these cases it would be best for the function to yield not an absolute 'true' or 'false' but a metric which measures the degree of agreement. A commonly used metric is given by:

$$\frac{A}{B}$$

where A is the number of properties for which there is an agreement and B is the number of properties in the list of property names to be tested.

With such a function we could think of testing several different interpretations of an ambiguous word, and accepting the interpretation which produces the best agreement figure. We shall not pursue this idea any further.

Exercise 8.1

Write and test the functions:
  (a) corresp(x,y);
  (b) has_prop(t,v,p);
  (c) is_gram(t,v);
  (d) is_noun(t);
  (e) is_verb(t);
  (f) is_adj(t);
  (g) agree(t1,t2,p);
  (h) agree_ntype(t1,t2);
  (i) agree_num(t1,t2);
  (j) agree_all(t1,t2,pl);
  (k) agree_metric(t1,t2,pl);

8.3 An improved ATN-based Parser

Earlier we provided examples of programs which represented an implementation of the ATN diagrams. The programming style was simple and direct but because it was based on the use of labels (to represent each node) and GOTO statements (to represent each arc) it was not structured, and therefore not suitable for the development of large and more complex ATNs. Here we will develop a better structure for these programs and at the same time we will try to preserve the close correspondence with the ATN diagrams which was the merit of the previous version of the programs.

The basic unit of any ATN-based algorithm is the 'node-test-and-branch'.

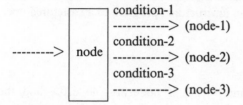

This was represented by an 'IF-then-GOTO' construct. One would like to replace this by a construct such as:

```
if      <condition-1> then <node-1-process>
elseif <condition-2> then <node-2-process>
elseif <condition-3> then <node-3-process>
else   <fail>
endif;
```

Unfortunately nodes 1, 2 and 3 do not represent unique and separate processes, since the pathways onwards from these nodes are not necessarily distinct. If we left the algorithm as shown above we would need to write the <node-1-process> as a complete procedure in its own right which was capable of processing all possible continuations from that point onwards. In many cases, however, the continuation from two different nodes will come together and become identical. We will have lost the advantage of sharing code for such cases and have a combinatorial explosion on our hands. If they do combine, however, and there is a failure at some later node, the procedure would not know which one of several possible starting points to backtrack to. We shall call this 'the continuation problem'.

One solution is to write the algorithm as a single function in which the node identification is a parameter. We can then call the function itself (recursively) with the continuation node as an argument. The function below has an argument 'node-id' which is a numerical flag indicating the node concerned. The different values which it may have are represented symbolically by <node_0>, <node_1>, <node_2> etc.

```
define parse(intext,node_id);
if node_id = <node_0> then
    if    <condition_1> then parse(tl(intext),node_1);
    elseif <condition_2> then parse(tl(intext),node_2);
    elseif <condition_3> then parse(tl(intext),node_3);
    else  <fail>;
    endif;
elseif node_id = <node_1> then
    if    <condition-4> then parse(tl(intext),node_4);
    ......etc......
    ......etc......
enddefine;
```

Computer scientists will recognise this as a version of the Ashcroft-Manna technique for the conversion of an unstructured program to a structured one.

Dealing with Back-tracking

The trouble with this algorithm is that if node_id=<node_0> and the <condition-1> test is successful then control will pass to the continuation associated with its arc irrevocably, and will not back-track and try other possibilities (say <condition_2>) if it fails at a later point. An additional variation in the algorithm cures this fault and provides for automatic back-tracking in the event of subsequent failure, thus:

```
/* the parse algorithm with provision for back-tracking */


define parse(intext,node_id);
if    node_id = <node_1> then
    if    (<condition_1> and parse(tl(intext),node_1)) then true;
    elseif (<condition_2> and parse(tl(intext),node_2)) then true;
    elseif (<condition_3> and parse(tl(intext),node_3)) then true;
    else  <fail>
    endif;
elseif  node_id = <node_2> then
    if    (<condition_4> and parse(tl(intext),node_4)) then true;

    ......etc.......
enddefine;
```

Prog. 8.1. The parsing algorithm with back-tracking.

Notice that what had been the continuation, the 'parse(tl(intext),node_id)' expression, has now been included (by conjunction) in the condition test, and must therefore be defined so that it yields a truth value. This construct ensures that at any node a test for a successful continuation is included in the condition test before an arc is selected. If the continuation fails at some later point, there is a back-track from that arc and the intext is restored to its original status. In effect the traversal of the arc, and of all subsequent arcs from then onwards, is tested before the algorithm commits itself to that arc.

Dealing with Side-effects

We now turn to the problem of generating side-effects, which is crucial to the construction of the internal text (or representation). There are two problems about handling side-effects properly.

The first is that whatever side-effects are created must be deleted if the parse fails (i.e. the back-tracking problem again). The second is that the generation of a side-effect often requires information from more than one level of the parse process. For example, when we are dealing with a single word such as 'dog' we will be able to discover from the dictionary that it is a physical object, that it is animate, is singular, is a four-legged animal, and so on. What we will not know at that level of the analysis is whether it is the active agent or the passive recipient of some action. We do not know whether it is the subject or the object of the sentence. That kind of information is only available at a higher level, when we are processing the pattern of the sentence as a whole. Without such information we cannot ensure that the subject of a sentence agrees with the verb with respect to number and person. The test for agreement is therefore impossible at the level of tracing arcs associated with particular word types, and yet it is at this level that the information is available about the number and person of the nouns and verbs.

The basic trick to overcome these difficulties is to let each level in the parsing process generate its own 'local' side-effect (which we shall call a 'register'). The exact form of this register is not important at present. These local registers should then be passed, as the results of each sub-process, back to the parent process which calls them, and which is dealing with the higher level of the analysis. It can then accept the information provided by its subordinate processes and slot these results into its own register. If a subordinate process fails, however, the higher process will ignore the local registers supplied by these failed sub-processes. The mechanism requires each process at each level to create its own register rather than simply updating an existing global register (or 'blackboard').

The function 'parse' should leave three results:

(1) 'true'
(2) register
(3) remainder of intext

or:

(1) 'false'
(2) nil
(3) original intext

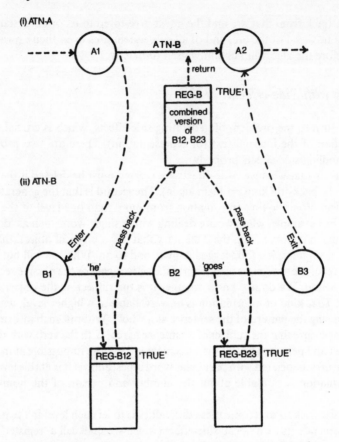

The sub-processes pass back their registers and these are combined to produce an overall register.

Fig. 8.1. The traversal of an ATN with side-effects.

Figure 8.1 illustrates the traversal of an ATN which we shall call ATN-1. ATN-1 is a high level ATN in that its arcs are labelled by the names of lower level ATNs. To traverse the arc (A1)-(A2) successfully it must call the function ATN-2. It passes down to this function the text of the sentence to be parsed.

To complete the traversal of ATN-2 successfully the two arcs (B1)-(B2) and (B2)-(B3) must be traced. In order to traverse the first of these, (B1)-(B2), a test for the word 'he' must be applied, and if successful a local register (reg-B12) is updated with the information '3rd person, singular'. This is passed back to the parent function ATN-2 together with the result 'true' and the remainder of the sentence with 'he' bitten off. ATN-2 then tries the second arc (B2)-(B3). To do this a test for the verb 'goes' is applied, and if successful the local register reg-B23 containing the information '3rd person, singular' is passed back to ATN-2 along with 'true' and the remainder of the sentence with 'goes' bitten off.

ATN-2 can then test the two registers reg-B12 and reg-B23 for agreement, and if it finds agreement it passes back to ATN-1 its register reg-A12 containing the information '3rd person singular' together with 'true' and the remainder of the text with both 'he' and 'goes' bitten off. If ATN-2 fails in any of these tests it passes back the results 'fail', 'nil' and the text in its original form. All the registers reg-A12, reg-B12 and reg-B23, being local to ATN-2 and its subordinate functions, are wiped out as though they never existed.

Note that the results left by these functions are the same three results which we used in the previous version of the ATN algorithm except that we have substituted 'register' for 'internal text'. The register, being a data structure of some kind, could contain the internal text as one of its elements.

Another factor to be watched is that the function places the results on the stack in the correct sequence so that the truth value lies under the other two. This means that we can remove the other two and assign these to some local variable for subsequent processing, and still leave the truth value on the stack for the condition test. We can then write:

```
if
(parse(intext,node_id)->remainder->register)
        then ....
```

and go on to process remainder and register as we wish.

This makes it possible to write:

```
if
  (
  (arc1-test(intext)->rem1->reg1)
   and
  (parse(rem1,1)     ->rem2->reg2)
   and
  (agreement(reg1,reg2)->reg)
  )
then
    true; reg; rem2;
else
    false; nil; intext;
endif;
```

Note that the call of 'parse' is processing the remainder (rem1) left by the 'arc1-test' function. As an illustration (without agreement testing) let us define an ATN for the simple grammar:

```
s :- np, vp
np :- det,?*adj,noun
vp :- vg,?np,?pp
vg :- ?*aux,verb
```

where s = sentence, np = noun phrase, det = determiner, adj = adjective, vg = verb group, vp = verb phrase, pp = prepositional phrase, aux = auxiliary verb, ? = optional, * = possibly repeated.

Let the register be a simple list. Let the update consist simply of appending a sublist with structure [<property> <data>] to the list, where <property> is a name such as 'agent', 'object' or 'instrument' and 'data' is a word from the input text. More complicated registers could be constructed by using information from the dictionary structure discussed in section 8.2.

The ATN for the parsing of a noun phrase (np) is:

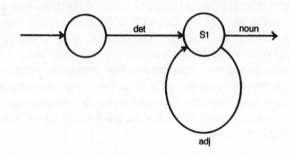

Fig. 8.2. ATN for a noun phrase (simplified grammar).

```
define parse_np(intext,node_id);
vars reg remainder;              /* create a new register */
nil->reg;
if node_id=0 then
   if (isdet(hd(intext)) and      /* test for determiner   */
   (parse_np(tl(intext),1) ->remainder->reg)) /* continue from node-1 */
      then true; reg; remainder;    /* leave the register as result */
   else
           false; nil; intext;     /* else a nil register and failure */
   endif;
elseif node_id=1 then
   if isnoun(hd(intext)) then
           lst_append([%"entity",hd(intext)%],reg) ->reg; /* update the register */
      true; reg; tl(intext);              /* and exit if noun */
   elseif isadj(hd(intext)) and
           (parse_np(tl(intext),1)           /* continue again from node-1 */
                 ->remainder->reg)
           then true; reg; remainder;       /* then exit */
   else false; nil; intext;
   endif;
endif;
enddefine;
```

Prog. 8.2. The noun phrase program.

The ATN for a verb group (vg) is:

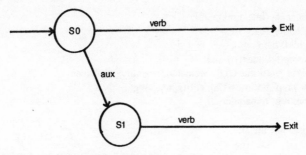

Fig. 8.3. ATN for a verb group (simplified grammar).

```
define parse_vg(intext,node_id);
vars reg remainder;
nil->reg;
if node_id=0 then
    if ((isaux(hd(intext))) and (parse_vg(tl(intext),1)->remainder->reg)) then
        true; reg; remainder;
    elseif (isverb(hd(intext))) then
        lst_append([%"act",hd(intext)%],reg)->reg;
        true; reg; tl(intext);
    else    false; nil; intext;
    endif;
elseif node_id=1 then
    if (isverb(hd(intext))) then
        lst_append([%"act",hd(intext)%],reg)->reg;
        true; reg; tl(intext);
    else    false; nil; intext;
    endif;
else        false; nil; intext;
endif;
enddefine;
```

Prog. 8.3. The verb group program.

The ATN for a prepositional phrase is:

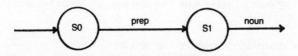

Fig. 8.4. ATN for a prepositional phrase (simplified grammar).

In this case the node identifier is redundant and we include it simply to maintain a constant function format.

```
define parse_pp(intext,node_id);
vars reg entity_reg;
if node_id=0 then
    if ((isprep(hd(intext))) and
        (parse_np(tl(intext),0)->remainder->entity_reg)) then
        [%"prep",hd(intext)%]::entity_reg->reg;
        true; reg; remainder;
    else
        false; nil; intext;
    endif;
else
        false; nil; intext;
endif;
enddefine;
```

Prog. 8.4. The prepositional phrase program.

The ATN for a verb phrase is:

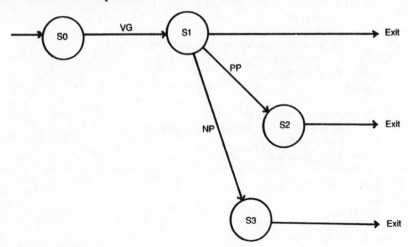

Fig. 8.5. ATN for a verb phrase (simplified grammar).

```
define parse_vp(intext,node_id);
vars act_reg obj_reg remainder;
if node_id=0 then
    if (parse_vg(intext,0)->remainder->act_reg) and null(remainder) then
        true; act_reg; nil;
    elseif
        (parse_vg(intext,0)->remainder->act_reg) and
        (parse_np(remainder,0)->remainder->obj_reg)
        then
```

```
            "object"::obj_reg->obj_reg;
                true; act_reg<>obj_reg; remainder;
        elseif
                (parse_vg(intext,0)->remainder->act_reg) and
                (parse_pp(remainder,0)->remainder->obj_reg)
                then
                true; act_reg<>obj_reg; remainder;
            else false; nil; intext;
            endif;
        else false; nil; intext;
        endif;
    enddefine;
```

Prog. 8.5. The verb phrase program.

The ATN for a sentence is:

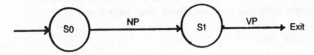

Fig. 8.6. ATN for a sentence (simplified grammar).

```
    define parse_sent(intext,node_id);
    vars subj_reg verb_reg remainder;
    if (parse_np(intext,0)->remainder->subj_reg) and
        (parse_vp(remainder,0)->remainder->verb_reg  /*...*/ )
        then
        "subj"::hd(subj_reg)->hd(subj_reg);
        true; subj_reg<>verb_reg; remainder;
    else
        false; nil; intext;
    endif;
    enddefine;
```

Prog. 8.6. The sentence program.

8.4 The Structure of a Dictionary

The following structure illustrates the possible contents of a usable dictionary.

```
[
[dog [gram noun] [ntype count] [num sing] [entity physobj] [anim animate] ]
[dogs [gram noun] [ntype count] [num plural] [entity physobj] [anim animate] ]
[house [gram noun] [ntype count] [num plural] [entity physobj] ]
[house [gram verb] [tense presinf] [aspect imperfect] ]
[man [gram noun] [ntype count] [num sing] [entity physobj] [anim animate] [hum human] ]
[men [gram noun] [ntype count] [num plural] [entity physobj] [anim animate] [hum human] ]
```

```
[big [gram adj] ]
[water [gram noun] [ntype mass] ]
[few [gram adj] [adjtype quant] [ntype count] [num plural] ]
[less [gram adj] [adjtype quant] [ntype mass] ]
[the [gram det] [dettype definite] ]
[a [gram det] [dettype indefinite] [num sing] [ntype count] ]
[run [gram verb] [tense presinf] [aspect imperfect] ]
[ran [gram verb] [tense past] [aspect perf] ]
[will [gram verb] [auxverb aux] [tense fut] ]
[is [gram verb] [auxverb aux] [tense pres] [num sing] ]
[are [gram verb] [auxverb aux] [tense pres] [num plural] ]
[was [gram verb] [auxverb aux] [tense past] [aspect perfect] [num sing] ]
[were [gram verb] [auxverb aux] [tense past] [aspect perfect] [num plural] ]
[have [gram verb] [auxverb aux] [tense pres] ]
[has [gram verb] [auxverb aux] [tense pres] ]
[having [gram verb] [auxverb aux] [tense pres] [aspect imperfect] ]
[being [gram verb] [auxverb aux] [tense pres] [aspect imperfect] ]
[had [gram verb] [auxverb aux] [tense past] [aspect perfect] ]
]
     -> gvar_dict;
```

We have given it the name 'gvar_dict' for 'global variable dictionary'.

8.5 Unification

Consider the two patterns '(a+b)-c' and '(x+y)-z'. We can all see that they correspond as patterns, even although the individual elements are not identical. We can make a temporary correspondence or substitution (a to x), (b to y) and (c to z) and declare the patterns to be equivalent. Afterwards a, b, c, x, y, z resume their anonymity. They have no identity in these patterns except as place holders. In some patterns an anonymous identifier might occur in more than one place. In such cases the substitution must be uniform. If we substitute an 'a' for an 'x' at one point in the pattern we must not substitute another identifier for 'x' anywhere else in the pattern. When two identifiers have been made to correspond in this way we shall say that they have been 'unified'.

Consider now the patterns:

(a+3)-c

and

(x+4)-z

An attempt to match these patterns would succeed only if $3=4$. We might deem this inappropriate, and we will normally operate with the rule that fixed values cannot be unified. If, however, we had the patterns:

(a+3) - c

and

(x+y)-z

we might quite reasonably decide that $y=3$, in which case we would say that 'y' was 'instantiated to 3'. Instantiation can be regarded as the temporary assignment of a value to a variable.

In Prolog, identifiers which are variable names are distinguished from others by being written in upper case characters, or at least having the first character of their name in upper case. We shall adopt the same idea here, and note in passing that the 'destword' function in POP11 which was discussed in section 5.2 provides us with a mechanism for recognising such variable names so long as they are POP11 'words' (see Appendix). Any variable which is capable of being instantiated will be called a 'formal parameter' or just 'a formal'. Other identifiers are assumed to be fixed values just like numbers.

Unification and instantiation are easy to implement, but there is a complication. After a matching procedure has been completed, or if it is abandoned at some intermediate point because of some evident failure to match, all unifications and instantiations which brought about that matching procedure must be deleted to restore the formals to their unadulterated state, and make them available for any alternative unification or instantiation which might be required of them. Note that it is not all unifications and instantiations which must be deleted, just those established within the context of the process just completed or abandoned. This is the problem of back-track yet again.

For the purposes of illustration we shall now invent a simple unification/ instantiation mechanism. In later sections we shall use it to develop some interesting matching algorithms.

The basis of our approach is a record structure which we shall call 'x_formal'. This is defined in POP11:

```
recordclass x_formal f_label f_val f_ref;
```

That is, it has four subelements.

'f_label' is the first element, and it has as its value a word which is the identifier (upper case) for the formal in question.

'f_val' is the element which stores the value of the formal, i.e. to which it is instantiated (or 'undef' if it is not instantiated)

'f_ref' is a pointer field to other formals with which it has been unified. This should also be initialised to 'undef'.

Next we define a function 'f_unify' which unifies a pair of formals (f1 and f2)

```
define f_unify(f1,f2);
f1->f2.f_ref;
f2->f1.f_ref;
true;
enddefine;
```

This function assumes that each of the two formals is not already unified. The function should contain a test to check that each has the value 'undef' assigned to its pointer field. If f_unify is able to unify f1 and f2 it should return the result 'true', and if it fails it should return the result 'false'. We leave these modifications to the reader. Next we define a function which instantiates a formal (f) to a fixed value (x).

```
define f_instant(x,f);
x->f.f_val;
true;
enddefine;
```

Again this should test the arguments to make sure that they are of the correct type and only return the result 'true' if instantiation is achieved.

Next we define a function 'f_match(x,y)' which examines and compares two arbitrary arguments. If they are both fixed values the result is the result of the test (x=y). If one is an uninstantiated formal and the other is a fixed value, it performs the 'f_instant' function on them. If both are non-unified formals it performs the 'f_unify' function on them. If both are unified formals it returns 'true' if they are unified to each other. If both are instantiated it returns 'true' if they are instantiated to the same value. The result in every case is a truth value. We leave the reader to implement this function.

Lastly we must implement a function which will de_instantiate and de_unify any formal:

```
define f_release(f):
"undef"->f.f_ref;
"undef"->f.f_val;
enddefine;
```

8.6 Matching Structures with Unification

We can now apply the functions we have defined in section 8.5 to the problem of matching lists of elements. Let the two lists be list1 and list2 such that:

```
list1 = [line X Y]
list2 = [line 123 456]
```

X and Y are formals so that list1 is part of a definition of something and list2 is part of an actual bit of internal text. We want to see if the internal text 'fits' the definition. What we would like to write is:

```
define list_match(list1,list2);
if null(list1) then true;                ;;; a match if both null
elseif f_match(hd(list1),hd(list2))      ;;; try matching heads
  then list_match(tl(list1),tl(list2));  ;;; if ok try the tails
else false;
endif;
enddefine;
```

But this would fail to release the formals which had been bound during an unsuccessful attempt to match. It also assumes that the two lists are of equal length.

Therefore the function must, at the very beginning, test the lengths of the lists and fail if they are of unequal lengths. It must also construct a list of all formals which it binds as it goes along. If the function fails, it should release all formals which it has bound (by applist(bound_list, release)) and return nil; false. If it succeeds, it should return its list of bound formals and 'true'. It goes something like this:

```
define list_match(list1,list2);
vars bound list3 result;
if not(length(list1)=length(list2)) then nil; false; return; endif;;
                              ;;;checks for equal length
nil->bound;                   ;;;initialises the bound-list
if null(list1) then bound;true;   ;;;if both null the true
elseif f_match(hd(list1),hd(list2))   ;;;if heads match
  then
    hd(list1)::bound->bound;       ;;;add heads to bound list
    hd(list2)::bound->bound;
    list_match(tl(list1),tl(list2))   ;;;and try the tails (recursion)
              ->list3->result;   ;;;and get the result (truthval)
    bound<>list3->bound;           ;;;add to the bound list
    if result then bound; true;   ;;;if ok then return the bound list
    else applist(bound,release);   ;;;else abandon the bound list
        nil; false;
    endif;
  else nil; false;
  endif;
enddefine;
```

Let us now take the matching process a step further by trying to match the definition list [line X Y] with one of a list of lists. This time the function should return three results: the list of bound formals, the address of the matching sublist in 'struct' and the truth value indicating success or failure. If it fails, the value of the second result is 'undef' and the list of bound formals is nil.

```
define struct_match(list,struct);
vars bound address;
if null(struct) then false; "undef" nil; return; endif;
if list_match(list,hd(struct))->bound->address then bound; address; true;
else struct_match(list,tl(struct));
endif;
enddefine;
```

We leave to the reader the exercise of writing the function which completes the set. It will compare a structure to a structure. Note that it must retain the bound list of formals from each successful match found and release them all if a failure occurs at any time.

8.7 General Unification

In section 8.5 we assumed that fixed values would never be unified. We also assumed that formal parameters would be unified only two at a time.

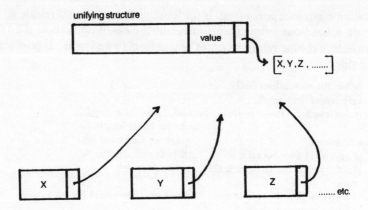

Fig. 8.7. General unification.

These restrictions are not necessary, although they are appropriate in many circumstances. A more general approach to unification would not have these restrictions and it is of interest to see how it might be implemented.

Previously the formal parameters each had a single pointer field which was either 'undef' or pointed at the single formal with which it had been unified. An alternative would be to introduce a third structure to link the two (or more) elements. The arrangement is shown diagrammatically in figure 8.7.

Here X and Y are both elements which have been unified and the 'unifying structure' is the third structure introduced when the unification is established. X and Y both carry pointers to this link record, and the link record has a pointer to each of the unified elements. These pointers can be held in a list so that more than two elements can be unified by a single link.

Multiple unification is very hard to handle correctly and it is usually inappropriate anyway. The mechanism suggested, however, has one important advantage over the simple mechanism suggested in 8.5. The link record can be used to store properties of the link itself. In section 23.3, for example, we will suggest that a 'possible' flag be appended to an instantiation, and in section 25.5 we will have need of a similar arrangement.

CHAPTER 9

A Grammar of English

9.1 Caveat

A definitive grammar of English does not exist. For a reasonably complete grammar from an authoritative source the reader is referred to *A Grammar of Contemporary English* by Quirk, Greenbaum, Leech and Svartvik (Longmans 1972). The grammar provided here is only a small subset of a full grammar but it is more complete than anything we have considered hitherto, and it may suffice for student exercises. It should be recognised, however, that no matter how authoritative a grammar may be it will still be subject to constant improvement and amendment.

The major defect of this grammar is the fact that it does not handle all agreements properly. As a result it will sometimes accept an ungrammatical sentence. It may also on occasion reject a sentence which is grammatical. The reader is invited to experiment with it to discover its shortcomings and to amend it accordingly.

9.2 Notation

In this grammar we have modified our notation slightly with the intention of improving readability and making the listing of the grammar much more compact.

The slash '/' has been replaced by the semi-colon ';' and wherever possible this has only been introduced at the end of a line. The exception is when it occurs inside a bracket. The angle brackets have been omitted, and a comma has been used to separate items which are to be 'anded'. This is permissible because we do not intend to include the comma as a terminal symbol in the grammar. The '*' symbol prefixes an item which may be repeated, and the '?' prefixes an item which may be omitted. Brackets have been used to disambiguate expressions with mixed 'and' and 'or' logical operators. At certain points we have inserted a list of terminal symbols (words) rather than try to invent a grammatical category for them. Sometimes the list is too long for complete enumeration. On those occasions we have inserted the symbol '..' to indicate that the list is not complete.

For those who find the FSD notation more readable we have provided diagrams to support the more cryptic BNF-like notation. To clarify things we provide some examples below in the old and the new notation:

Example 9.1

OLD NOTATION

noun-phrase:-<noun-group> / <noun-group><prep-phrase-list>
prep-phrase-list:-<prep-phrase> / <prep-phrase><prep-phrase-list>

If we replace   <noun-phrase> by <np>
                 <noun-group> by <ng>
                 <prep-phrase> by <pp>
                 <prep-phrase-list> by <ppl>

we have the grammar:

np :- <ng> / <ng><ppl>
ppl:- <pp> / <pp><ppl>

NEW NOTATION

np:-ng,?*pp

Example 9.2

OLD NOTATION

sent:- decl-sent / imper-sent / quest

NEW NOTATION

sent:- decl-sent;
     imper-sent;
     quest.

Example 9.3

NEW NOTATION (only)

adj-gp:-?*emph,(quant;m-quant)

This means that an adjective-group consists of zero or n emphasisers (e.g. 'very') *and* (',') then (*either* a quantifier *or* (';') a mass-quantifier).

9.3 Glossary

* = possibly repeated
? = possibly absent
; = or
, = and

.. = the list is not complete
adj = adjective
adj-gp = adjective group
adv = adverb
adv-ph = adverbial phrase
decl-sent = declarative sentence
de-emph = de-emphasiser (e.g. 'too')
ed = the past participle of a verb (e.g. 'broken')
emph = emphasiser (e.g. 'very')
fut = future and/or modal
        (will; shall; should; would; cannot; can; must)
imper-sent = imperative sentence
inf-vp = infinitive verb phrase (e.g. 'to build a house')
ing = present participle of a verb (e.g. 'walking')
ing-gp = 'ing' group
ing-ph = 'ing' phrase
intr-vg = intransitive verb group
ment = mental state noun (e.g. 'anger')
m-n = mass noun
modif = modifier (e.g. 'enough')
m-quant = mass quantifier (e.g. 'much')
n = noun
ng = noun group
np = noun phrase
num = number
ord = ordinal (e.g. 'first')
p-adj = 'people' adjective i.e. applicable only to people
pl-n = plural noun
pp = prepositional phrase
prep = preposition
pres-inf = present infinitive verb (e.g. 'move')
pres-2ndpers = a verb group in present 2nd person
pron = pronoun
prop = proper noun
quant = quantifier (e.g. 'many', 'some')
quest = question
q-vg = question verb group
rel-comp = relative comparison
preposition (e.g. 'like', 'as')
rel-dir = relative direction preposition (e.g. 'up', 'in')
rel-loc = relative location preposition (e.g. 'near')
rel-quant = relative quantifier (e.g. 'more')
rel-tim = relative time preposition (e.g. 'after')
sent = sentence

s-n = singular noun
st-vg = stative verb group (e.g. 'know')
tr-vg = transitive and bi-transitive verb group
vg = verb group
vp = verb phrase

9.4 The Grammar

sent:- decl-sent;
     imper-sent;
     quest.
decl-sent:- np,vp;
         ing-ph, decl-sent;
         adv-ph, decl-sent.
np:- ng,?*pp
ng:-?(the;those;these;his;her;my;..), ?*adj-gp, pl-n;
   (our;the;..), ?*adj-gp, p-adj;
   (a;an;the;that;his;her;my;..), ?*adj-gp, s-n;
   pron;
   ?*adj-gp, prop;
   ?(the;his;her;my;..), ?*adj-gp, (ment;ing;m-n);
adj-gp:- ?*emph, adj;
      ?*emph, adv, (ed;ing);
      ?*emph, n, ed;
      ?*emph, ed;
      ?*emph, (quant;m-quant);
      ord;
      ?*ord, num;
      ?*m-quant, m-n;
      ?*n, ed;
      ?*n, ing;
vg:- (do;does;did), ?not, pres-inf;
   pres-inf;
   ed;
   (have;has;had), ?not, been, ?not, (ed;ing);
   (have;has;had), ?not, ed;
   (am;are;is;was;were), ?not, (ed;ing);
   (am;are;is;..), ?not, being, ?not, ed;
   fut, ?not, pres-inf;
   fut, ?not, have, ?not, ed;
   fut, ?not, have, ?not, been, ?not, (ed;ing);
   fut, ?not, be, ?not, (ed;ing);
   fut, ?not, be, ?not, being, ?not, ed.

adv-ph:- rel-tim, (ing;decl-sent);
     prep, np;
     rel-dir;
     (in;with), ment;
     ?(by;with;of), ing-ph;
     ?*emph, adv;
     ?de-emph, adv;
     ?rel-quant, adv;
     emph, much, rel-quant, adv;
     adv, enough;
     to, inf-vp;
     almost, adv, enough;
vp:- ?*adv-ph, (am;are;is;was;were), adj-ph, ?*adv-ph;
   ?*adv-ph, intr-vg, ?*adv-ph;
   ?*adv-ph, st-vg, ?*adv-ph, ?decl-sent;
   ?*adv-ph, st-vg, ?*adv-ph, np, ?np
imper_sent:- ?do, pres-2ndpers, ?adv, ?(pp;np), ?pp, ?adv
quest:-(why;who;when;..),q-vb,?(np;pp),?adv
quest:-(why;who;when;..),is, it, that, decl-sent
q_vb:-(am;are;is;was;were), np;
     ed, np;
     (have;has;had), np, ?not, been, ?not, (ed;ing);
     (have;has;had), np, ?not, ed;
     (am;are;is;was;were), np, ?not, (ed;ing);
     (am;are;is;..), np, ?not, being, ?not, ed;
     fut,np, ?not, pres_inf;
     fut,np, ?not, have, ?not, ed;
     fut, np, ?not, be, ?not, (ed;ing);
     fut, np, ?not, be, ?not, being, ?not, ed.

9.5 Test Sentences

These sentences are offered to the reader as examples for testing the grammar. Optional expressions have been placed in brackets.
1. *John kicked Bill.*
2. *John was kicked (by Bill) (in anger) (in the kitchen).*
3. *John died (quickly) (after the play) (as the result of taking poison).*
4. *Having taken poison, John died.*
5. *(Being insane), John took his own life.*
6. *Having been mistaken for a policeman John laughed heartily.*
7. *For a long time John thought of writing a book.*
8. *Behind the door there was a large man waiting for me.*
9. *That John was mistaken for a policeman surprised us all.*

10. *John thought that Bill was stupid.*
11. *John thought Bill stupid.*
12. *She always stays in bed on Sunday mornings.*
13. *It is necessary to pay the rent once per week.*
14. *I just love those roses.*
15. *He completely forgot about the lecture.*
16. *I doubt quite seriously that John came yesterday.*
17. *I did not do that.*
18. *When John took the book he forgot to sign the register.*
19. *It is strange that John is coming.*
20. *Big honest Joe kept the money in his pocket.*
21. *John went to the pictures with Mary.*
22. *I would hate for John to lose it.*
23. *Everyone prefers you to drive slowly.*
24. *He is eager to please.*
25. *He is easy to please.*
26. *Some people prefer driving slowly.*
27. *He is going to jump.*
28. *The doctor agreed to examine John.*
29. *Walking is a very pleasant way to spend an afternoon.*
30. *Going to the bank, John deposited 100 pounds.*
31. *Lots of green water was pouring over the stern.*
32. *The grim faced tight lipped hard riding cowboys rounded up the cattle.*
33. *The boy we all liked came to dinner.*
34. *The boy who had read the book put his hand up.*
35. *The largest of the boys put his hand up.*
36. *Jack and Jill went up the hill.*
37. *Jack went up the hill and Jill went down the hill.*
38. *For every man there should be two questions to be answered.*
39. *They spoke to the boy who is a pupil at the school.*
40. *Johnston, the largest of the men, refused to answer.*
41. *Jones, then a student, was unable to pay.*
42. *They elected as chairman the only person who had not spoken.*
43. *I liked the book but hated the film.*
44. *He was a man who, unaccountably, had few friends.*
45. *Happily, they came home safely.*
46. *It is certain that he will not will approve.*
47. *Having a car, he drove to London.*
48. *While watching the film he began to smell burning.*
49. *The lady, who was by this time able to tell who had interrupted, spoke directly to the offending person.*
50. *You can never hear what he is saying.*

9.6 The Grammar as ATN Diagrams

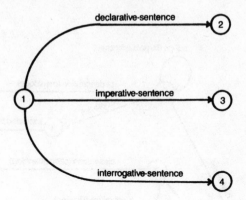

Fig. 9.1. ATN for a sentence.

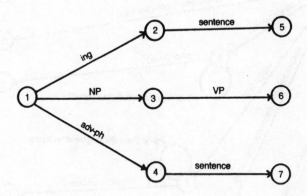

Fig. 9.2. ATN for a declarative sentence.

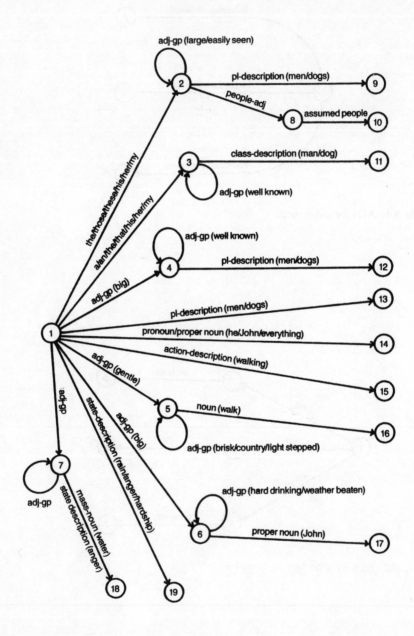

Fig. 9.3. ATN for a noun-group.

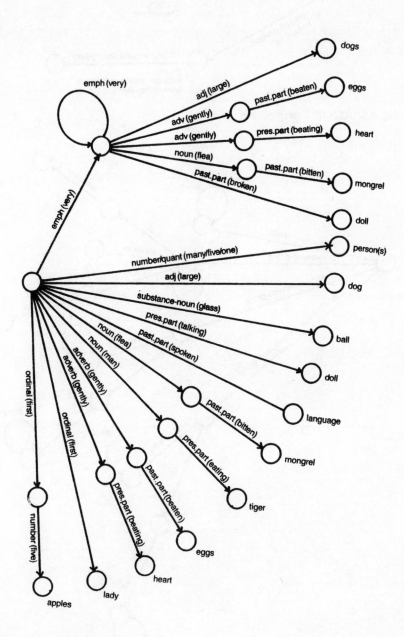

Fig. 9.4. ATN for an adj-group.

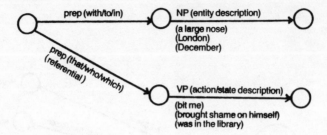

Fig. 9.5. ATN for a prep-phrase.

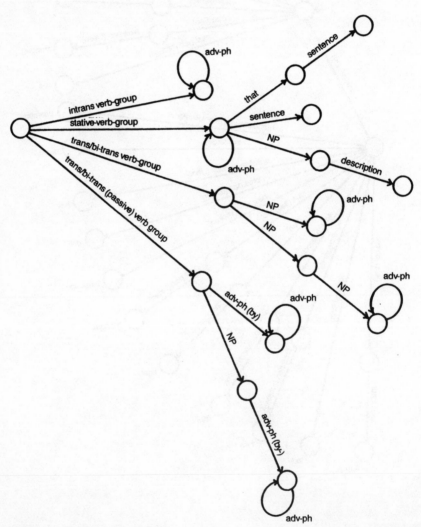

Fig. 9.6. ATN for a verb-phrase.

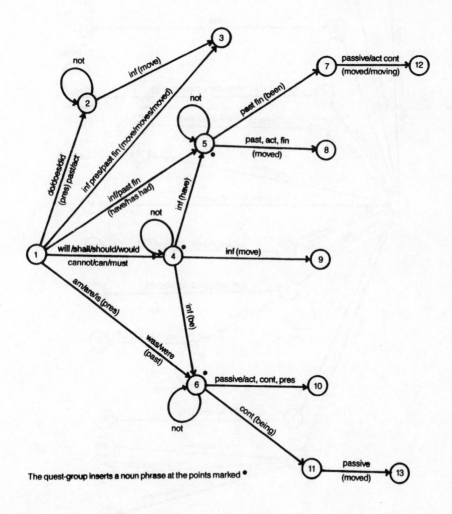

Fig. 9.7. ATN for a verb-group and quest-group.

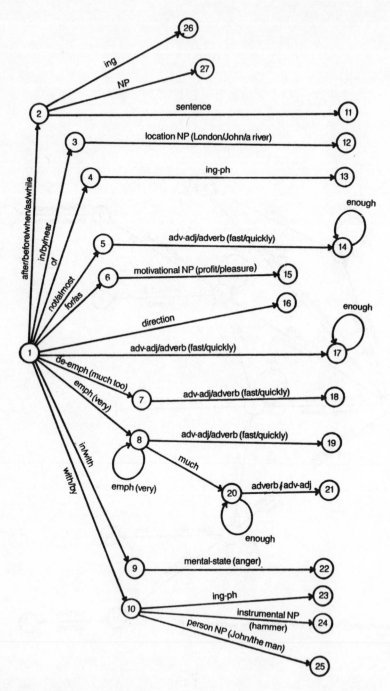

Fig. 9.8. ATN for an adv-phrase.

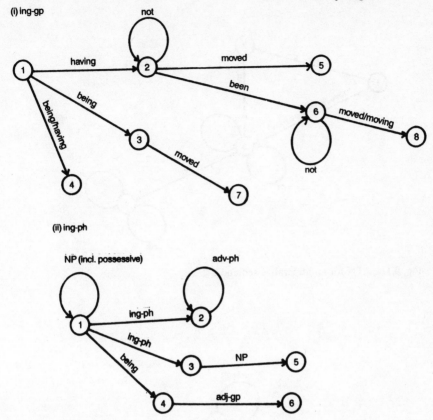

(i) ing-gp

(ii) ing-ph

Fig. 9.9. ATNs for an ing-group and an ing-phrase.

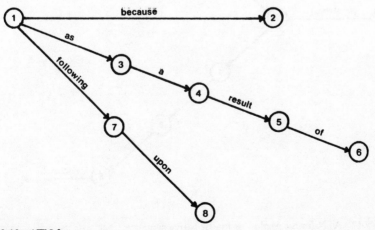

Fig. 9.10. ATN for a conseq.

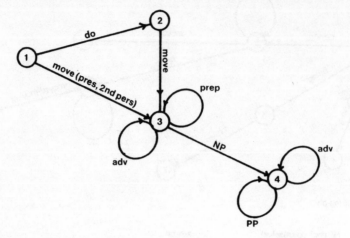

Fig. 9.11. ATN for an imperative sentence.

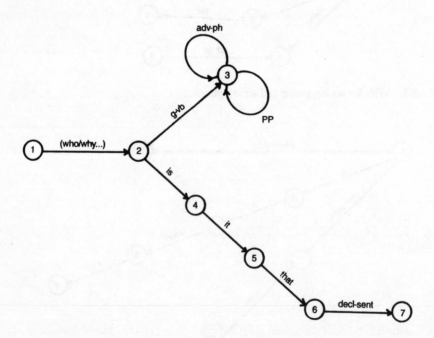

Fig. 9.12. ATN for a question or interrogative sentence.

CHAPTER 10

From Syntax to Semantics

10.1 A Review

The micro-graphics world illustrated several features and techniques which are widely applicable:

(a) The translation of natural English into some other form of representation which was more useful. By 'more useful' we mean that the new form of representation can be processed readily to create some desirable end product (in our case a screen display). The form of representation was provided by an (assumed) existing system, and so we could concentrate upon the translation problem.

(b) The development of a specialised grammar (specifically for the subset of English involved) using both BNF and ATN notation.

(c) The realisation of an ATN in the form of a program (POP11 and Prolog), with side-effects which are the way the internal text or representational form is generated.

(d) The problem of ambiguity and the need for 'back-tracking'. How back-tracking can be achieved by means of recursion.

(e) Reference and the object of reference being a segment of the internal representation.

(f) The need to identify and isolate a segment of internal representation and label it as the object of reference (or referent). We note that this ability to 'lasso' an arbitrary segment of code in the internal representation is of fundamental importance and requires complicated pattern-matching facilities. The entities identified in this way could be objects or actions.

(g) The techniques of pattern matching and the need for recursive (back-tracking) mechanisms. The idea of instantiation.

(h) We noted that as there was an increase in the complexity of the subset of natural language being tackled, there was a requirement for a corresponding increase in the complexity of the representational form. This was evident as we introduced progressively the representation of colour, movement, objects which undergo changes of shape and form, and the notion of object-histories extending over time.

(i) We introduced the idea of time-stamps, and noted that the properties of relative time were preserved (locally) for an entity when we copied and re-located it in absolute time.

(j) We introduced the idea of a 'concept' as a segment of internal representation for which the parameters had not been assigned specific values. We described this as a 'generic' representation — that is, capable of generating any specific example of the concept by the assignment of particular values to these parameters and by adding additional non-standard properties.

(k) We discussed the tense of verbs in terms of the time-stamps already introduced.

(l) We discussed the structure of a noun phrase, first in terms of the micro-graphics world but also in general terms.

(m) We have developed a general grammar for a significant subset of English which is not confined to the requirements of the micro-graphics world.

10.2 NL System Applications

The micro-graphics world allowed us to avoid asking the most important question of all. What do we require of an NL system?

NL systems have been developed for many applications including:

(a) Translation from one natural language to another.

(b) Processing natural language descriptions (newspaper reports) and reducing these to a standardised format which is appropriate for a conventional information retrieval system.

(c) The reduction of scientific reports to a standardised form for the same purpose.

(d) Processing natural language queries to an information retrieval system or database system and mapping these into a conventional query language.

(e) Processing student answers to questions posed by a computerised assessment system, and matching these answers to standard answers supplied by the author of the assessment system.

(f) Processing natural language statements in order to produce a paraphrase of the original statement (also in natural language).

(g) Conducting a dialogue with people in order to elicit information.

(h) The control of robotic devices in natural language.

Some of these applications are intensely practical and some are of purely academic interest. In each case the form of internal representation used is different and designed specifically for the application.

Although some of the systems actually developed have been moderately successful, the general goal of achieving a human-like performance remains beyond the current state of the art. One of the best known and successful systems yet developed was that due to Winograd. It was essentially a robot control application with a very restricted domain of objects which required manipulation. In it every reference is identified as a reference to some object within the domain.

Winograd himself has pointed out the limitations of his system. For example, it has no way of dealing with objects which do not exist within the domain, such as imaginary objects. Winograd's own example is the statement 'I want to own the fastest car in the world'. The simple-minded representation of this is to search the list of representations of all cars in the world and select the fastest as the referent. Yet the speaker is not referring to that car, he is actually referring to a car in his own imagination which is faster than the (currently) fastest car.

Charniak attempted to apply the techniques which Winograd had developed to another domain of discourse — the understanding of children's stories. He found that the techniques were totally inappropriate, and in a very influential thesis analysed the reasons for the failure of the techniques to transfer to another domain. The main reason was that an NL system requires the kind of understanding of its domain possessed by humans. In the case of the simple 'blocks world' used by Winograd there was not much to understand. But in the case of the children's stories the domain was the real world, and the wealth of information required for a proper understanding was overwhelming. In the real world people do not say exactly what they mean. They refer obliquely to things and expect others to make the appropriate deductions, and this comes so naturally to humans that we often overlook the fact that it is so.

The history of NL processing is a story of optimism giving way to a realisation that the volume of information, and the capacity to process that information required by a human-like system, is very much greater than had been anticipated.

In the early stages of NL processing, workers in the field limited their goals. It was felt that topics such as metaphor, beliefs and intentions could be excluded as unnecessary complications, at least in the first instance. It has turned out that trying to produce a human-like system without these aspects is like trying to ride a stationary bicycle. It may seem that the movement of the bicycle is an unnecessary complication, but without it the problem is actually insoluble.

We can achieve limited success for limited goals. We can write an 'intelligent' front end system for a database, or process newspaper reports into standard form, but these systems do not match human performance. The essence of human performance is its flexibility. When we provide a human with some information there is no artificial limit on the way that information will be used. The human can choose to behave like a robot, translate the statement into another natural language, paraphrase the statement, match it to another statement which means the same thing, parse it, answer the statement with another, or ignore the statement altogether. A system which can mimic only one of these behaviours is not human-like. The only way for a system to behave in a human-like way is to process the natural language in the same way as a human would do. This does not mean that the actual mechanism of the computer system (in hardware terms) must be exactly the same as that of the human brain. It merely means that the mechanism must be an analogue of the human brain processes.

It is clear that the way humans represent the meaning of a statement is much more complex and much more general in its applicability than anything we have looked at yet.

When a human chooses to behave in a particular way in response to a statement, he or she does so for some reason. Motivation is involved. It may be the desire to please the speaker, or to insult the speaker or impress some other bystander. Without some analogue of such motivation a computerised NL system could not choose an appropriate response.

It is not clear that we actually want to create such a system. The limited and specialised goals of database access, robotic control, question answering etc. may be quite sufficient for our purposes. But the history of natural language processing has also been a record of dissatisfaction with current systems and continuing efforts to improve performance — to make the systems more human-like.

The successful achievement of that goal may not result in a system which we would actually want to use, but may provide us with a better understanding of ourselves.

10.3 An Outline of the next Chapters

In the next few chapters of the book we shall examine a number of techniques which have been used by various research workers. They are introduced not in chronological order but in order of increasing semantic complexity. Each technique has its uses, and if the reader is bent on practical implementations he or she should select and adapt the technique which is most appropriate to the application in mind. There is no sense in developing a system which is more complex than is actually necessary.

The progression of techniques not only exhibits a steady increase in semantic complexity but a steady decrease in the importance of syntactical analysis. It also represents a progression towards a more human-like capability.

Part 2

CHAPTER 11

Case Grammar

11.1 Case: Syntax or Semantics?

It is considered ungrammatical to say or write:

'I done it'
'You goes'
'She did it to he'

The notion of 'case' was introduced into traditional grammars to describe this phenomenon and give precision to the restrictions which render these statements ungrammatical. Three cases were recognised — the subjective, objective and genitive (or possessive). For example, the pronoun 'I' is always associated with the subject of a sentence. 'Me' is always associated with the object of a sentence and 'mine' is the genitive form. In this type of analysis 'case' is a syntactical phenomenon.

More recently, however, an argument has been developed for a notion of 'case' which is associated with some role which an entity is playing in the events or situation described. As such, 'case' is a semi-semantic notion, and the role refers to the entities which are identified as the meanings of various noun phrases in a sentence rather than to individual nouns. In this form of analysis the main verb determines the various case roles which can be associated with the nouns or noun phrases in the sentence.

Consider for example the two sentences:

S1 'I did it'
S2 'It was done by me'.

Traditionally, in S1 'I' has subjective case and in S2 'me' has the objective case. But, in S1 'I' is the agent and in S2 'me' is also the agent (i.e. the person doing the action).

11.2 Traditional (or Syntactical) Case Classifications

A sentence with a transitive verb has, in its simplest form, the pattern:

<subject> <verb> <object>

The main noun in the noun phrase which corresponds to the <subject> slot is said have the subjective case. The importance of case, for syntactic analysis, lies in the fact that when pronouns are used they must be used in the form which agrees with the case slot they fill.

subject = I, we, he, she, they, who
object = me, us, him, her, them, who(m)
genitive = my, our, his, her, their, whose

The possessive or genitive case can also be recognised in nouns, so that we have such phrases as 'the boy's book'. Here the word 'boy's' has the genitive case. If the verb has passive voice the pattern is:

<subject> <passive-verb> by <object>

The subjective form 'I' is used in both the sentences 'I kicked the boy' and 'I was kicked by the boy' even although in one sentence 'I' is carrying out the action and in the second sentence 'I' is the recipient of the action. This is why we describe this type of case analysis as syntactic.

Where the verb is intransitive the surface structure pattern does not contain an object. The simplest pattern is:

<subject> <verb>   e.g. 'John slept'

The name 'subject', which is the case of the noun which precedes the verb, indicates that it is the main subject of discourse. It is also the focus of attention.

Although the early notion of case was intended to be purely syntactical, we can see in the notion of focus, and in the distinction between transitive and intransitive verbs, some notion of semantics creeping in. The difference between a transitive and an intransitive verb is that the first is associated with some action being done to something, while the second is associated with some action which does not require the participation of another entity. The genitive case (or possessive) also has some hint of semantics about it, although the emphasis is on the form of word to be used, not the role which it is playing. These might be thought of as very 'broad brush' semantic properties.

We will not develop the discussion of traditional surface structure case classifications any further because it has not played a significant role in the development of NL-systems. It should be noted, however, that the identification of the correct surface structure case of a noun has often been used as a stepping stone to the identification of the more semantically based case classification.

11.3 Semantic Case Classifications

In this type of case analysis we are concerned with the roles which various entities are playing with respect to the meaning of a sentence. We are concerned with whether a person is the active 'agent' of an action or the passive recipient (or 'experiencer') of that action. We also note that sometimes an entity is an 'instrument' participating in some action without being the causative agent.

These descriptions 'agent', 'experiencer' and 'instrument' are examples of case classifications. A list of possible cases is given below. For each example the noun shown in capital letters is the one with the case being discussed. Various authorities have suggested several different case categories and an agreed set of case classifications appears to be elusive. The list below includes some from different sources.

Agent. The entity is the animate causative agent which causes the events described. Although it is not explicitly indicated, there is an assumption that the action is deliberate. This assumption can be removed by inserting an adverb such as 'accidentally' or made explicit by means of the adverb 'deliberately'.

> e.g. JOHN killed Bill.

Experiencer. The entity is the target of some action, the object to which the action is done. That is, its position changes, or its condition or state of existence is modified in some way as a result of the action taken.

> e.g. John killed BILL.
> BILL died.

Instrument. The entity is the means by which the action is carried out or is the immediate stimulus for the action.

> e.g. John killed Bill with a KNIFE.
> A HAMMER broke the window.

Result. The entity came into existence as a result of the action taken.

> e.g. John built a HOUSE.

Dative. The entity is being given something.

> e.g. John gave a book to BILL.

Comitative. The entity accompanies something.

> e.g. John went to the pictures with MARY.

Goal. The entity is the target location of some movement.

> e.g. John went to LONDON.

Source. The entity is the location from which some motion took place.

> e.g. John came from LONDON.

Other case classifications have been suggested. These include: counter-agent, patient, beneficiary, force, vehicle, material, referent, range, causal-actant, theme, donor, and many others. The multiplicity of these testifies to the fact that no classification scheme for case has been shown to be entirely satisfactory.

11.4 Case-frames

The basic method of determining the case of an entity depends upon the idea that each verb has a predisposition to be associated with particular cases. From this we get the notion of a 'case-frame' — a structure which has slots available into which various entities can be slotted if they have the right syntactical and semantic properties. The idea is analogous to chemical bonds. A molecule has a predisposition to bond with other molecules (or atoms or ions etc) if they are in the correct position and have the correct form (cf. syntactical properties) and if they have the correct chemical properties (cf. semantic properties). While each molecule has unique chemical properties of its own we can identify classes of molecules which have similar bonding characteristics, and the same is true of verbs. We can identify classes of verbs which appear to share a common case-frame structure.

In the description which follows we shall distinguish between the syntactical case and the semantic case by prefixing these with syn- and sem- respectively.

Case-frame 1

---

verbs: kill, hit, smash, break, hurt,

----

sem-agent = syn-subject (if animate) (active voice)
else   = by <agent> (passive voice)

----

sem-experiencer = syn-object (active voice)
else   = syn-subject (passive voice)

----

sem-instrument = syn-subject (if not animate)
else   = with <instrument>

The case frame above is somewhat cryptic. The explanation is as follows. In any sentence containing the verbs 'kill', 'hit', 'smash' etc. the noun phrase associated with the 'agent' case will be found to be the grammatical subject (in an active voice sentence). If, on the other hand, the sentence has the passive voice (e.g. 'He was killed by John') then the agent case will be found to be associated with the noun phrase preceded by the preposition 'by'.

The 'experiencer' case will be associated with the grammatical object in an active voice sentence, and with the grammatical subject in the passive voice sentence.

The 'instrumental' case is associated with the grammatical subject in an active voice sentence, if that subject is inanimate, for example 'A hammer broke the window'. It is also often introduced by the preposition 'with', (e.g. 'John broke the window with a hammer'). The instrumental case presents particular difficulties and the reader will immediately begin to see possible objections to this analysis. In the sentence 'John was killed by a bus' our analysis would suggest that the bus was the agent, whereas in the sentence 'John was killed by Bill with a bus', the analysis casts the bus in the role of instrument. It is clearly possible for an entity to be both agent and instrument simultaneously. The problem has been discussed extensively in the research literature, and to date no completely satisfactory solution has emerged.

The basic idea is that the case frame will be implemented as a data structure which is associated with each verb classification. Associated with each slot in the frame will be the conditions which should be true of any entity which fills the slot. Since these properties often refer to syntactic properties, it is anticipated that the case-frame analysis will follow upon a syntactical analysis, during which each noun phrase will have its syntactical category determined and tacked on to it.

For comparison we provide a second case-frame, this time for verbs which are intransitive and therefore do not normally take a grammatical object.

Case-frame 2

---

verbs: die, sleep, weep, cry, smile,

----

sem-experiencer = syn-subject (active voice)

----

sem-location = to <location noun>

Here again the reader might raise objections. While one does not normally 'die something', or 'sleep something', one does from time to time encounter sentences such as 'He died a quick death' or 'He slept a dreamless sleep'. Both of these constructions suggest a more active role than that of 'experiencer' for 'he'. We can also have such constructions as 'He died of poison', which is equivalent to 'He was killed by poison'. This appears to justify the role of 'experiencer' for 'he'. These problems are the result of trying to force a case-frame analysis on a set of verbs as though all members of the set were in this respect identical. In fact all are different in meaning, and therefore possess subtle differences of case dependency which will show up if we seek them out. We shall return to an analysis of the deficiencies of case-grammar in section 11.5.

The prepositions (by, in, on, to, beside, above,...) indicate locative case, but since some of these prepositions also denote other relationships in other circumstances this is not always helpful. One can invent sentences in which the locative case is indicated by the preposition 'in' but in which the same preposition is used for other purposes, e.g.:

'John kicked Bill in a rage, in the kitchen, in our house, in Aberdeen, in December, in a flash, in the stomach, in defiance of my instructions, in full sight of everyone, in my book.'

'He hit the girl with his hand'.
'He hit the girl with red hair.'

It is clear from these examples that the prepositions 'in' and 'with' cannot be accepted as an unambiguous indicator of the locative case or the instrumental case. It also indicates the extent to which we must rely upon examination of the semantic properties of each entity in order to determine its case. Similar examples could be generated for every other preposition.

In most case-frame based systems the case-frame includes slots for:

Tense of the verb (present/past/future/infinitive),
Aspect (perfect/imperfect or continuing/completed),
Mood of the sentence (imperative/declarative/question),
Modality (actual/possible),
Voice (active/passive).

These factors, which are often carried by auxiliary verbs, are interrelated to the case-slots. For example a transitive verb with passive voice does not need to have an agent but must have an experiencer, (e.g. 'John was killed').

Although, as we have hinted, a case grammar does not provide a good foundation for an NL-system, it has been included here because it represents an important stage in the development of more useful techniques, and because an examination of the reasons why it is unsatisfactory provides a clue to the nature of more promising approaches. It is also the case that the notion of case can be used to augment some other formalism to produce an improved system overall. One of the difficulties often found with an ATN grammar is the problem of dealing with prepositional phrases. The extreme example we gave above for the preposition 'in' shows how much ambiguity is often associated with prepositional phrases. A case-frame for the verb can indicate a predisposition for certain prepositional phrases. The verb 'to blame' for example has a potential case-slot for a prepositional phrase beginning with 'on', (e.g. 'He blamed the failure on Joe').

The diagram below illustrates the way a case-frame can be used along with a simple ATN.

The dotted-line arrows are intended to indicate the creation and update of data structures as a side-effect of traversing certain arcs. The traversal of the verb arc creates the appropriate case-frame. Since this does not exist at the time the first np-arc is traversed, traversal of the first np-arc merely creates a data structure representing the 'subject' case. After the case-frame has been created the traversal of other arcs can update its case-slots directly.

An alternative approach involves the use of 'demons'. These are functions which are placed within each case-slot. When the case-frame is created these are activated one at a time, and each begins to seek out the entity which fits its conditions best. This is a powerful technique which has a number of applications.

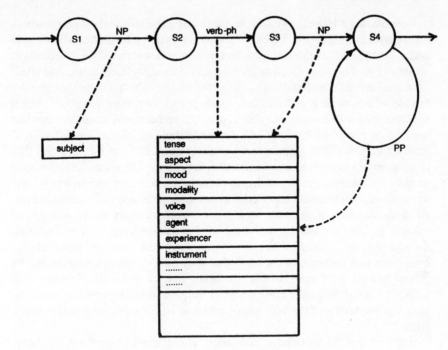

Fig. 11.1. The creation and update of registers as an ATN is traversed.

11.5 Why a Case Grammar is unsatisfactory

One argument against case grammar can be summarised as follows. A grammar consists of a set of categories within which all words are classified, and a set of grammatical patterns or sentence-patterns which are allowable with respect to these categories. The idea is crucially dependent upon all words within a single grammatical category behaving in exactly the same way with respect to the patterns. It should be possible to replace any word in a pattern by another word in the same grammatical category, without rendering the sentence ungrammatical (although the meaning may be and probably will be changed).

The cases of a case grammar are semantic categories. They relate, not to the words involved, but to what the words mean, and the roles played by the entities associated with those meanings within the overall interpretation of a sentence. The idea is based upon the notion that actions can be categorised with respect to these roles, so that we can identify role-patterns just as we identify grammatical patterns, and that we can categorise verbs according to those patterns.

It is arguable that the meanings of words, and particularly of verbs, are much more complex than can be captured by a set of role-patterns, and that therefore we can never define a universally satisfactory set of case-frames which are tied to verbs alone.

Role-playing is intimately concerned with cause and effect relationships which form chains linking events. Verbs are the main way that information about cause and effect chains is communicated, but in some cases some of the information is carried by, or is implicit in, a noun. Consider, for example, the cause-and-effect information (and therefore the role-slot information) which is communicated by the use of nouns such as 'fertiliser', 'poison' and 'computer program'. When these are used within a sentence they convey information which would otherwise need to be conveyed by the verb. An understanding of the word 'fertiliser' involves knowing that plants grow by taking nutrient from the soil, and that placing certain materials in the soil aids this process. The noun 'fertiliser' may identify the material concerned, but understanding would be incomplete if it did not contain the additional knowledge about the actions and their consequences. An understanding of the verb 'to fertilise' involves exactly the same items of knowledge, even though the verb is the label of the action and not the material. To a large extent, therefore, the two words, noun and verb, can substitute for each other in a sentence in the sense that they indicate the roles which can be played, provided the other words are chosen to make good the elements each lacks. The case-frame idea, however, in its simplest form, is dependent upon the idea that the verb and the verb alone carries or conveys the information about roles.

In the set of verbs provided as examples of case-frame 1 transitive verbs above, we might have been tempted to include the verb 'to poison' (on purely semantic grounds). It has, after all, a similarity to 'hit', 'hurt' and 'kill'. We can use it in similar sentence patterns:

'John killed Bill'
'John poisoned Bill'
'John killed Bill with arsenic'
'John poisoned Bill with arsenic'
'Arsenic killed Bill'
'Arsenic poisoned Bill'

Consider, however, the sentence (S1) 'John poisoned Bill's drink'. There is no equivalent for 'kill'. The sentence (S2) 'John killed Bill's drink' may be grammatical but it is semantically anomalous and 'drink' has a different case ('experiencer?'). We can have (S3) 'John put poison in Bill's drink'.

In these sentences we have empirical evidence that 'to poison' is to be classified in a different way from 'to kill'. But our argument goes further.

In the case of the two sentences S1 and S3 most people would agree that they have very similar if not identical meanings. However in S1 'Bill's drink' fills the experiencer case-slot, while in the latter Bill's drink fills the location case-slot. The difference is due to the fact that in one sentence much of the cause-and-effect information is carried by the verb 'poisoned' whereas in the other the same information is carried by the noun 'poison'. That is, the verb 'poisoned' conveys the same information as 'put poison in'. We might therefore (taking liberties with the grammar) describe the group of words 'put poison in' as the 'verb' of the second sentence, and this new composite verb would have the same case-slots as the verb 'to poison'.

The meaning of 'to poison' covers both the act of placing a poisonous substance in a suitable medium for ingestion, and the possible consequences which follow. If the syn-object is animate then it is assumed that the consequences have occurred; if the syn-object is inanimate then the verb is taken as describing the action of placing the poisonous substance in some medium identified by the syn-object.

The semantic representation of 'to poison' must therefore have a structure which in simplified form has the following ingredients:

The actors in this play:

    <agent A>
    <poisonous substance B>
    <medium C>
    <experiencer D>

The action:

    <A causes B to enter C>
    <D causes C and B to enter D>
    <entry of B into D causes D to be sick>
    <D dies>

From this 'scenario' we can identify the uninstantiated elements (actors) A,B,C and D. There must, therefore, be possible case-bonds for each of these, and so the case-frame structure emerges as a consequence of the semantic structure. Note, however, that the information contained in this scenario can be communicated both by the verb 'to poison' and the noun 'poison'. For case grammar to be effective in capturing the semantic content of a sentence, it would need to take into account the information content of the nouns involved, not just that of the verbs.

Basically case-frame 1 above is telling a little story. It says that someone (the agent) did something (the action — no case-slot) to something (the experiencer), possibly by causing something (the instrument) to cause the action to happen to the experiencer. We could add other elements to the story, such as that the action took place somewhere (the location) and so on. The frame with its blank slots tells that basic stereotyped story, and the filling in of the various case-slots fleshes it out and particularises it. What that story lacks, however, is any suggestion of detail, and any sense of consequence. It could be argued that we erred in placing the verb 'to kill' and the verb 'to poison' in the same case-category. There are other verbs for which a common case-category is harder to invalidate. Consider, for example, the verbs 'to hurt' and 'to kill'.

'John hurt Bill'
'John killed Bill'

and for (almost) every other sentence structure involving 'hurt' the word 'kill'
can be substituted without loss of grammatical sense and without destroying the
case-slot pattern. Consider however 'John was hurt until screaming'. The
sentence is somewhat contrived, but its meaning is clear enough. The question to
be asked concerns the correct case classification for 'screaming' in the case-frame
of 'hurt', and whether there can be any equivalent case-slot associated with
'killed'. Hurting can continue over a period of time 'until' some condition or
event; death is an instantaneous event even although it may be preceded by a
period of approach to death.

Case grammar is unsatisfactory because it simply does not go far enough in
the analysis of the semantic structure of the units it tries to characterise. A case-
frame is really a syntactical device trying to accommodate semantic information.
Case-frames are too rigid, and cannot accommodate the changes which are
necessary to deal with exceptional circumstances. A case grammar identifies the
case-slots associated with a verb, but does not make use of the information about
roles which can be associated with other words.

A case-frame representation of a 'story' is rather like someone telling us the
plot of a film by saying: 'It had a poor fast-shooting good guy, a rich bad guy,
a beautiful widow who owned a ranch, two wild Indians, a corrupt sheriff and an
amazingly intelligent horse'. No doubt we can fill in the blanks for ourselves
without too much difficulty, but as a narrative it leaves something to be desired.

Earlier we made an analogy between case grammars and the idea of chemical
bonding between molecules. The classification of chemicals based on ideas of
bonding has been extremely successful. That classification scheme, however, is
based upon a well-established theory of molecular structure. The bonding
characteristics of a chemical are a consequence of its structure.

A case grammar is similar to an empirical law of bonding which is not
illuminated by having an underlying theory. As a consequence we may be
tempted to classify in the same way two examples of 'case' which are actually
different although they may have superficial similarities. Likewise we may be
tempted to separate two verbs because they have some different characteristics
with respect to their case-frame although they have an underlying similarity.
Later we shall develop an argument in favour of the scenario approach to
semantic representation. It is of interest to note here, however, that the scenario
approach can explain the existence of case-slots.

In spite of the limitations of case grammars, they have been a spawning
ground for a number of very interesting NL-systems.

CHAPTER 12

Frame-Based Systems

12.1 The Terrorist Attack

The idea of a case-frame described in the last section can be extended. Instead of considering the case structure of a single sentence, we might consider the case structure of an entire narrative. Many stories are fairly stereotyped (like our cowboy film described in section 11.5). In these circumstances, provided others are well aware of the standard storyline, it is sufficient merely to identify the role-playing participants and associate them with their stereotyped roles.

One possible application for such an approach concerns the need to condense large volumes of text into a more accessible form. People involved in medical or biological research, for example, are required to read enormous numbers of research papers which are often of a stereotyped form. (e.g. The effect of <chemical-reagent> on <biological-tissue>). Likewise news agencies and industrial and financial analysts are also required to read large volumes of text which can be structured into a standardised form. The recognition of the standardised form of many reports has led to the development of systems which 'understand' various classified texts in terms of a standardised 'frame'.

For example, a frame developed for reading newspaper reports on terrorist outrages might identify certain role-playing participants and certain attributes and factors, e.g.

    date
    time
    terrorists
        number
        nationality
        faction
        leader
        cause
    locus of attack
        vehicle/building
        country (origin)
        country (via)
        country (ending)
    hostages
        number
        nationality

    leader
      threat
    deadline
      date
      time
    demands
      money
      release of
      escape vehicle
    negotiator
      name
      country
    result
      compliance/resistance
    date
    time
    enforcement agency
    death of
    injury of
    release of

The text is scanned, and the slots in the standardised frame are filled in with the details as they are discovered. The data identified could then be stored in a database for later retrieval or collation with other such stories.

Consider the following example:

> *Early on Monday morning three terrorists seized control of the Ruritanian embassy in Utopia. They are holding the ambassador and 19 of his staff hostage, and are demanding the release of 10 prisoners held by the Ruritanians. They have threatened to kill their hostages and blow up the building at midnight on Wednesday if their demands are not met. Government soldiers have surrounded the building, and the Chief of Police is attempting to negotiate the release of the hostages. In a telephone message from the embassy the ambassador has said that the hostages are not being badly treated, but that he feared that the terrorists would carry out their threat if the prisoners were not released. The names of the terrorists are unknown but it is suspected that they are members of the RFF (Ruritanian Freedom Fighters).*

Once the case-slots in the frame have been filled in the system could answer questions — if these are related to the standard items in the frame — and it could match two such stories by recognising that they were concerned with the same event (by matching the information in the forms). We might describe this as reporting by form filling.

The analysis of the complete problem would consume more time and space than we can afford here, but we can do two things to help the reader towards a solution — we can show that the problem is a modified form of the 'front-end system', and we can provide a solution for a small part of the complete problem, leaving the reader to complete the process.

Note that although a ready-made representational language does not exist initially we have provided such a representational language by creating a 'frame'. To see that that is the case we should look again at the micro-graphics problem. The graphics language could be regarded as consisting of a frame:

```
point
   name:
   coordinate-1:
   coordinate-2:
line
   point-1:
   point-2:
```

and when we process the natural language text we 'understand it' by filling in the appropriate slots in the frames above. Of course we must be able to add more and more examples of these frames as we proceed, and it may be necessary to add more slots for colours, time-stamps etc. We should not be confused, however, by the fact that the frame format looks rather different from the graphics language statement format. They are functionally or logically identical with respect to the information stored, and since they both have a fixed format it would be a trivial task to write a program to translate from one to the other.

The second part of our partial solution requires us to write a grammar from the terrorist story text which will relate it to the slots in the frame above.

Consider the first sentence, which we shall term a 'seizure sentence'. A seizure sentence tells us what was seized and who did the seizing. It may also tell us where and/or when the seizure took place.

We shall use the dot notation ... to indicate that we have not exhausted all the possible patterns.

The grammar might look like this:

```
qss:- <when-id>ss
qss:- ss/<when-id>
qss:- <where-id>ss
qss:- ss<where-id> .
   ...
```

where ss = seizure sentence and qss stands for 'qualified seizure sentence'. There are at least four alternative patterns. More can be added by having both a <when-id> and a <where-id> in the same sentence.

```
where-id:- in <town>
where-id:- in <country>
when-id:- <daytime><datetime>
when-id:- <daytime>
```

when-id:- <datetime>
daytime:- at <clocktime> / early / late
clocktime:-integer.integer / noon / midnight
datetime:-today / last night / on <weekday>
weekday:- Monday / Tuesday / Wednesday / ...
town:- London / Paris / New York / ...
country:- America / Lebanon / Italy / ...
ss:-<qual-ter-agent><seize-verb><seized-obj>
ss:-<seized-obj><passive-seize-verb> by <qual-ter-agent>
ss:-<seized-obj><passive-seize-verb>
seize-verb:- seized / grabbed / took control of / ...
passive-seize-verb:- was seized / was grabbed / ...
qual-ter-agent:- <number><ter-agent>
qual-ter-agent:- <nationality><ter-agent>
qual-ter-agent:-ter-agent
ter-agent:- terrorists / <adj>terrorists
ter-agent:- men / <adj> men
ter-agent:- freedom fighters / ...
adj:- armed / hooded / masked / ...
number:- <integer> / many / a group of / ...
nationality:- Ruritanian / Utopian / ...
seized-obj:-<building> / <vehicle>
building:- <name> building / control tower / embassy / ...
vehicle:- airliner / liner / train / bus / ...

Exercise 12.1

As explained above, it is our intention only to give an indication of how a
solution to this problem might be developed. The reader might care to refine this
grammar and add other types of sentence. The exercise might be best suited to
a small team, with each member taking a different kind of sentence for analysis.
These would include:
  (a) the threat sentence (or phrase),
  (b) the 'storming the building' sentence (or phrase),
  (c) the hostage treatment sentence (or phrase), and so on.
  When a sentence type is successfully matched against the pattern described in
the grammar, the appropriate frame slots are filled in as a 'side-effect'. When a
word such as 'embassy' is encountered, then another 'side-effect' would be to call
up an 'embassy' frame which would have a structure such as:

embassy-frame:
    country of ownership:
    country of location:

city of location:
ambassador's name:
attache name:
number of staff:
...

This would augment the existing frame and introduce an augmentation to the grammar containing patterns for such stock phrases as 'a senior attache at the embassy said ...'

The final stage in this exercise is to construct a program which will process the frame(s) and produce a summary of the narrative. Such a system does not need to process every sentence in the text successfully. Sentences which do not correspond to the grammar can be ignored. It is usually sufficient to get a 'gist' of the narrative to be able to produce a reasonable summary.

12.2 Frames within Frames and Inheritance

The example we used in the previous section was confined mainly to one frame. It is possible, however, to use several frames at the same time to obtain a much richer representation, and we hinted at this with the mention of the 'embassy frame'. The embassy frame is an example of an 'object frame'. An object frame contains slots for the normal properties of a particular type of object. When we are filling in the slots of a frame we might find that the appropriate slot-filler is another frame, possibly an object frame. This augments the grammar and generates another set of slots to be filled.

One feature of object frames is that objects can usually be classified in a hierarchical structure. An Alsatian, a Corgie, an Airedale and a Spaniel are all examples of the concept 'dog'. A dog is an example of the concept 'animal', and so on.

The frames which are associated with these objects can be organised into a hierarchical data structure as shown in Figure 12.1. In these circumstances it is normal to assume that all the subordinate entities in a hierarchy possess all of the properties shown for their common superior entity, at all levels in the hierarchy. Only those properties which are peculiar to a given entity are shown explicitly, and it is assumed that these are also shared by the entities below it in the hierarchy. This property of a hierarchical structure is called the 'inheritance property'. That is, all entities 'inherit' all properties from their parents (automatically). While it may add a degree of complexity to the processing of frames, the inheritance property allows a very great saving of data storage, and in the labour involved in creating new frames. If we wish to add a new object frame to our collection (say for a 'Dalmatian'), it is sufficient to indicate that it is one of the class 'dog' instead of repeating all of the properties which are common to dogs. We need only add the information that a Dalmatian is white

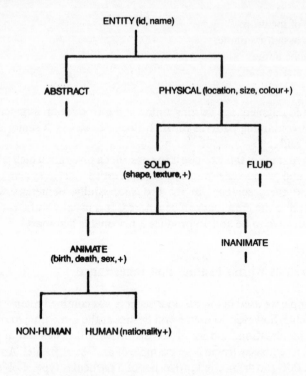

The "+" symbol indicates that the list of properties is extended by all those belonging to the parental node. Thus a human entity has the properties (nationality, sex, birth, death, shape, texture, location, size, colour, id, name)

Fig. 12.1. A hierarchical data structure with 'inheritance'.

with black spots and is often called 'a blotting paper dog'. To construct the hierarchy each object frame should be provided with two extra slots. The first is for 'classification' and the second is for 'examples'. These are in effect the pointers to the superior entity and the inferior entities respectively.

Special languages have been developed to facilitate the use of frames, of which the best known is FRL (Frame Representation Language). These languages, however, are not widely available, and the construction of a frame hierarchy (and the primitive procedures for handling frames) is a useful exercise.

12.3 Demons

In section 11.4 we described briefly the idea of embedding functions within the case-slots of a case-frame. These functions would then be activated and seek out the appropriate entity to act as a case-slot filler. The idea has particular relevance to frame-hierarchies, and the functions, or 'demons' as they are sometimes called, can be used for many purposes. In particular they can be activated whenever a case-frame is accessed in any way, with one set for update operations and another for retrieval operations. These can solve the problem of dealing with inheritance, since on accessing a frame the appropriate demon will be fired, and access its superior frames to retrieve the properties it should inherit, without these being explicitly contained in the first frame.

In a programming language such as Pascal it is not possible to handle the names of functions in the same way as data, but in languages such as POP11, LISP and Prolog this is commonplace. Given the facilities of these languages it is easy to insert into a frame the name of a function which is to be called whenever the frame is processed.

12.4 Thematic and Narrative Frames

We began the discussion of frames with a study of case grammar, and the idea of a case-frame which stored all the case-slots belonging to particular verbs. We noted that there were two kinds of case to be considered, those based on syntactic phenomena and those based on more semantic ideas. We have now progressed to frames which provide a standard set of slots for entities and properties associated with a 'theme' such as the terrorist attack the.ne. Frames of this type are often called 'thematic frames' to distinguish them from the next type we shall study — 'narrative frames'. Narrative frames are often also called 'scripts', and these are the topic of the next section.

CHAPTER 13

Scripts and Plans

13.1 From Frames to Scripts

Although frame-based systems such as the one described in the previous chapter are often entertaining to create, and can serve a useful purpose, most people would agree that they are unsatisfactory as a model for human natural language processing. Of course we all take advantage of the cliches used in news reports to cut the intellectual effort involved in understanding, but the frame-based system would be lost without them. It does not 'understand' the text in the same way that the small child reading the Peter and Jane story understands the text. Such a child builds an internal representation of the narrative which is dynamic and which conforms to the elementary laws of the physical world. If the story says *'Peter throws the ball'*, the child can visualise the ball describing a parabolic curve, rising and then falling. When the story says *'Rover catches the ball'*, the child visualises the dog catching the ball in its mouth. In other words the 'world knowledge' of the child is much richer than that provided by the simple frame data structure. He or she knows some facts concerning the way certain events 'cause' other events.

The frame-based system works because the humans who use it know the pattern of events involved in a terrorist hijack story. They fill in for themselves the connecting links between the bare facts stored in the frame. They know that the terrorists plan and execute the hijack. They know that the hostages are unwilling participants and would escape if possible. They know that the negotiators are in a dilemma, and could overpower the terrorists quite easily if they did not care about the consequences to the hostages, and so on. The frame-based system has no knowledge of the chronology of events, no knowledge of the motivation of the participants, no knowledge of the causation of events and therefore no knowledge of the implications of the events. It cannot fill in gaps in the story from its imagination and knowledge of the world.

In recognition of some of these deficiencies of frame-based systems another type of system, based on so-called 'scripts', has been developed.

13.2 Scripts

A script is still tied to stereotyped events, but it contains within it a representation of the chronology and causation involved. It tells a basic storyline, with blanks to be completed as an actual story is processed. Scripts can be somewhat complex, and a typical script will contain other simpler scripts within it (like subroutines). The difference between a script (or narrative frame) and a thematic frame as described in section 12.1 is not a sharp one. It is rather a difference of degree of detail, and hence of richness and of representational power.

A script which describes a student going to a college lecture might be structured as follows:

---

lecture script

---

players: student, lecturer
props: chair, notebook, pen, bag, desk, lecture room, college
time-of-occurrence: times-of-operation of college
location: location of college
event-sequence:
first: enter-lecture-room(student) script (**)
then: find-empty-desk script
then: sit-at-desk script
then: take-out-notebook script
then: enter-lecture-room (lecturer) script
then: give-lecture(lecturer) script
     take-notes(student) script (*)
then : ask-question(student,lecturer) script
finally: leave-lecture-room script

---

* = main concept
** = header

Each of the sub-scripts will be laid out in similar fashion. Sub-scripts will have sub-sub-scripts, and so on until primitive operations are used which require no further explanation. Primitive operations might involve the contact of pen on paper, the movement of the pen, the speaking of the lecturer and so on.

The idea underlying the use of scripts is that when one is invoked, as the script above might be by the sentence: 'John went to a lecture' the system (like a human) knows or anticipates all the remainder of the script. We do not need to be told that the lecturer spoke, that the students took notes etc. A script provides more information than a frame, and for that reason is more complex. Given the information — 'John went to a lecture' — both a frame- and a script-based system might then ask the question 'What did he use to write with?', but only the script would know that the act of writing would normally takes place after the act of entering the lecture room. A script therefore represents a standard or typical scenario, and if no other information is provided it can be assumed that the scenario has taken place according to expectations. An important feature of a script is that certain participants and props are assumed to be present even if there is no mention of them in the narrative. In fact the opposite is the case; the absence of an anticipated participant calls for comment rather than the reverse.

The events described by a script can be blocked by obstacles, as in the sentence 'John went to a lecture but the lecturer did not turn up'. Scripts should therefore be capable of modification as a story unfolds.

The most interesting implementations of the scripts idea also make use of the theory of conceptual dependencies, which we discuss in Chapter 14. We will, therefore, reserve the description of an implementation of scripts until Chapter 15.

13.3 Triggers

One of the major problems associated with the use of scripts is that of providing the system with triggers to invoke and terminate appropriate scripts. The simplest method of invoking a script is to associate each script with a keyword. In our example the word 'lecture' would be a suitable trigger. In many cases, however, the trigger word is a verb. Another possible trigger is a 'precondition'. In our example a suitable precondition would be that 'John' is a student studying for examinations. Additional possible triggers are associated with locations and the use of 'instruments'. 'University' or 'college' would be a suitable location trigger in our example, but there does not appear to be an obvious instrument to act as trigger in this example.

In principle then, the text is scanned for a keyword trigger. The appropriate script is invoked and the text is processed in order to find fillers for its slots. As the slots are updated, demons will be fired, and if the filler for a slot has particular significance another script may be activated, and the process continued. The updating of certain slots may act as a trigger which closes the script (e.g. the time of leaving the lecture). The system will then return to filling in the slots of any script which was active when the current script was activated — rather as control returns to the main program after a subroutine call.

13.4 Plans

Scripts represent one of the most promising lines of development in natural language processing, but there is something ad hoc about the approach which is unsatisfactory. Scripts have been developed for a number of scenarios, often associated with stereotyped social activities in the USA such as a visit to a restaurant or a supermarket. There are, however, some limitations to their use, particularly when the events of a narrative are not stereotyped. Consider the following text for example:

'John went down to the river and gazed at the inviting hills beyond the wide stretch of water. He resolved to go the following week to a lecture on canoe building.'

Now the lecture script will not contain anything about canoes, because there is no reason to select this topic for special mention from all the other possible topics. Likewise it has nothing about rivers or hills. Conversely, if we could devise a script about 'inviting hills' it is unlikely that we would think it appropriate to include within it anything about canoes, and a canoe script is unlikely to contain information about lectures. But we can all understand the connection between the first and the second sentences. The link lies in the obvious plan which John is formulating to get across the water. The scenario described, however, has no ready-made script to act as a support for our system. Recognising this, those who introduced the idea of scripts have also introduced the idea of 'plans'.

Representations for plans have been developed for a number of situations. A basic plan to 'go somewhere' might consist of a number of sub-plans involving various possible methods of transportation. A script can be thought of as a stereotyped sequence of events which is related to implicit plans designed to achieve some overall major plan. A plan is a more high-level organisation of a narrative, and is more general in that it will fit a rather wider set of circumstances. We can therefore develop systems which use plans as the basic method of understanding, and take the occasional short cut if a suitable script is available.

It is not appropriate at this stage for us to develop a script-based system because we have not yet discussed the primitive actions in terms of which the scripts and their sub-scripts must ultimately be represented. These are the subject of the next chapter. It is interesting to note, however, that with the idea of plans we have introduced the idea of explicit representation of motivation — an idea which has profound implications.

CHAPTER 14

Conceptual Dependencies

14.1 The Theory of Conceptual Dependencies

The theory of conceptual dependencies has been influential, and has been used as the foundation for a number of interesting systems which have achieved a limited measure of success. Although it has an ad hoc flavour which is philosophically unsatisfactory, it addresses important questions of meaning and interpretation which have largely been avoided by many other NL systems.

The theory is based upon the idea that the meaning of statements can be analysed in terms of three basic types of mental construct. These are *acts, picture producers* (PP), and *states*. These three constructs are the building bricks of the theory. They are combined to produce structures known as 'conceptualisations' and the relationships between the various components are called 'conceptual dependencies'. We shall describe each component in turn and then consider the theory as a whole.

14.2 The Eleven Primitive Acts

The theory of conceptual dependencies suggests that there are eleven 'primitive acts'. The description 'primitive' indicates that they do not require analysis into more fundamental actions, and they do not require explanation. These acts consist mainly of the moving about of ideas and physical objects. The actions described by, or associated with, the use of particular verbs are then analysed in terms of these primitive acts, and in most cases they can be shown to be equivalent to one or more of the primitive acts, perhaps with the value of one or more of the case-slots predefined. If the primitive acts are thought of as the 'atoms' of meaning, then the actions associated with the verbs can be thought of as the 'molecules' of the system. The case-slots or 'dependencies' which are associated with each verb emerge as a property conferred upon them by their 'molecular structure'.

The primitive acts each have three basic case-slots — the *agent*, the *object* and the *direction*. The direction is subdivided into 'from' and 'to' case-slots. In some cases both do not apply.

Every primitive act can also be extended by adding an instrumental case which is often another primitive act. Thus a person might INGEST a glass of milk, where the instrument is the primitive act of physically transferring (or PTRANS-

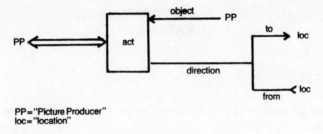

PP = "Picture Producer"
loc = "location"

Fig. 14.1. The basic case-slots in CD theory.

ing) the glass to his lips. In some instances we have used expressions such as 'mindof(X)'. This is intended to indicate the conscious mind of a person or animal. The nature and number of primitive acts described by this theory have varied over a period of years as the theory was refined, tested and modified. A recent count places the number at eleven.

The eleven primitive acts are:

(1) MOVE

This is the movement by a person or animal of a part of its own anatomy. That is, it moves its hand, or some other part of itself, to a new position. The case-slots associated with this act are:

MOVE:
    the agent   : A
    the object moved   : partof(A)
    the direction
        where from   : B
        where to   : C

(2) PROPEL

This is the act of causing something (other than oneself) to move to a new position. The case-slots are:

PROPEL:
    the agent   : A
    the object propelled : B
    the direction
        where from   : C
        where to   : D
    the instrument   : a MOVE act

another PROPEL act

a GRASP act

(3) INGEST

This is the act associated with the assimilation of food or drink. The case-slots are:

INGEST:
the agent   : A
the object ingested   : B
the direction
where from   : C
where to   : inside(A)
mouthof(A)
etc.

the instrument: a PTRANS act

(4) EXPEL

This is the act associated with the elimination of material from the body (e.g. blood, faeces, urine, air, etc.). The case-slots are:

EXPEL:
the agent   : A
the material expelled   : B
the direction
where from   : inside(A)
where to   : C
the instrument   : a PROPEL act
a MOVE act

(5) GRASP

This is the act associated with the grasping of an object in the hand, or in some other way. The case-slots are:

GRASP:
the agent   : A
the object grasped   : B
the direction
where from   : C

where to	: the hand of A
the instrument	: a MOVE act

(6) *ATRANS*

This is the act associated with an 'abstract' transfer from one state to another. A typical example is provided by the sale of goods from one person to another. In some cases the object itself does not move at all (e.g. a house) but the object has been 'transferred' from the ownership of one person to the ownership of another. The case-slots are:

ATRANS
the agent	: A
the object transferred	: B
the direction	
where from	: C
where to	: D
the instrument	: a PTRANS act
	an MTRANS act
	a MOVE act

(7) *PTRANS*

This is the act associated with the physical transfer of an object (including the movement of itself) from one place to another. The case-slots are:

PTRANS:
the agent	: A
the object moved	: B
the direction	
where from	: C
where to	: D
the instrument	: a MOVE act
	a PROPEL act

(8) *SPEAK*

The nature of this act is obvious from its name. The case-slots are:

SPEAK:
the agent	: A
the object (thing spoken)	: B

the direction	
where from	: A
where to	: C
the instrument	: a MOVE act (one's mouth)

(9) ATTEND

This act is the converse of SPEAK. It is associated with the reception of some communication. The case slots are:

ATTEND:

the agent	: A
the object (sense organ)	: B
the direction	
where from	: C
where to	: A

(10) MTRANS

This is the act associated with the transfer of ideas or information from one person to another. The case-slots are:

MTRANS:

the agent	: A
the object (information)	: B
the direction	
where from (medium)	: C
where to	: mindof(D)
the instrument	: a SPEAK act
	an ATTEND act

(11) MBUILD

This act is associated with the mental construction or working out of ideas from simpler ideas leading to decisions. The case-slots are:

MBUILD

the agent	: A
the object	
input	: B
output	: C

the direction
where from	: memory(A)
where to	: mindof(A)
the instrument	: an MTRANS act

That completes the list of primitive acts.

14.3 Picture producers (PP)

The strange name 'picture producers' arises from the notion that many mental constructs trigger a pictorial visualisation in our minds. A picture producer (or PP) corresponds both to the generic concept structure which we have described in previous sections and to specific examples of these concepts. Many nouns are associated with PPs, but not all nouns. A concept such as 'honesty' is not a PP. (It is not clear how a concept such as 'honesty' is represented in the theory of conceptual dependencies.) Being a concrete entity, a PP can be the agent of an act.

A PP can be implemented as a record structure or frame with slots for its properties. These properties may be states. The idea is very similar if not identical to the object-frames described in section 12.2.

14.4 States

A state is a condition or property of the world. Something being in a particular location is a state. Something having a particular colour is a state. Someone being in a particular emotional condition is a state.

A state can be represented by a record structure with two elements : the name of the state (or 'state-id') and the value (or 'state-val'). The terminology is that proposed by those who developed the theory of conceptual dependencies (CD), but a 'state' in CD terminology appears to be identical to a 'property' which has a 'property name' and a 'property value', rather in the same way as we suggested for the dictionary structure in section 8.5.

The record which represents a state can itself be the value of one of the properties of a PP or one of the case-slot values of an act. For example, to indicate that a PP has a particular location we might give it a property:

state-id = LOC (for location), and
state-val = London.

This data structure could be assigned as the slot filler for the 'where to' case-slot of a primitive act.

The theory identifies states corresponding to (or having the property names) length, colour, light intensity, mass and speed. It also identifies states of control, part(of), ownership, containment and proximity.

To deal with emotional states of mind, CD theory has introduced the concept of 'mental location' (MLOC) and defines an arbitrary numeric scale of values ranging from –10 to 10 (catatonic to ecstatic). The act of pleasing someone is therefore represented as an act which causes (DO) an increase of the numeric value of that person's mental state (ATRANS from MLOC -1 to MLOC +1 (say)).

Other mental states which also have their numeric scales of values are 'anger', 'fear', 'disgust' and 'surprise'. The theory also includes states such as 'health', 'hunger', consciousness' and several others.

The arbitrary nature of these states and their numeric scales of values is one of the most unsatisfactory aspects of the theory, but at least it represents an attempt to tackle these problems in a fairly direct way.

14.5 Implementation: from Input Text to Conceptualisation

Various mechanisms for getting from the original input text to the internal representation (or conceptualisation) have been tried. Some have used special parsers and others have abandoned the process of parsing altogether. We shall describe one possible method in outline only.

The basic data structures are:

(1) INLIST: the input text.
(2) CSTACK: a stack of conceptualisations. It is initially empty.
(3) RSTACK: a stack of 'requests'. The RSTACK is also initially empty.
(4) LEXICON: a list of all the words which the system can handle. Each word is associated with a PACKET.
(5) PACKETS: a set of requests.
(6) REQUEST: a demon, or function (see section 12.3) which can be stored and fired when required. A request has the form:-

TEST: a condition which must be true for the request to be granted;
ASSIGN: a set of variables and values. If the request is granted the values are assigned to these variables;
NEXT-PACKET: a list of further requests, which are loaded if the first request is granted (and after the assignment of the variable values).

The text-processing algorithm is as follows:

while inlist is not empty
    Remove the first word of inlist and assign it to x.
Look up x in the lexicon, extract its packet and place the packet on RSTACK,
    while (RSTACK is not empty) and
        (there is a request there which can be fired)
            Look for a request with test-condition = true;
            if found then

```
            assign the variable values
            and carry out any other actions requested
            remove the packet from RSTACK
            add its next-packets to RSTACK
    endwhile;
endwhile;
```

Note that in carrying out the actions indicated by the request, the system may place a conceptual dependency structure on the CSTACK. It can also access and modify the values assigned to the variables within conceptual dependencies already on the CSTACK. The CSTACK therefore provides a mechanism for communication between processing handling different parts of a statement — the same facilities provided by the side-effects of our ATN processing technique. When processing is completed, the contents of the CSTACK will represent the meaning of the statement.

The real work of the process (analogous to the side-effects of our ATN processing) is therefore carried out by the requests, which vary from word to word in the lexicon (just as the side-effects varied from arc to arc of the ATN).

An example of the packet associated with the word 'went' (adapted from *Inside Computer Understanding* by Schank and Riesbeck) is shown below. Go-var1, go-var2 and go-var3 are local variables (within PTRANS). Part-of-speech, subject and conceptual-dep are global variables which are updated as processing is carried out. The variable conceptual-dep is always set equal to the most recent conceptual dependency analysed.

```
    PACKET for "WENT"
---------------------------------------(start of "went")
    TEST: ---
    ASSIGN:
        part-of-speech := verb
        conceptual-dep := PTRANS
                        agent := go-var1
                        object:= go-var1
                        to := go-var2
                        from := go-var3
        go-var1 := subject
        go-var2 := nil
        go-var3 := nil

    NEXT-PACKET
        --------------------------------(start of "to")
    TEST (next-word = "to")
    ASSIGN: ----
    NEXT-PACKET
        --------------------------------(start of "np")
```

```
        TEST: (part-of-speech = np)
        ASSIGN:
          go-var2 := conceptual-dep

        TEST: (next-word = "home")
        ASSIGN: go-var2 := "house".
        -----------------------------(end of "np")
      --------------------------------(end of "to")
    ---------------------------------------(end of "went")
```

Note that this could be translated into the program:

```
define went;
  part-of-speech := "verb";
  v1 := subject;
  v2 := nil;
  v3 := nil;
  conceptual-dep := PTRANS(v1,v1,v2,v3);  *
  if next-word(inlist) = "to" then
    *
    if part-of-speech = np then
        v2 := conceptual-dep;  **
    endif;
  else
    if next-word(inlist) = "home"
        v2 := "house";
    endif;
  endif; enddefine;
```

At the points marked '*' the program is entering a new 'request'. At the point
marked '**' the value of the conceptual-dependency which is assigned to v2 is the
conceptual dependency belonging to the noun phrase (np).

The way this system behaves is complex and difficult to understand because
of the number of variables, and the way these are updated at different times by
procedures which are themselves dependent upon the other words in the
sentence being processed. It is important to note, however, that the idea of a
parser has almost vanished from the system. Syntactical information is
embedded in the packet associated with each word. Each 'knows' what words
and syntactical structures to expect in its immediate vicinity, and provides the
system with this local information as it is required. Note that the series of packets
given in the illustration are testing for two possible sequences of words:

    went to <somewhere>
    went home

The tests involved in the 'requests' correspond logically to the tests carried out
in an ATN before deciding which arc should be followed. The updates of the
variables correspond to the side-effects generated when an arc is traced.

14.6 The 'DO' Act

To the eleven primitive acts is added a twelfth general purpose act called DO. It simply means 'to cause something to happen' and is often used in conjunction with the primitive acts by making one of these fill its object case-slot. That is.

```
DO
    the agent        : A
    the object       : another act
                       or a state
    the instrument   : a MOVE act
                       a PTRANS act
                       etc.
```

14.7 Tense in Conceptual Dependencies

To simplify things we have omitted any mention of tense. The conceptualisation structure can be extended to include additional case-slots, one of which would be a tense parameter. The requests associated with the package for any given verb can include a request to insert an appropriate tense value.

14.8 Examples of Conceptual Dependencies

In section 14.5 we provided an example of the 'package' which is used for the verb 'went'. This package creates and places in the CSTACK a conceptualisation with the structure PTRANS(agent,object,from,to), so that the representation of the sentence 'John went to London' would be:

```
PTRANS
    (agent=John
    object=John
    from= ?
    to=London)
```

We also stated in section 14.1 that the basic idea in CD theory is to interpret the meaning of verbs (and other words) in terms of the primitive objects (PPs), acts and states. To illustrate this we provide below some examples of sentences and their interpretation in these terms. Most are adapted from examples given by Schank and Riesbeck.

    (a) *John took a plane to London*

```
PTRANS
    agent = John
    object = John
```

from = ?
to = London
instrument =
   PROPEL
      agent = plane
      object = plane
      from = ?
      to = London
   and
   PTRANS
      agent = John
      object = John
      from = ?
      to = plane

(i.e. John went to London by placing himself on a plane which propelled itself to London)

  (b) *John drank a glass of milk*

INGEST
   agent = John
   object = milk
   from = glass
   to = mouth of John
   instrument =
      PTRANS
         agent = John
         object = glass
         from = table
         to = mouth of John
         instrument =
            MOVE
               agent = John
               object = hand of John
               from = ?
               to = glass
            and
            GRASP
               agent = John
               object = glass
               from = ?
               to = hand of John

(i.e. John drank a glass of milk by moving the glass to his mouth by moving his hand to the glass and grasping the glass)

The reader will recognise the alarming complexity of this structure, and the fact that some additional instrumental or intermediate acts have been omitted. For example, after grasping the glass and moving his hand to his mouth (thus transporting the glass to his mouth) John tipped the glass so that the milk flowed into his mouth, and then he swallowed...etc.

(c) *John decided to go to London*

```
MBUILD
   agent = John
   object
      input = ?
      output = PTRANS
                  agent = John
                  object = John
                  from = ?
                  to = London
      from = memory
      to = conscious mind
```

(d) *John told Mary the story*

```
MTRANS
   agent = John
   object = story
   from = John
   to = Mary
   instrument =
      SPEAK
         agent = John
         object = story
         from = mind of John
         to = ?
      and
      ATTEND
         agent = Mary
         object = ears
         from = John
         to = mind of Mary
```

14.9 Some Thoughts on CD Theory

It is easy to be critical of CD theory. The description provided here is necessarily brief and inadequate. It is intended only to give a flavour of the system, and does not do justice to the very real success which the approach has achieved in producing, for example, good paraphrases of the input text. It is not recommended, however, that the reader try to reproduce a working system for CD theory.

The criticisms which have been levelled at CD theory tend to be generated by a distaste for the clumsy representations it produces and the almost complete absence of mathematical elegance. Two things need to be said in its defence, however. Firstly it represents a frontal attack on the real problem of NL processing. It asks the right questions of itself. It tries to produce a representation of the actual meaning of a statement. It recognises the importance of motivation (or 'mental states'). It recognises that events are linked causally and can be chained together to produce an overall result. Secondly by demonstrating its own limitations it has drawn attention to the need for contextual information and knowledge about the knowledge of others. When the system was put through its paces and was asked questions about the sentences it was processing, it tended to give answers which were much more detailed than a human would give. For example, if such a system processed the statement 'John fell in the water and was drowned', and was then asked why John died, it tended to give a string of answers such as:

because he could not breath
because his air supply was blocked
because his mouth was under water
because he was immersed in water
and
because he could not float
and
because the water was deeper than his height
because ...

In other words it would print a very detailed list of cause and effect in terms of primitive acts. A human, on the other hand, would know that the list was of little interest to another human, because it was common knowledge. The interesting information is that which cannot be assumed to be common knowledge — that John fell in the water. The rest can be taken for granted. This clearly points up the need for an NL processing system to have some idea of what others (as well as itself) know about.

It is suggested that we should ignore the clumsy notation and terminology and the crude numerical scale representing mental states and the like. Whatever method we use to represent the meaning of a statement, it will require a notation or symbolism of some kind. What form it takes is of less importance than the things it attempts to represent. The important aspect of CD theory is the fact that it tackles the representation of the important factors, and correctly relegates syntactical analysis to the role of an aid in the achievement of understanding. The function of language is, after all, to transmit understanding from one person to another. The grammatical elegance of our words (or lack of it) is of secondary importance.

CHAPTER 15

Conceptual Dependencies and Scripts

15.1 The Need for Scripts

The success of the conceptual dependencies theory when applied to the processing of individual sentences, and its failure to deal adequately with more extended narrative, drew attention to the need for scripts. The use of scripts provides a mechanism for representing the implicit or underlying world knowledge of a person, which does not always find expression in spoken or written narrative. Consider the small fragment of narrative below:

'John decided to take Mary to see a film. They drove to the centre of town in his car. He found that he had forgotten his wallet. They went for a walk in the park.'

To an NL-system which has not been provided with the appropriate world knowledge, these four sentences would appear to be about completely dissociated actions. The knowledge essential to an understanding of this narrative, which is not given explicitly, is:

That films are shown in cinemas.
That cinemas are often located near the centre of town.
That money must be paid to gain entry to a cinema.
That a wallet is a container for money.
That parks can usually be entered without payment.

When we tell a story we can assume that our human listeners have all this information before we start. The story therefore consists simply of markers and signposts which enables the listener to select from memory the appropriate sets of knowledge, and guide them through the structure of that knowledge as through a labyrinth of alternative passageways. For an NL-system, however, this knowledge must be provided explicitly, and scripts provide us with the means to do this.

15.2 Implementing Scripts with Conceptual Dependency Structures

In section 14.5 we described the algorithm for translating the input text into a conceptual dependency structure. The input to that process is provided in the form of a list INLIST, and the output is produced in the form of a list (CSTACK) which contains a number of 'CD-FORMS' or conceptual dependency structures.

The INLIST is processed word by word in left to right order. Each word is looked up in the 'lexicon', and the corresponding 'packet' is extracted. The packet contains a number of 'requests' (which are in fact demons or functions) which, when activated, construct new CD-FORMs, or modify existing CD-FORMs, or insert the completed forms into the CSTACK. Let us call this process the 'TX-CD process' (text to conceptual dependency process).

The next part of the overall process is to assign unique identifiers to the objects or 'picture producers' (PPs) represented in the CD-FORMs. World knowledge about PPs is provided by a structure called the PP-memory. This is a lookup table which for each PP provides information about its properties: (class of object, physical object, human, ...) It also describes it in functional terms (what it is used for). This represents its usual role in a script. For example, a 'chair' is an object used by people for sitting on. This information is held in the form of CD-FORM structures with formal parameters where these cannot be identified. The problem is therefore to take the PPs identified by the TX-CD process and assign to each either a unique new identifier (a 'token') or the identifier of an existing PP, which has already been analysed, or of one which is a special 'world knowledge' PP (that is, a PP corresponding to some known unique entity such as 'Mount Everest' or 'Henry VIII'). These will be held in the PP-memory.

Assigning tokens to PPs involves the resolution of references. This in turn requires the matching of CD-FORMs in order to unify the representations of PPs. In some cases resolution cannot be completed until the next stage of the overall process. For the most part, however, this part of the process takes as input the CSTACK and outputs the CSTACK with a token appended to each PP. Let us call this part of the process the 'PP-ID process' (PP identifier process).

The last part of the overall process introduces scripts. It has a dictionary of scripts, and its first task is to select the appropriate script, or set of scripts, for the narrative being analysed, based on the part already analysed. The second task is to predict what further scripts are likely to be required. The third task is to instantiate the PPs identified in the narrative by the PP-ID process with the roles in the scripts.

Once again we have the insertion of entities into case-slots, but now the case-slots are part of a rather larger scenario and the construction of these scenarios is rather more flexible and data driven. Let us call this part of the overall process the 'SC-APP process' (script application process).

The complete process therefore consists of the function calls:

TX-CD(INLIST) => CSTACK
PP-ID(CLIST) => CSTACK + tokens
SC-APP(CLIST+TOKENS) => script + instantiations

Part 3

CHAPTER 16

Outstanding Problems

16.1 From Optimism to Pessimism

The various techniques which we have examined in the first two parts of this book can, at best, be regarded as only partial solutions to the problem of natural language processing. A feeling of optimism which was prevalent among research workers some years ago has given way to disillusion, and in some quarters to frank pessimism. It is ironic that this should occur just when there is unprecedented publicity for all things related to artificial intelligence, and the goal of the 'Fifth Generation Computer' is attracting significant financial backing. A large proportion of the effort which is at present going into natural language processing systems is being directed at producing practical implementations of well-established techniques. Those engaged in this work know well enough that the results produced fall short of true natural language processing, but those funding the work seem satisfied with what they are getting — commercially viable products and useful user-friendly systems. They are, perhaps understandably, not too concerned with the philosophical unease which pervades the theoretical side of the work.

Alongside the flourishing exploitation of established techniques, a fundamental rethink of the approach to natural language processing is currently in progress among research workers. It is recognised that in order to progress we must backtrack to a more elementary level, and develop a theory of semantic representation which is not over simplified by being restricted to a limited context or 'micro-world'.

In this book the intention is to examine both aspects, and in this third part we shall look at some of the problems for which no solutions yet exist, and try to develop the outlines of possible solutions.

16.2 Micro-worlds and the Real World

In the early 1970s some excitement was generated by the relative success of systems which deal with a simplified environment ('micro-worlds'). The micrographics example which we described in Part 1 is an example of a micro-world. In it, every object can be associated with a particular identifier, every allowable process is predefined, every concept is concrete. Processes which could be carried out on entities were defined in procedural terms and included the procedures which had to be carried out beforehand. In one well-known system which used a 'blocks world' (a simulated table top covered by simulated wooden blocks of different shapes and colours) the process corresponding to the placement of one block on top of another included the program code to clear the top surface of the receiving block if that was necessary.

At that time many research workers felt that all we needed to do was to analyse and produce systems for an increasing number of specialised micro-worlds, until these gradually accounted for most aspects of the real world. Sadly this optimism has proved unfounded, and it is now realised that micro-worlds of this kind omit many important aspects of natural language understanding. The reader will recall Winograd's discussion of the problem when dealing with a sentence such as 'I want to own the fastest car in the world'. A simple-minded extension of the micro-world approach would find the referent for the phrase 'fastest car in the world', by searching a database of all cars in the world and selecting the one which was the fastest. Humans usually interpret this sentence by assuming that the speaker wishes to create a new car which is faster than the fastest existing car. That is because they know about how people behave, about how records are set, about the technicalities of using the Bonville Salt Flats in Utah for a record-breaking attempt, and the kudos which comes from *building* the fastest car as opposed to mere ownership. Note how the idea of human motivation has crept into the discussion, and the vacuous interpretation of the sentence if we leave it out.

In many a micro-world system, the relationship between objects — such as one object 'owning' another — is represented by a simple predicate 'owns(X,Y)', meaning 'X owns Y'. Such knowledge can be stored within the system, and when asked the question 'Who owns Y?' the system will correctly respond 'X'. This does not constitute evidence that the concept of ownership is understood. Ownership is actually a very complex concept indeed, which many people have difficulty in understanding fully. It involves a social contract between the person owning the object and the rest of humanity. Sometimes that contract is made concrete in terms of a codified law, which is enforced by government, and sometimes it is an informal contract which is respected by all who wish to conform to the social norms of society. Consider, for example, the different kinds of ownership involved in owning a country, owning a child, owning a house (outright), owning a house (under mortgage), owning a house (rented to others), owning a book, owning a chair (at a public meeting — e.g. someone saying 'That's my chair' when someone else tries to sit in it), and owning your own hand. Consider the different processes required to transfer ownership, and the impossibility of doing so if the object in question is 'my hand'. Consider how those who do not own something recognise and respect the ownership of objects by others (in all the different cases listed above). Consider also the sanctions available to punish those who do not respect ownership rights. Can we say that a system (human or computer) understands 'ownership' if that system is not aware of all these implications and nuances?

This argument does not prevent us from representing ownership formally by means of the predicate own(X,Y). But it should help us to realise that we cannot leave it at that. We must be able to relate that simple representation to other facts in an extraordinarily complex way. The complications usually involve issues of human motivation.

Thus far, the micro-world approach has tended to avoid this issue. Many who develop NLP systems concede the point made above, but continue to use the simplified representation while waving a hand at the problem. Somehow or other the additional information is supposed to be added on later, like some trivial detail. That is not good enough.

Another aspect of the micro-world approach which gives some disquiet is the tendency to define objects in terms of their properties in a rather inflexible way. A man does not cease to be a man if he loses his legs. The identity of an entity is not simply a function of its properties.

16.3 Naive Physics

'Naive physics' is the term used to describe everyday knowledge of the physical behaviour of the world. We all learn at an early age that things fall down if not supported, that fluids have no shape of their own, that some objects (like a piece of string) can be used to pull things along but not to push them, that when a moving object collides with another object the second tends to move away. We discover the heft of objects in our hand. We relate the physical appearance of an object to the tactile sensation of texture. The term 'naive physics' distinguishes this type of knowledge from the more formal knowledge of physics which some of us acquire at school or college. Natural language processing depends upon knowledge of naive physics, since this is knowledge which can be assumed common to almost all humans. Such an assumption is implicit in the meanings of words. For example, the verb 'to fall' does not mean 'to reduce in altitude'. When we use the word 'fall' we expect our fellows to understand the spontaneous aspect of falling, and the direction of the movement, and that (eventually, at least) the falling object will make contact with something.

In most existing NLP systems the entities involved have nice regular geometrical shapes. It is particularly difficult to find an adequate way of representing the shape of things which do not have a regular or geometrical form. Even worse is the problem of representing shapeless entities like a quantity of water. Should we distinguish between physical objects which have a size, shape and location, and 'stuff', like wood, water and plastic, which does not have these properties but instead contributes to the properties of objects like 'a tree', 'a lake' and 'a watch'.

Recently some efforts have been made to represent the behaviour of liquids by means of a kind of finite element analysis, in which a body of water is subdivided into regular particulate units and the behaviour of an aggregation of these is computed as the result of the interaction of each element with its fellows and with their surroundings. On conventional computers such systems produce entertaining graphics of water pouring etc, but they require the services of non-conventional parallel machines to produce these results in real-time. Perhaps, in time, we will have the services of such equipment for the development of NLP systems, but it is unrealistic to think that we will be able to make use of such techniques in the short term. Humans, however, probably do have facilities for visualising the behaviour of fluids which are not unlike this kind of simulation.

The problem of representing fluids and irregular shapes is a severe obstacle for NLP systems.

16.4 Real Dialogues and Bad Grammar

Scene: In a telephone box. Jack is phoning his girlfriend.
　　Jack: 'What would you like to do tonight then? Film?'
　　Jill: 'Mm...'
　　Jack: 'Good at the Odeon.'
　　Jill: 'Who is it?'
　　Jack: 'Humphrey Bogart.'
　　Jill: 'Oh no!'
　　Jack: 'Well — how about a walk?'
　　Jill: 'It's raining!'
　　Jack: 'Dancing?'
　　Jill: 'We danced on Tuesday.'
　　Jack: 'Well what, then?'
　　Jill: ...
　　Jack: 'Come on then. Eh?'
　　Jill: 'My hair is a mess.'
　　Jack: 'What's the matter?'

... and so on.

The reader will recognise the authenticity of this dialogue, particularly in comparison with most of the dialogues in the current literature concerning NLP systems. The reader will also have no difficulty in following the drift of the conversation, and will already have formed the opinion that Jack is not doing too well.

Consider now how many of the statements in the dialogue are not grammatical sentences. Several of the statements have no verb; two have a dangling conjunction ('then'); several consist of exactly one word ('Film?' and 'Dancing?') and two contain words which have no dictionary entry ('Mm...' and 'Eh?'). Consider also the amount of background knowledge of people and the world which is necessary to see a relevant connection between 'Come on then. Eh?' and 'My hair is a mess'. Without the knowledge that people may grow weary of an activity which they would normally find entertaining, if they do it too frequently, there is no way to understand the connection between 'Dancing?' and 'We danced on Tuesday'.

The moral of this is:

(1) Real people do not always converse in well-formed grammatical sentences.

(2) The connection between statements in a real dialogue is often not explicit, but relies heavily upon people sharing common background knowledge which carries the hidden connection.

(3) The hidden connection often has a good deal to do with human psychology, and less to do with the physical world.

(4) An NLP system which relies upon a strict syntactical analysis is doomed to failure before it starts if an attempt is made to process real dialogues.

16.5 Repetitive Operations

It is not too difficult to see how we could represent a sequence of events extending over a period of time. We discussed this in Chapter 4 when we dealt with time-stamps and object histories. There is a problem, however, in dealing with sequences of events which occur repetitively, or which occur several times at unpredictable times. If we say of someone 'He plays tennis' we do not necessarily mean that he plays the game continuously, or even that he is engaged in a game at that precise moment. We usually mean that he is able to play the game, that he has played several games in the past, and that he continues to play from time to time.

How exactly can we represent the notion behind the words 'from time to time'?

In programming we are accustomed to using a looping mechanism to represent repetitive or iterative operations, but that technique clearly will not do in this case. Each game of tennis is a separate event and might be referenced separately in order, say, to provide information about different opponents. There is also the implication that the person concerned has the appropriate equipment, can be expected to play the game again in the future, and might be a suitable person to ask to make up a pair for a doubles match.

There is also the problem of how we can represent a single game, with each rally consisting of one serve and zero to N returns. Again each stroke is a separate event and requires a separate representation. Again looping mechanisms will not do. The number of strokes in a rally is potentially infinite, however, and so we cannot suppose that we can provide an actual representation of each. These are difficult issues which have not been tackled by any NLP to date. We will discuss possible solutions later, in Chapter 22.

16.6 Metaphor

In elementary school lessons on language we learn about 'figures of speech'. The sentence *'He was a lion in the fight'* is described as an example of a 'metaphor', while the sentence *'He was like a lion in the fight'* is described as being a 'simile'. 'Hyperbole' is the deliberate use of exaggeration, as in 'there were millions of people with red rosettes at the football match yesterday'.

Here, by the term 'metaphor', we mean any figurative use of language which does not rely upon the literal meaning of the words for its interpretation. Used in this way the term embraces simile.

In the early days of NLP, metaphor was viewed as a complication we could do without. It was put on one side until the 'main' problems of NLP were solved. The remarkable thing about it, however, is that humans find metaphor so easy to deal with. More recently the realisation has dawned that metaphor is just the most spectacular and visible characteristic of language, among many which give a clue to some of its hidden mechanisms. The use of adjectives which do not quite fit the known properties of the entity in question is another. *'Millions of people'* is usually taken to mean *'a very large number of people'* not literally *'millions'*.

The common characteristic of this use of language is that some of the properties normally associated with the use of certain words, in certain contexts, are inappropriate and are simply ignored. There is a relationship between this aspect of language usage and the point made earlier about a man not ceasing to be a man just because he has lost his legs. The deletion or ignoring of properties normally associated with something, when the occasion demands, is a basic element of the way we think and organise our view of the world, and the way we use language is a direct consequence of the way we think.

Metaphor is also fundamental to the way language develops and changes. When circumstances change, and a novel situation demands a novel word to describe it, we often adapt a word from a more familiar situation on the basis that there is some shared characteristic. When such a use of language is first introduced it is considered a 'metaphor' and may attract literary acclaim. Later, when the same words are used in the same way by many people, it becomes a 'cliché'. Later still, the new meaning may be formally adopted and find its way into established dictionaries. For example, when electric storage cells were first invented the term 'battery' meant a collection of large guns which fired together. When applied to the new-fangled electric storage cells it drew upon that aspect of the conventional meaning which was suggestive of a source of great power. Words behave like an amoeba. They can stretch into new shapes and develop strange lobes to embrace new usages. And they can also split in two.

An understanding of metaphor, then, is fundamental to an understanding of language, and an NLP system (in the fullest sense of the term) which cannot explain the mechanism of metaphor has failed.

16.7 Spatial Relationships

It may seem strange to include spatial relationships in a list of outstanding problems, because there have been a number of systems developed which appear to solve this problem quite successfully. It is relatively simple to define a number of predicates such as *above(X, Y)* (which is interpreted as meaning that the object 'X' is above the object 'Y') and *on_top(X, Y)*, *in_contact(X, Y)*, *below(X, Y)* and *behind(X, Y)* which all have similar meanings. These can be related by rules stated in the form:

'above(X, Y)' and *'in_contact(X, Y)'* implies *'on_top(X, Y)'*

or any similar logical notation. Many rules of this kind could be constructed so that the implications of any expression of spatial relationship can be reexpressed in terms of other spatial relationships. Thus the implications of a statement about spatial relationships can be inferred. This appears to be a neat solution to the problem of representing spatial relationships until we dig deeper into the nature of the problem. Consider the set of predicates and rules shown below:

'right_of(X, Y)' implies *'left_of(Y, X)'*
'right_of(X, Y)' and *'right_of(Y, Z)'* implies *'right_of(X, Z)'*

If we used these to represent the positions of persons sitting at a dinner table we would find some anomalies if the table was round. At such a table, if we keep placing people 'to the right' we will eventually place someone 'to the left' of the first person who sat down. This appears to infringe the rules stated above. The rules above simply do not deal properly with the notion of 'to the right of' when it is applied in the context of a circular table. Does this mean that we must create a separate logic suitable for each shape of table?

There is also the problem of correctly interpreting statements such as *'on the side of the picture'*. Does this mean within the picture itself but not in the centre, or does it mean adhering to the outside of the picture frame? Does *'behind X'* mean on the far side of X so that it is occluded by X, or does it mean to the rear of X?

What is obvious is that the simple-minded approach outlined above is inadequate.

CHAPTER 17

The Meaning of Meaning

17.1 Internal Representation and Predictions

When a person hears a statement, he or she translates it into an internal representation of some kind. At its simplest level, this representation is descriptive of some aspect of the world about us. If the statement is *'your book is lying on the table in the room next door'* the internal structure which is formed would contain the representation of an entity <book>, of an entity <table> and of two entities <room-1> and <room-2>. The speaker and the hearer will also be represented as two entities <speaker> and <hearer>. Both will be represented as being <inside room-1> and the table and book will be represented as being <inside room-2>. The two rooms will be represented as being <adjacent> and the book will be represented as being <on the table>.

We have placed angle brackets round the representations of entities to indicate that we do not want to get bogged down at present in the detail of exactly how these things are represented.

The hearer will then be able to process this composite representation and make predictions about hypothetical situations. For example, if the person concerned goes into the room next door, the book will brought into view and can thus be obtained. The speaker will have a similar representation and this representation, or *model*, will include a representation of the hearer's representation. It will also include a representation of the hearer's motivation, that is, his wanting to obtain the book. Based on this guess about what is going on in the hearer's mind, the speaker will predict that the hearer will take action to find the book or at least express gratitude for the information which makes this possible. If such action is not observed, the speaker may conclude that the hearer has either not heard or not understood the statement.

This somewhat complicated description summarises the nature of a conversation. Two people engaged in a conversation are constantly constructing representations of the meanings of the statements made by each other, and they also form representations of each other's representations. The internal condition of another person's mind is for all of us an important piece of information. In an environment which is constantly being changed by the actions of other people, we would be in dire straits if we had no idea what to expect of other people's behaviour.

Understanding then, requires two activities: the construction of an internal representation, and the processing of the representation to make appropriate predictions.

17.2 Context and Implications

The phrase 'appropriate predictions' is used advisedly. There are many predictions which could be made from any such representation, most of which would be irrelevant. For example, if the room next door was to be filled with water, then the book would get wet. If the book is very heavy then the table may be damaged, and so on. These predictions might become appropriate however, if we have additional information which provides a context for the statement. For example, we may know that there is a burst water pipe in the room next door, or we may know that the table in the room next door is at present being glued together and is not capable of bearing heavy weights. The internal representation constructed by the person who 'understands' the statement will include a representation of the context. The context will determine which of the possible predictions are relevant. The inclusion of information about the context, far from being an unnecessary complication, is the only hope we have of avoiding the embarrassment of dealing with an infinity of possible predictions.

We shall call these relevant predictions the 'implications of the statement'. It is our contention that people do not understand a statement (as we do) unless they are aware of the implications (of which we are aware).

17.3 Multiple Meanings and Partial Meaning

Different persons will have different experience and, in consequence, different contextual information available to them. They will be aware, therefore, of different implications for any given statement. It may be supposed that the person who utters a statement, or who writes it for others to read, is the true arbiter of its meaning, but there are circumstances where this is not so. It is easy to envisage a scenario where a speaker addressing a meeting might make a statement which, to his surprise, causes instant panic or hilarity in his audience because it has some implication of which he was unaware. In such a case he might be described as not (fully) understanding what he has just said. The parenthetic 'fully' is important, and suggests the notion of partial understanding and therefore of partial meaning.

Since we have no reason to suppose that any one person is in a privileged position in this respect, it follows that any given statement may have several different and equally valid 'meanings'. At the same time, although each person may be aware of a unique set of implications in the context of their unique experience, each will be aware to some extent of how much of that experience is common to many people. They will therefore be aware of how much of their interpretation is shared. This judgement about what is shared is what we regard as the meaning of a statement. We do not expect others to understand our unique and innermost thoughts, but we do expect a degree of common understanding, and it is this that serves as the 'meaning' used in communication. It is easy to see how misunderstandings can arise.

17.4 Uniformity of Representational Form

Another thing emerges from this example. The contextual information which affects the internal representation of a statement may not have been gained by hearing other statements. It may have been the result of direct observation.

It has been found that people are sometimes unable to distinguish between the representation they construct as the result of visual observation and that generated by processing linguistic utterances. In laboratory experiments, witnesses to a motor accident (on film) were asked the questions:

(1) 'Did you see broken glass on the road after the two cars SMASHED INTO one another', and
(2) 'Did you see broken glass on the road after the two cars HIT each other'.

They were more inclined to say 'yes' to question (1), although in the film there had been no broken glass at all. The mental representation of a 'smash' is more likely to generate an inference of broken glass than a mere 'hit', and this inference influenced the answers. The witnesses seemed unaware that they had allowed an inference based on linguistic clues to modify what they thought they had actually seen.

If the two types of information can be combined, then they must be constructed from the same kind of constructional units. We deduce that the internal representation formed when we 'understand' a linguistic statement is made of the same kind of stuff as our other mental constructs, and that the information which is derived from several different sources can be integrated into a single form. In other words, we do not have a special kind of semantic representation which is used only in the processing of language. Language processing makes use of the mental processes and representations which are associated with intelligent behaviour, and which were developed long before the ability to use language.

17.5 Perception

We perceive the world by means of our senses, and our view of the world is governed by the physical characteristics of those senses and by the processing which we carry out upon the data input. Sensory stimulations generated by sight, hearing, smell, taste and touch are recorded and stored as exact images. They are called *eidetic* images. Under normal circumstances, however, the information is only accessible to us in that form for a very short length of time. During that time it is processed.

'Perceptions' are the results obtained by processing sensory data. Much of this processing is more or less automatic, being to a large extent 'hard-wired' or 'firm-wired' into our sensory systems.

An important aspect of this processing is the identification of 'features'. In vision, the features associated with shape consist of lines, edges, corners, etc. Processing is fast and unconscious, so that we are not aware that what we see is actually a collection of these features and a mosaic of colours. What we perceive are entities such as people and other objects. We also appear to have standard templates for the purposes of recognising and distinguishing specific and important patterns, such as that associated with the human face.

Our perceptual apparatus is extremely poor at determining absolute values, but is extremely efficient at detecting subtle differences. Thus most of us can tell that two musical notes are not identical with amazing discrimination, but are poor at identifying the absolute pitch of one note. We are able to detect the motion of objects which we would overlook completely if they remained still. Encoding is in the form of change and difference. We remember faces in terms of the way they differ from a standard template pattern.

In general we classify entities by the properties they share and we distinguish individual members of a class by the differences between them and the standard for their class.

17.6 Memory

There are at least three types of memory store involved in human cognition.

Naturalistic memory traces. There is evidence which suggests that eidetic memory traces persist in the brain indefinitely for all persons, but although they might be physically present, they become 'forgotten' after a very short time and can no longer be retrieved (normally). People with so-called 'photographic memories' appear able to access precise details of past experiences, so that at a later time they can 'read' from their memory trace information of which they were not consciously aware at the time of the actual experience. For most practical purposes, however, we can ignore the existence of eidetic or naturalistic memory.

Episodic memory. Our memory of past events, or 'episodes', is normally recalled in a degraded form with details deleted and, as the example of the traffic accident witnesses shows, details concocted from our knowledge of what 'ought' to have happened. When asked to recall sentences read to them a short time before, people are often unable to recall the exact wording, but are usually able to paraphrase the sentences. What gets remembered is the meaning of the statement. Meaningless data is much more difficult to commit to memory than meaningful data. Episodic memory, therefore, is a trace of past experience, filtered and interpreted in terms of its significance.

Semantic memory. Semantic memory is a store of 'concepts' in which the memory traces of events and entities have been analysed and classified to become 'general knowledge'. In semantic memory even more detail has been lost, and what is retained is a compendium of several experiences and observations which have been classified and associated to form concepts. A concept represents a class of perceptions. Concepts are associated with other concepts for ease of retrieval.

General knowledge. Two of the most important aspects of general knowledge are:

(a) the ability to recognise the classification of a specific entity, which may never have been observed before, by virtue of the properties it shares with other, known entities. This allows us to predict some of its less obvious properties (e.g. whether it is likely to be dangerous).

(b) the ability to predict the occurrence of events on the basis of events currently or recently observed. This is done by abstracting the patterns of 'causation' from the trace of past events. 'Causation' is the way in which events of one type follow upon events of another. Current events can then be matched with these past experiences and classified so that the likely outcome of events can be predicted.

Concept organisation. To build an effective semantic memory it is necessary to process the episodic memory and to organise and classify what is found there. It is likely that such classification is multi-dimensional, so that a single experience or episode will be classified along with similar experiences according to different criteria. For example, episodic concepts could be classified on the basis of similarity of outcome, similarity of cause, similarity of entities involved and, perhaps most important of all, similarity of emotional effect on ourselves.

Other concepts are associated with distinct objects which could be classified by their shared attributes, such as having the property 'edible'. Evidence for this is provided by patients who have suffered brain damage (e.g. as the result of a stroke) and who are sometimes found to have lost, selectively, the ability to use a particular class of words, such as the class of words associated with the 'edible' property, or with verbs of action (i.e. not including the verb 'to be'). Since this loss is associated with damage to a particular location in the brain, the obvious conclusion is that for a given patient that location had been part of the 'index-table' or 'classification' structure. By analogy, if we delete a node in a tree structure we lose all of its subordinate nodes. Such an organisation of memory would be helpful for a speaker in finding appropriate words to match his or her meaning.

The everyday experiences of a typical adult are not usually greatly different from other past experiences. The memory trace of these experiences is therefore quickly analysed and subsumed within existing concepts in semantic memory.

However, completely fresh types of experience, particularly those associated with charged emotions, do not fit easily with past experiences and may trigger the formation of a new concept. In such a case, the 'general' case is based on only one example, and therefore retains much of the detail of that example. Slowly, as other examples of that kind are added, the particular details of the first experience (that is, those which are peculiar to that experience), are deleted, while the aspects of the experience which it has in common with others (those which characterise the concept) are reinforced. The concept gradually becomes more general and loses specific detail. Unique experiences remain etched in some detail in our memories, since no other experience of that kind is available to generalise it.

17.7 Labelling Concepts and Learning new Concepts

Labelling a concept. It is possible to label concepts symbolically. The symbol used could be a visual pattern, a gesture, a sound or a word. A label is used like an index in a filing system to access the concept. A language is a system of symbols together with rules governing their use.

Any concept can be labelled linguistically, and many can be described by patterns of lingistic symbols. In this way we can transfer concepts to each other verbally without the need for direct experience. Not all concepts can be described adequately by language, however. Motor actions, such as the actions necessary to achieve a parallel turn in skiing, or a good golf swing, can often defeat efforts to analyse them linguistically. The only effective way to have a mental concept corresponding to these things is to have them encoded within the mind in terms of the muscular patterns necessary to achieve them.

Learning a new concept. Learning the meaning of a new word may mean identifying a concept which we already have and simply indexing it by that word. For example, most people will have seen and noticed the vertical and horizontal strips of wood in a window which separate and hold the panes of glass. These strips will be part of the concept 'window', and they will also constitute a concept in their own right in the minds of most people. Perhaps not so many people have a word-label for this concept. When told that the correct term is 'astragal' they are able to append it to the existing concept.

On other occasions the learning of a new word-label may mean constructing a new concept from an assortment of existing structures in semantic memory. As an example of this, let us invent a new word and a concept to go with it.

'Glunging'. An example of 'glunging' takes place when the driver of a car decides to overtake the car in front, pulls out, and is almost irrevocably committed to the manoeuvre when another oncoming car appears round the bend ahead. Our glunging driver breaks dramatically and aborts the overtake procedure, suffering as he does so a mixture of fear and embarrassment.

Glunging also takes place when a man decides to proposition a woman at a party, and after launching himself on his 'lead in' patter suddenly realises that she is his boss's wife, and has to extract himself from the situation in some confusion.

The reader should now be in a position to think of other situations not involving motor car driving or parties to which the term 'glunging' might be applied.

We now share an understanding as to what 'glunging' means. Our ideas may not coincide exactly, but the degree of common knowledge will suffice to allow communication. To an extent this account will have modified the reader's semantic memory store, so that he or she now has a concept which was not there before. Previously the constituent parts of the 'glunging' concept were dispersed through several other concepts, and were obscured by detail. It is unlikely that it was recognised as a concept in its own right. But now it has been identified and labelled. Language not only labels concepts but modifies our view of the world.

The concept 'to glunge' has a structure roughly as follows:

There exists an entity PERSON. PERSON is in a state of indecision. PERSON wants to take some ACTION but is inhibited by fear of some ADVERSE CONSEQUENCE and by the disapproval of others which might accrue if the venture fails and therefore appears stupid. At length the PERSON decides, impetuously, to take the ACTION. At a point when there is almost no chance of taking an alternative course of action, ADVERSE CONSEQUENCE suddenly appears certain. The PERSON aborts the ACTION in circumstances where it is fairly obvious to others that PERSON has blundered. The PERSON suffers embarrassment in consequence.

The words in upper case represent parameters which can be replaced by specific identifiers or descriptions to suit the particular circumstances. By replacing the parameters with specific values the concept above could generate all possible examples of glunging. Hence, it is a 'generic' structure. This is strictly analogous with our concept 'triangle', used in the micro-graphics example, which could generate all possible examples of 'triangle' by giving the parameters (vertex coordinates) the full range of numeric values. In the notation of predicate calculus we would have:

glunge(<person>,<action>,<adverse consequence>)

To use the verb 'to glunge' in natural English, we need to invent a grammatical structure for it so that the various parametric values can be attached conveniently. We might describe our first example of glunging above with these words:

'He glunged the overtaking of the car away from a head on collision'.

In the second case we would say:

'He glunged a pass at the woman away from an entanglement with his boss's wife.'

The structure is <person> glunge <action> away from
<adverse consequence>.

'To glunge' has some similarities with the verb 'to abort', but has overtones of embarrassment and absurdity.

Note the use of the words 'away from' in this structure. They play an important but subordinate role. They help to identify the role of the entity corresponding to the formal parameter which follows them. They trigger an action, which is to evaluate or process the description of the entity which follows, and then to fit that description into the role-slot provided by the verb 'to glunge'. In a similar way the word 'the' in the phrase 'the man' triggers a search for some previous mention of an entity 'man', so that the new description of that entity can be linked to the past description. These considerations suggest that certain words are labels not for passively descriptive concepts but for active processes or 'functions'.

17.8 Types of Concept

We note that concepts exhibit the characteristics of:
   (a) entities
   (b) episodes
   (c) functions

A given concept may incorporate more than one of these characteristics, being partly descriptive of some entity, partly episodic and partly functional. The concept 'tennis ball' for example, involves a description of a physical object but also a description of a typical tennis match (episodic). The concept which is labelled by the word 'and' describes a single (conjoined) entity and also triggers a search for two entities which are to be conjoined.

Roughly speaking, 'entity' concepts are associated with nouns, episodic concepts are associated with verbs, and functional concepts are associated with prepositions and conjunctions. We shall argue later, however, that this association with nouns, verbs and prepositions is imprecise, and that, for example, some nouns are as 'episodic' as many verbs.

Meaning and Communication

18.1 The Nature of Communication

The basic function of language is to communicate. The ability to communicate, however, is not confined to the use of language. We communicate with others by means of facial expressions, body positions, drawing attention by pointing, and so on.

We all have a mental 'model' of our environment. It includes a representation of the physical objects around us and their likely behaviour. Our immediate sensory experiences are changing continuously but our model, being an interpreted version of our sensory images, is stored in episodic memory and is relatively stable. This model enables us to take appropriate actions and, for example, to sit on a chair which, at the moment of sitting, is behind us and therefore out of view. It enables us to walk about in a completely dark room without falling over the furniture, provided we have had a prior look at the room. It would be a confusing world to live in if our model of it changed with our changing sensory perceptions.

Along with the model of our immediate surroundings we have a more general model of the world at large. The experience on which this model is based is acquired over a longer time span, and the model itself is stored in semantic memory. It is 'general knowledge'.

When we communicate we enrich the internal representation of others with respect to the environment. If we draw their attention to some phenomenon, a representation of that phenomenon will be added to their internal model of the world about them. If we describe to others a place known to us but not to the hearers, a representation of that place will be added, after due processing, to their world model. For them it now 'exists' in their model, perhaps not as vividly as would be the case if they had seen it for themselves but it 'exists' nevertheless. It is in this way that we can all build up a model of the world which includes countries and places of which we have no direct experience.

Our episodic memory will have a record of the experience of being told facts. Our semantic memory will store the knowledge which results from that experience. Eventually we forget about the actual experience of being told, but we retain the general knowledge: if asked why it is that we are so sure a certain country exists, even though we have never visited it, we are perhaps unable to recall the many occasions on which we encountered indirect evidence of its existence.

The things we communicate about are not confined to simple facts which people might have observed for themselves. If we describe something in a story, our audience will construct a model of a fictitious environment which will enable them to understand the significance of the actions in the story. They will enrich the fictitious environment with their general knowledge of the world. They will be aware, however, that the model is fictitious. Humans are able to handle many models simultaneously without confusion.

Communication is also concerned with transmitting information about our own emotional states. If we frown, others will be able to enrich their model of their immediate surroundings with the knowledge that we are unhappy about something. This makes it easier for them to predict our likely behaviour.

18.2 Symbolic Communication and Concepts

We can tell a story by means of a series of isolated words. For example: DOG. MAN. BIT. HOSPITAL. RABIES. TEST. OK. RELIEVED. On reading these words, the reader can extract from semantic memory the concepts associated with each word. Each concept will have a large number of associated 'scenarios' or schematic episodes. A 'hospital' for example, is more than a large building. The representation includes the scenario of people being injured or falling ill, being taken there in an ambulance, being treated, and finally, it is hoped, being cured. It includes the representation of doctors and nurses etc.

Each concept labelled by words in the list above is the centre of a similar cluster of scenarios. The concepts associated with each word will differ from person to person, but will contain a core of similar material. For example, the word 'hospital' has for each of us particular associations concerning particular occasions in our past. However, as explained in section 17.3, we do not expect others to share all of these associations, and so when we use the word 'hospital' we do not use these (personal) associations to form the predictions we make about how another person will interpret our words. The common core of associations may be ill-defined, but it is this common core which permits communication. It is a kind of bargain or contract we strike with our fellows. Occasionally there will be misunderstandings when we assume someone has an association which they do not have, but for the most part communication flows freely.

Some of the scenarios associated with a word will also be associated with other words in the list. For example, the concept labelled by the word 'hospital' will be associated with people becoming ill, and the concept labelled by the word 'rabies' will have a similar association. These overlapping scenarios will be matched and therefore 'confirmed' as important to the story being told. Others, which have no commonality, will be held in abeyance until the story appears to require their use. In this way the words in the list generate a 'context' for each other which determines the appropriate implications. The concept labelled by the word 'test',

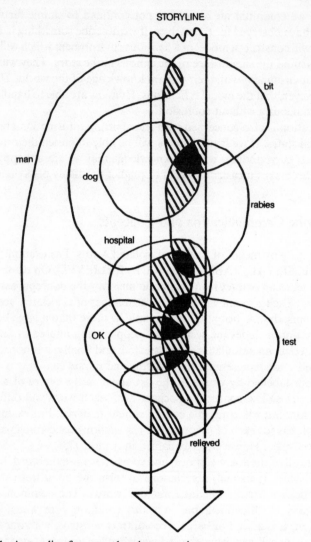

Fig. 18.1. A storyline from overlapping scenarios.

for example, will have associations with examinations and schools. Such associations will not have relevance to the story told in the words above, because no other word in the list labels a concept with similar associations. But it does have associations with medical tests and these are shared by the other words in the collection. In this way the reader can construct a series of scenarios which appear to represent the story told by the set of words.

If we deliberately jumble the words, the story is still discernible although with difficulty and with more possibility for ambiguity (e.g. HOSPITAL. DOG. TEST. RELIEVED. MAN. BIT. RABIES. OK). There is more ambiguity because the chronological sequence of events is not represented. The dog might have been bitten by the man, for example, or even by the hospital. Nevertheless if we give the most likely scenarios preference to the least likely, the story is still more or less as before.

From this example it would appear that word order is an aid to understanding, but is not a necessary element of communication. The main message is carried by the words which label concepts and by their associations. Our ability to fit these word-meanings together in a sensible way, based on our knowledge of the world, is what makes communication possible.

If we not only sequence the words in chronological order, but provide additional clues to the way the concepts associated with the words are to be linked, the story becomes even more easily understood.

A dog bit a man.
The man was taken to hospital.
Rabies was suspected.
A test was made.
The result showed that he was OK.
The man was relieved.

The additional words and the grammatical structure of the sentences allow us to link the scenarios together and slot entities such as *dog* and *man* into the correct roles. The verb in each sentence and its form (active or passive) helps us to identify the role positions. For example, the entity preceding the verb is responsible for the action (in active voice), and a phrase such as *'a man'* indicates that we are talking about one arbitrary example of the class of men, not the whole of mankind. Grammatical structure is therefore an aid to understanding. Placing sentences in a particular sequence gives an indication of the chronological sequence of events. These aids, however, are very imperfect, and the main reason why communication is possible in this symbolic form is that humans know what is reasonable.

In past years the development of natural language processing was hindered by the idea that the grammatical structure of sentences and their meaning were two separate issues. Evidence for this was produced in the form of examples of sentences which were meaningful but ungrammatical, and sentences which were grammatical but 'nonsensical'. What seemed to have been overlooked at that time was the notion of partial meaning. If a sentence which is both meaningful and grammatical is modified so that it is no longer grammatical, then it has lost some, but not all of its meaning. If the important concept-labelling words in the sentence are replaced by others, with the same grammatical classification but with different (and anomalous) associated scenarios, then it has lost even more meaning, but not all of its meaning. Even if such a sentence appears to have no meaning (i.e. it is 'nonsensical') it is invariably possible to create a context which supplies the missing overlap of scenarios and gives the sentence some meaning.

These considerations lead us to suggest that the grammatical structure of a sentence is a meaning bearing symbolism, and that syntax is a sub-topic of semantics.

18.3 The Construction Kit Analogy

A statement made in communication can be regarded as a 'construction kit' for an internal representation of some aspect of the world, real or imaginary. Some of the words are labels for the constructional units, other words (and the order of the words) carry information about how the constructional units are to be put together.

There is a very close analogy with a child's modelling kit. The kit provides the child with constructional units and with instructions about how to put them together. Individual instructions perform the same role as some words in a natural language sentence. For example, some of the instructions are entirely devoted to part recognition and establish the names for these, e.g. *'The wing panels will be found in the plastic bag. The leading edge is the more rounded edge.'* Certain instructions are devoted to the method for joining these, e.g. *'Glue the butt end of the wing panel into the groove on the side of the fuselage with the leading edge forwards.'* The sequence of instructions indicates the chronological sequence in which the instructions should be carried out. However, if the instructions are lost, it is often still possible to put the pieces together in roughly the correct pattern, provided that the person doing it uses his or her common sense. In the same way we might still be able to interpret the story correctly if the words (all nouns) are jumbled.

18.4 The Importance of Models of Models in Communication

The idea that our internal models contain representations of other people's models is very important. It is this that enables us to predict the likely behaviour of others. Since mankind is essentially a social animal, required to cohabit and cooperate with the most intelligent (and the most dangerous) animal known (man himself), that ability is crucial to our survival.

Knowledge of physical objects can be gained by direct observation, but knowledge of the internal model of another person can only be gained by that person communicating the information to us by facial expression, by other body symbols, and, most important of all, by language. It is not surprising, therefore, to find that language abounds with allusions, direct and indirect, to thoughts, attitudes and emotions. The obvious examples are expressions such as:

I think that ...
I wish ...
He wants to ...

They are going to ...
She knows that ...

and so on. But this kind of information is not carried by such obvious candidates alone. We are all familiar with sets of expressions such as:

'I am of independent mind.'
'You are hard to convince.'
'He is a stubborn fool.'

To some extent these all describe the same kind of human behaviour. The real difference between them is the way they provide clues about someone's attitude to such behaviour, and how that depends upon the person whose behaviour is described. Indeed it is sometimes hard to find a form of words to describe something which does not carry some connotation about the speaker's value judgements. That is not an accident.

18.5 Imperative Statements and Questions

There are, however, even more subtle ways of making hidden allusions to internal models. Consider the three sentences:

The door is open.
Shut the door!
Is the door open?

The first, said with a flat tone of voice, is a straightforward example of a 'construction kit' statement. The speaker gives the hearer a kit to construct a representation of a door standing open. The hearer can then take such action as he feels appropriate. The second statement is also an example of a construction kit communication, but in this case the model is more extensive and includes details about the speaker's attitude to the door being open. It can be interpreted thus:

The door is open.
I want it shut.
If you do not shut it I will be annoyed.

The first statement can be made to carry the same information as the second, by changing the tone of voice to indicate the speaker's irritation.

The third statement is also a construction kit communication, but in this case it describes the speaker's model and indicates that in that model the state of the door is unknown. The interpretation is as follows:

There is a door.
In my model its state is unknown.
I would like to be able to complete my model.

If you supply the information I will be pleased.

The first statement could be made to mean the same as the third by a change in the voice inflection, (that is by adding additional information about the speaker's internal model).

18.6 Summary

This analysis shows several things:

(1) The construction kit theory of communication holds for imperative statements and questions as well as for simple descriptive statements.

(2) Information about internal models is carried in subtle ways by very many statements.

(3) An important aspect of internal models is the indication of emotional state and predicted emotional state.

(4) Any attempt to develop a natural language processing system for the general case, as distinct from a restricted domain such as our micro-graphics world, will be doomed to failure if it does not attempt to represent the internal models of people.

CHAPTER 19

Causation

19.1 The Nature of Causation

It was the 18th-century philosopher David Hume who first drew attention to the fact that no one has ever directly observed a causal connection, or as he described it 'a necessary connection', between two events. Experience tells us that certain events are usually immediately followed by certain others, and the experience sets up in us an anticipation of such consequences. To say that one event 'causes' another, however, is not to offer an explanation; it is simply a handy way of describing our observations. Why does one magnet attract another? We can offer descriptions at atomic and even sub-atomic levels, and we can model the attraction in mathematical terms so that we can predict the behaviour of magnets with very great accuracy, but we are still faced with a basic lack of explanation as to why one magnetic pole attracts another of opposite polarity. Indeed the very ideas of 'attraction' and 'magnetic pole' are human inventions created to organise our thoughts about these phenomena.

Psychological experiments have shown that people have a tendency to assume a causal connection between any two relatively rare events if one happens immediately before the other. If the juxtaposition of such events is repeated the impression of causal connection is strengthened. Just as we are disposed to see our world in terms of 'entities' rather than in terms of a confused collection of patches of colour, so we tend to perceive a chronological sequence of isolated events as a single extended event. Causation is perceptual 'glue' which combines several events to form one. It is a product of the human mind which renders predictable that which is otherwise unpredictable.

19.2 Notation

Let us represent the causal connection between any two events X and Y by the notation 'X --> Y'. Sometimes it is helpful to provide a graphical representation of causal connections. When it is appropriate we shall use the notation illustrated in Figure 19.1.

Fig. 19.1. A diagrammatic representation of causal links.

19.3 The Transitivity of Causal Connections

Causation is transitive. That is, if we observe that (X causes Y) and (Y causes Z), we can infer that (X causes Z), or in the new notation:

(X --> Y) and (Y --> Z) =>> (X --> Z)

or more succinctly:

(X --> Y --> Z) =>> (X --> Z)

where =>> means 'implies'.

Furthermore we can, if the situation warrants it, insert extra events between A and Z to give:

(A --> B --> C --> D --> .... Z)

We have been using the term 'event' rather loosely so far. If we return to the ideas introduced in section 4.3, where we discussed object-histories of objects in the micro-graphics world, we can represent our view of the world as a chronological sequence of 'states'. A state is a condition of the world perceived at some particular time or over a particular period of time. The expression (A --> B --> C --> D ... Z) should then be interpreted as a sequence of causally linked states (rather than events). A causal connection exists between states if we find that we can use the observation of one state to predict (with reasonable confidence) the future observation of the other.

19.4 Causal Links and Time-stamps

When we speak about causation, we are sometimes discussing a general rule which applies to all occasions. For example *'Disease causes death'*. On other occasions we are speaking of a particular set of circumstances, e.g. *'The King's death was caused by Bubonic Plague'*.

The second case is the more interesting because the states concerned, which represent the King alive (A), and the King dead (Z), have, presumably, actually been observed and will have particular time-stamps. We are saying that (in our opinion) certain other states intervened between A and Z to form a causally linked chain of states (A, B, C, ... Z) where B, C, etc. are states describing the King catching Bubonic Plague, developing a temperature, and so on. We are saying that each state in the chain was directly responsible for the next, and that these causal links (or connections) actually happened at particular moments in time. Something which happened at a particular moment in time can be represented as a state (since it represents a perceived condition of the world). It follows that a causal connection can be represented by a 'state'.

This is an important conclusion because it means that a causal connection can itself be the causal precursor or the consequence of some other state. In other words a 'cause' can cause a 'cause'. To implement our representation we can use a predicate 'cause(X,Y)', or a data structure of type 'cause' with elements holding pointers to X and Y. It does not matter which. What we cannot do, however, is to provide a representation of X with a simple pointer (labelled 'cause') to Y (or vice versa). The representation of the causal link between X and Y must be independent of the representations X and Y so that it can have its own identity and its own time-stamp.

A causal connection of the type *'Disease causes death'* is timeless (has a formal parameter as its time-stamp) and is analogous to the generic structures we introduced to deal with concepts. It can be used to generate an infinite set of particular examples of causal links.

When we say *'X caused Y'* it could be the case that X has been observed and Y is being inferred. It could also be the case that Y has been observed and X is being inferred (as in forensic science). It is also possible that both X and Y have been observed and we are asserting that it is our perception that there was a causal link between them. The interpretation of this last type is interesting because it introduces the idea of hypothetical situations. We are in fact asserting that if X had not occurred, Y would not have occurred (at the time that it did occur). The implication is that we must be able to represent hypothetical states.

19.5 Types of Causal Link

There appear to be several different types of causal connection, but because a 'cause' can cause a 'cause' a single type of representation of causal linkage can be used for all of those types.

Multiple causes

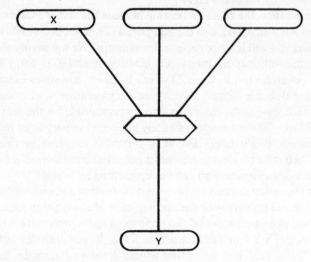

Fig. 19.2. X contributes to the cause of Y.

Gating. This is really a disguised form of the multiple cause condition, where most of the multiple causes are normally present and one remaining condition (state) is caused by X. We can reduce the complexity of the representation, however, as illustrated in fig 19.3.

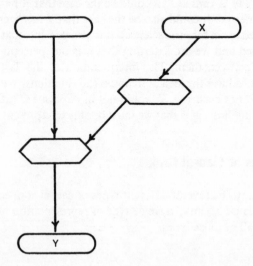

Fig. 19.3. X allows Y.

Negative gating. For this form of representation we need to be able to negate states.

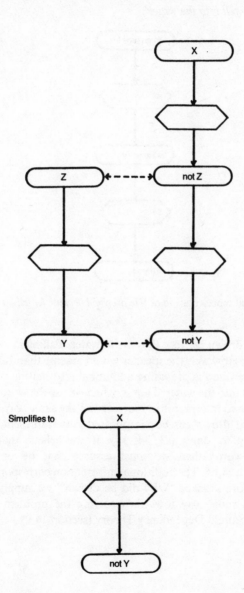

Fig. 19.4. X prevents Y.

19.6 Ignoring Causal Links

In many cases causal links are implicit in the use of certain words, and the speaker is concerned to add additional information which extends the causal chain, or inserts additional links into it. An example we have already used is *'He drowned because he fell into the water'.*

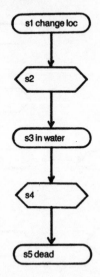

Fig. 19.5. A graphical representation of *'He drowned because he fell into the water'.*

Actually people drown because they *are in* water. Falling in is not by itself a cause of drowning. However, the speaker would assume that this simple fact is known to the hearer, and is providing additional information which indicates how the person got into the water. That is, when we use the word 'drowned' we expect other people to interpret it in more or less the same way as we do. The meaning of the word 'drown' can be paraphrased by the representation in Figure 19.5 corresponding to states (s3, s4, s5). If we believe that the speaker understands our words then we must assume that he or she has the representation of s3, s4, s5. The additional information corresponds to states s1 and s2, and therefore if asked 'Why did he drown?' we supply s1, s2 as the answer. This goes some way towards resolving the problem noted in our discussion of Conceptual Dependency Theory (section 14.9).

19.7 Summary

We have developed arguments which support the following conclusions:

(1) Causation is a product of human perception.
(2) Causation is transitive.
(3) Our representation should allow causal chains to be extended and additional links to be inserted.
(4) We require the representation of negated states.
(5) We require the representation of hypothetical states.
(6) We require the representation of other people's internal representations.
(7) A causal link can be represented as a state with its own time-stamp.
(8) A cause can cause a cause.

CHAPTER 20

The Representation of States

20.1 States and Perceptions

In Chapter 17 we discussed some aspects of human perception and the organisation of memory. We suggested that internal representations of the meaning of linguistic utterances made use of the same structures as other types of representation (section 17.4). The consequence is that our method of representation for states should lean heavily on the representation of perceptions. In fact a state is a perceptual 'snapshot' of the world (real or imaginary).

In this chapter we develop a method of representing states, taking the requirements discussed in Chapter 17 into account. The method will serve as a basis for discussion for the remainder of the book. It is by no means the only form of representation which we could have chosen, but unlike some of the exotic formalisms it does not call for a deep understanding of logic. Instead it is based upon simple data structures, and each state is represented by a record structure. We attempt below to determine the appropriate elements or fields of that record structure, and to do that we will return once more to the features of human perception.

State-id. Each state will have a unique identifier so that we can cross-reference it from other states in a perspicuous way.

Time-stamp. Each state will have a time-stamp. This will be represented by a formal parameter which may or may not be instantiated (see Chapter 8).

Channel. We have five senses through which our perceptions of the external world are filtered. These are sight, hearing, touch, taste and scent. When we perceive the world we are aware of which senses we are using, and so it is reasonable that our representation of state should have a parameter which records the sense involved. We will call that the *channel* of the perception (and of the state).

Aspect. Consider the sight channel. When we look at the world we are able to discriminate between and be aware of several different aspects of the scene. We recognise 'entities', we note their 'colour', their 'shape', their 'location', and so on. Each of these we shall refer to as an *aspect* of a perception.

Model. Consider the aspect of location. When we observe the location of an object we can think about it in terms of different frames of reference. We might use ourselves as the point of origin and think about the location of the object relative to ourselves in terms of some kind of polar coordinate system, or we might use a plan view of the scene. When children of a certain age are asked to sketch a house, they invariably sketch the house in vertical elevation and the garden in plan view. This is obviously not how they would see a house if they looked at it, or how it would appear in a photograph, but it does indicate how they 'perceive' it. We shall refer to a system of coordinates of this kind as a *model*.

Axis. When we talk about locations we refer only to a particular quantity like distance, height or depth. When we talk about the shape of an object, we talk about its height, thickness, width, length and so on. When we discuss a complex shape (like a face) we can compare it with some standard shape, like a template of a 'standard face'. We will also need some function which compares such shapes and provides a measure of difference which we shall call a *metric*. Always we are referring to a singular quantity which coincides with one axis of the coordinate system involved. For a quantity like area we use a model which has only one axis. Length and width are not distinguished one from another. We shall call this the *axis* of the perception. A metric is an axis. Various metrics have been proposed which measure, for example, the symmetry of a shape, the ratio of perimeter to area, and so on.

Value and relative value. We perceive the value of some quantity. As we indicated in section 17.5, human perceptions are poor with respect to absolute values and superb with respect to relative values or discrimination. Our representational technique will reflect that by providing each quantity value perceived with an individual identifier (a unique string). The relative measure of that value will be provided in terms relative to other identifiers (including 'standard values' — see section 7.7). Once we have identified the channel, aspect, model, and axis of a perception, and have two identifiers X and Y which indicate the positions of certain values on that axis, we can readily understand what the relationship X>Y means.

Reference. Finally we note that these properties (height, shape, size, distance etc.) all belong to some entity. We require some means of representing an entity, and each state which represents a property of that entity must be cross-referenced to it.

These, then, are the parameters which we suggest should be present in the representation of a state, so that we can write:

state(state-id,time-stamp,channel,aspect,model,axis,value,reference)

As we develop our argument we shall have cause to add more parameters to that set, but the basic set will not be changed. We shall call the set of four parameters (channel,aspect,model,axis) a *framework*.

The impressive thing about the way we, as humans, deal with complex descriptions of a scene is the speed and ease with which we can flip from one framework to another, or even maintain several different frameworks in operation at the same time.

The internal channel. We are aware of ourselves in a way that does not require the use of any of the normal sensory channels. To allow internal feeling to be represented we therefore introduce an additional channel which we shall call the 'internal channel'.

Entities. We noted earlier (in Chapter 4) that an entity is a manifestation of human perception, and that the identity of an entity is not dependent upon the set of properties it may have at any particular time. It has an object history and an existence which can outlast its physical disappearance. We could fit the representation of an entity into the framework idea, but it is simpler to provide a special state for the purpose. It will still have a state identifier and a time-stamp which indicates the period of time for which it is perceived by the person concerned. The state identifier becomes the identifier for the entity and it is often convenient to have a name for an entity. The representation structure is therefore:

state(state-id,time-stamp,'entity',entity-name)

Causal links. We discussed the representation of a causal link in Chapter 19, and concluded that it could be represented by means of a 'state'. Again the simplest method is to introduce a special kind of state for this purpose. It will have an identifier, a time-stamp, and two lists of state identifiers to indicate the set of states which comprise the cause, and the set of states which comprise the effect of the causal link. We will allow 'and' and 'or' connectors within the lists of states so that we can have contributing and alternative causes and effects. The representation has the form:

state(state-id,time-stamp,'cause',causing-state,effect-state)

20.2 Representations of Representations

We have remarked frequently that it is important that a formalism for representation should be capable of dealing with the representation of other people's representations. To this end we introduce a new structure which, for want of a better name, we shall call a *rep-box*.

A rep-box will be able to contain a variable number of states of all kinds and provide them with a common identity. We can think of it as a cardboard box into which we can put all of the states of some representation, and on the lid of the box we can write global information about the contents. This will include a relationship between the relative time-stamps on the state within the box and absolute 'now'. We can also indicate on the lid whether this is a real or a fictitious representation, and to whom the representation belongs.

We can think of the whole of the computer memory being one very large box which belongs to the computer itself. In a sense then all representations belong to it. (It can call itself 'me' or 'us'.) All other representations are held within that global box, and represent its representations of someone else's representation.

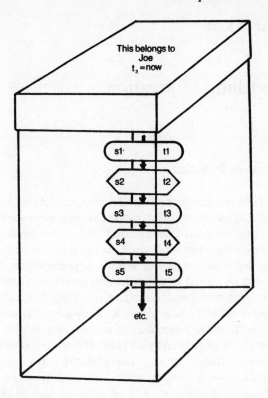

This belongs to
Joe
t_3 = now

s1   t1
s2   t2
s3   t3
s4   t4
s5   t5

etc.

Fig. 20.1. A 'rep-box'.

The representation of that 'someone else' will be an entity outside the box belonging to that person but within the computer's box.

We will develop this idea further in Chapter 22.

CHAPTER 21

Modelling Motivation

21.1 An Exercise in Robotics

The complexity of human emotions makes the thought of trying to model these in any explicit way a daunting task. The complexity may, however, be somewhat reduced by taking a rather unflattering and simplistic view of human nature. The result may be a form of representation which ignores many of the subtle nuances of human nature, but it will carry our system surprisingly far. In short, the human organism can be viewed as a gratification-seeking automaton.

Imagine that we have been asked to design a robot which will later be sent to some distant planet of which we have almost no knowledge. The environment in which it will find itself, and in which it must survive, may exhibit very strange phenomena and could be populated by all kinds of strange and possibly hostile life-forms. Let us assume that technology is available so that we can provide the robot with external sensors, eyes, ears etc., with which it can perceive its surroundings. However, we have no way of knowing how to program it to respond to the things it sees, hears, touches etc. since we do not know what they are or how they will behave. A strategy which we might adopt to solve this problem is as follows.

We can provide the robot with internal sensors. These can detect its oil pressure, its temperature and whatever else is appropriate to the innards of a robot. With these it can detect its inner condition. At least we know what *these* conditions should be for survival, and we can program it so that it can recognise when it is in a desirable condition and when it is in an undesirable condition. We will call these 'goals' and 'anti-goals' respectively. We can also arrange its sensors so that it will be able to detect when its inner conditions are changing for the better or the worse (towards goal state or towards anti-goal).

Next we provide it with something like a 'black-box flight recorder'. This records all its external and internal perceptions as they occur, and stores them together with indicators to show when the sequence of events recorded led to goal and to anti-goal conditions. Of course, events are unlikely to repeat themselves exactly, but if the robot can process and analyse its recordings so they can be classified by similarities, ignoring circumstances peculiar to each unique event, then there is some chance that it will be able to recognise history repeating itself and take action to select favourable outcomes and avoid unfavourable ones. From these records the robot could form for itself sequences of hypothetical but probable events, in order to predict the likely outcome from known starting conditions.

The formation of these chains could become too complex and time-consuming for real-time computation, and so it would be expedient to develop sub-goals which were known from previous experience to be conditions from which the main goal state was easily achieved. Some way would need to be found to label these sub-goals as 'desirable' in their own right. It would, for the same reason, be expedient to identify sub-anti-goals which should be avoided whenever possible. Note that we cannot identify the sub-goals in advance, since here on Earth we have no way of knowing what they will be. What we must arrange for is an automatic labelling of the sub-goals after they have been discovered.

Some behaviour patterns could be pre-programmed into the robot. These would be basic behaviour patterns such as that required to maintain its fuel supplies. For example, if the robot could recharge its batteries by means of solar panels, it could be pre-programmed to 'like' sunny places. That is, sunbathing would be a sub-goal. We would not need to give the robot any insight into why it liked these places, but other aspects of its behaviour would be learned and would adapt to the prevailing circumstances by trial and error. The pre-programmed 'chunks' of behaviour could be used along with learned 'chunks' to form the more complex behavioural patterns which would help it to survive.

If someone unaware of how the robot had been programmed was able to witness the robot's behaviour, they could be forgiven for thinking that the robot was driven by 'desire' for certain things. And such a person, who wanted to predict the behaviour of the robot, would be well advised to think in terms of 'desires' even if they knew about the internal program involved. The program would, after all, be extremely complex, and its precise behaviour would depend upon remembered data which was internal to the robot and was unknown to the observer. Trying to work things out from first principles would not be an efficient way of predicting the robot's behaviour in real-time.

The final touch, which would give the robot an almost human-like behaviour pattern, would be the ability to predict the behaviour of other organisms (i.e. people) based upon a similar model of their assumed 'desires'. Such a robot may well decide that helping others to achieve their 'desires' was the best way of achieving its own 'desires' (i.e. helping others was a sub-goal) and would, therefore, develop an analogue of altruistic behaviour.

We do not want to push this idea too far and suggest that this is actually how humans behave. It is merely a way of representing something which would otherwise be extremely elusive. Our robot may feel no inner sensations such as we feel, but its behaviour would make it look as if it did. It may seek its goals as an automaton without any awareness of a desire, but in our representation of its behaviour, our programs will identify goal states and will 'know' that the robot will try to achieve them. So 'desire' will not be represented by an actual feeling, but will instead become an inferred property of the programs which process the representations. We may not be able to create feelings, but we can write such programs.

This way of representing motivation is fundamental to the whole strategy we will develop in the next chapters. 'Goal' and 'anti-goal' states will be primitives of our representational scheme, and it is our contention that this simple mechanism is capable of supporting a representation of quite involved human social behaviour patterns such as those associated with the concepts 'duty', 'ownership', 'honesty' and 'flattery'.

21.2 Examples of Concepts involving Motivation

Many words contain hidden references to the mental states and motivations of people. We will try to illustrate this with a series of examples, and show how these representations can be constructed using 'goal' and 'anti-goal' states as primitives. Since the representations can become quite baroque, we will simplify them by showing only the relevant items. The notation <Sn....> is used to indicate a state. It is identified by its number 'Sn' where 'n' is an integer. A causal connection between S1 and S2 will be denoted S1->S2.

Example 1: likes

The representation of 'likes', as in 'John likes X', must identify X as the cause of John's potential happiness (in John's mind). Thus we have:

'John likes X'
rep

---
owner = <John>

<S1 agent>
<S2 X>
<S3 goal of agent>
<S4 S2->S3>

S2 and S4 are labelled 'potential', interpreted as *'John thinks that X causes him to achieve goal-state'*

It will be noted that this representation cannot distinguish between 'likes', 'desires' and similar words. A more adequate representation would make use of the representation of X. For example, if X = 'apples' then the representation of X would contain a description of X as something which people eat. This could be used to explain more fully how X would cause John to achieve his goal state by unifying John with the agent of the eating process. This is of course a very selfish form of liking.

Example 2: loves

The idea is that 'loves' is the unselfish counterpart of 'likes', i.e. *'If X loves Y then X wants to give pleasure to Y'*.

'X loves Y'

---
owner = X

<S1 X>
<S2 Y>
<S3 goal of Y>
<S4 goal of X>
<S5 S3->S4>

Or, *'Y being happy makes X happy'*.

Example 3: controls

The idea behind 'controls' is that one entity, X, can manipulate another, Y, in order to achieve the desired results of X.

'X controls Y'

---
owner =

    <S1 X>
    <S2 Y>
    <S3 some arbitrary state>
    <S4 goal of X>
    <S5 S3->S4>
    <S6 S2->S3>
    <S7 S1->S6>

Note the last element. It indicates that X causes Y to be the cause of the state causing X's goal state.

Example 4: accepts

The interpretation of 'accepts' here is concerned with the acceptance of a situation or a state of affairs, not the acceptance of a gift. That would require a different representation.

'X accepts Y'
---
owner =

<S1 X>
<S2 Y>
<S3 an arbitrary state of affairs>
<S4 goal of X>
<S5 not(S3->S4)>
<S6 S2->S3>
<S7 not S1 controls S2>

The idea here is that Y is causing a state S3 which is not causing X to achieve his goal state. Nevertheless, X does not seek to change this state of affairs (does not control Y).

A more subtle representation might include information about whether or not X was able to control Y if he wished (possible or not possible X control Y).

Example 5: owns

The word 'owns' is particularly difficult to represent because of the many different types of ownership which are possible (see section 16.2). The idea developed here is that ownership is a kind of social contract between the owner of something and the rest of humanity which accepts the owner's right to control the object 'owned'. This contract can be time limited so that it only lasts for the duration of a meeting (owning a chair) or for a lifetime (owning a leg). The acceptance by humanity may be limited to certain types of control. For example, parents 'own' their children but are not granted the power of life and death over them by society.

'X owns Y'
---
owner =

<S1 X>
<S2 Y>
<S3 humanity>
<S4 X controls Y>
<S5 S3 accepts S4>

For a representation of humanity we would require some of the ideas developed in Chapter 26.

Example 6: duty

Some will object strongly to the ideas we put forward here because they present a very poor view of human nature. The idea is that duty is a person's belief that certain behaviour is expected of them by society, and that should they fail to behave in this way society would disapprove. A more subtle representation might include the idea that the person concerned is not consciously aware of the details of this situation (or has forgotten) and is now aware only of a compulsion to serve humanity. He now seeks to please himself by this behaviour rather than humanity.

'X has a duty Y'

---

owner = X

<S1 X>
<S2 Y>
<S3 humanity>
<S4 an arbitrary state>
<S5 S1->S4> (S5 is identified with 'Y')
<S6 goal of S3>
<S7 S4->S6>
<S8 S3 loves S1>
<S9 S5->S8>
<S10 goal of X>
<S11 S8->S10>

Or, X takes action to bring about an arbitrary state which will cause the goal state of humanity to be achieved. The fact that X caused this state of affairs causes humanity to 'love' X. The goal of X is to have humanity loving him. If we dropped some of the intermediate causal links so that the achievement of humanity's goal was an end in itself for X (without the need for humanity to love him), we would have a less base interpretation of 'duty'.

Example 7: deceives

The idea here is that X causes Y to have a false idea about the true state of affairs (or at least what X believes to be true).

'X deceives Y about Z'

---

owner =

<S1 X>
<S2 Y>

```
<S3 an arbitrary state Z>
<S4      _____

          owner = Y
          <S5 not(S3)>
          _____
>
<S6 S1->S4>
_____
```

In other words, X causes Y to have a model (S4) in which the state (S5) is the opposite of the actual state of affairs (S3). A more complex definition might have X causing Y to believe that the achievement of some state will help him (Y) to achieve his goal, when it will actually help X to achieve his goal.

Example 8: ability

The idea is that X is able to cause certain things.

```
_____
'X has the ability Y to Z'
_____
owner =
<S1 X>
<S2 arbitrary state or set of states>
<S3 S1->S2 'Y'>
_____
```

Y is identified as the causal link between X and some arbitrary state Z. That is, X has the ability to bring about Z.

Example 9: flattery

```
_____
'X flatters Y'
_____
id = M1
owner = me

<S1 X>
<S2 Y>
<S3      _____

          id = M2
          owner = Y

          <S4      _____
```

```
         id = M3
         owner = X

         <S5 Y has the ability Z>
         <S6 X likes Z>
         _____
      > (end of S4)
      _____
  > (end of S3)
  <S5 S1->S3>
  _____
```

For clarification we have introduced identifiers for each representation (M1, M2 and M3). Y has a model (M2) in which he believes that X has a model (M3) in which X believes that Y has certain abilities, which X would like to have. That Y believes model (M2) was caused by X. Whether or not M2 is accurate is not shown here. Perhaps it should include 'X deceives Y about S5'.

With this we feel that we have plumbed the depths of the baser human attributes and leave the reader to try developing representations for such words as 'honesty', 'courage', 'trustworthiness' and 'intelligence'. It is fully accepted that these representations are simplistic travesties. What they do show, however, is that the representation of the ideas conveyed by these words is not entirely beyond the bounds of practicality. It also shows that complex definitions can be constructed from simpler ones, holding open the prospect that we may be able to teach a computer the meaning of such terms in words which it already understands.

CHAPTER 22

The Representation of Truth and Knowledge

22.1 Beliefs within Beliefs

What we are concerned with in this chapter are possible ways of representing the belief that a statement is true. We are not concerned with whether particular statements are true, or with the proper methods of deducing true statements from other true statements. The question is — how do the representations of the following statements differ from each other?

> *'John believes that Mary likes him.'*
> *'John knows that Mary likes him.'*
> *'John does not know that Mary likes him.'*
> *'John believes incorrectly that Mary likes him.'*

In section 20.2 we introduced a way of representing someone's internal representation (or beliefs) as a kind of box into which we place the representation of his/her representation. On the lid of the box we can write down who this representation belongs to (let us say 'John') and anything else which *we* believe to be true about it, including, perhaps, our belief that the contents of the box are incorrect (untrue) even if John believes the contents to be true. If the box belonging to John contains another box (containing, let us say, Mary's beliefs) then what is written on the top of the box is what John believes to be true about Mary's beliefs. If we want to represent what *we* think are Mary's beliefs then we must create yet another box, and place it outside the box belonging to John but inside our box (which is the whole system).

The closest we can come to the representation of an absolute truth is the representation of what *we* believe. If we have a representation of John's beliefs, and we want to represent the fact that we believe John's beliefs are true, then we can simply represent the same beliefs within our own box, and note the fact that the contents of John's box correspond to our own beliefs, i.e. *'John thinks X and we think X therefore John is correct'* (in our opinion).

Here, then, we have the difference between the representation of *'John thinks that Mary likes him'* and *'John knows that Mary likes him'*. For *'John thinks...'* we simply have John's box with the appropriate contents, whereas for *'John knows ...'* we have not only got John's box, but we have our own box containing a corresponding set of representations and an explicit note to the effect that they agree.

In dealing with a sentence such as *'John does not know that Mary likes him'* we can have our own 'box' with the the representation of Mary liking John. Elsewhere we have a representation of John's thoughts (John's 'box' within ours) and a third element which indicates that these do not agree. It appears that the agreement between 'boxes' should be represented explicitly so that it can be negated without actually representing the contents of 'John's box'.

It is obvious that boxes representing people's beliefs can be nested indefinitely in order to represent a statement such as *'John believes that Fred believes that Mary believes that ...'*

22.2 Representing the Knowing of Things not known to us

The idea of creating a correspondence between John's beliefs and ours, in order to indicate that John's beliefs are true, works well enough in many circumstances but comes to grief when we want to represent the information that John knows something which is not known to *us*. For example, *'John knows Mary's telephone number'*. It is not appropriate, even if we know what Mary's telephone number is, to replace the thing which John knows by the number in question, and it is impossible if we do not know what the number is. Knowing a telephone number is more than having a number in your head. The representation of the word 'telephone' must contain within it all the functionality of the device we call a 'telephone', and that representation will contain a representation of someone having something in their head (or in their box), an element X. The possession of this X will allow them to carry out a procedure on the telephone which will cause it to allow them to converse with the person at the other end of the telephone. Clearly we are leaning very heavily on our ability to represent causal links.

The difference between the two kinds of knowing is really the difference between *'Knowing THAT something is true'* and *'knowing HOW to do something'*. Because of the nature of a telephone, knowing a telephone number is equivalent to *'knowing how'*.

Representing something which someone knows and which we do not know can always be converted into the representation of something which produces results which are known to us. If I know that a friend knows all about advanced physics (which I do not), I know that he can pass examinations in physics (which I could not). I do not need to represent the knowledge in his head which enables him to do these things.

22.3 Negative Transportation

A particular problem which has been the subject of some controversy in linguistics is called the problem of 'negative transportation'. The term 'transportation' refers to the way in which the scope of negation appears to move from one level in a syntactic analysis to another level. The phenomenon is therefore seen by some as a problem for syntactic analysis. Consider the following sentences:

(1a) *He thought that he did NOT need to leave.*
(1b) *He did NOT think that he needed to leave.*
(2a) *He knew that he did NOT need to leave.*
(2b) *He did NOT know that he needed to leave.*

Most people agree that (1a) and (1b) mean the same thing, and most agree that (2a) and (2b) do not mean the same thing. This seems puzzling in view of the identical grammatical structures of the sentence pairs. Why should the scope of the negation appear in (1a) to extend over both the thinking and the needing, whereas in (2a) the scope of the negation covers only the knowing and not the needing, which remains as a positive assertion? Careful examination of (1a) and (1b) usually reveals, for some people, a subtle distinction in meaning, but the problem of the complete difference between the two types of negation in (2a) and (2b) remains.

The problem can be resolved, however, by resort to belief structure representation. Consider first the positive forms of these sentences:

(1a) *He thought that he needed to leave.*
(2a) *He knew that he needed to leave.*

In both cases we have a box with 'his' beliefs inside it. In the case of (2a) we have in addition our beliefs, which correspond to his.

The word 'know' carries within it a hidden reference to an additional representational structure of the thing which is known. Moreover the veracity of that additional structure is vouched for (by *us*). When we negate each sentence, the negation applies to the whole sentence (to John's beliefs); but certain elements escape negation by referring to something for which there exists other evidence of its truth. In the representation of sentence (2) the negative form (2a) *'he did not know that ...'*, the part of the representation which lies outside John's box (which belongs to *us*), escapes negation. Our representation then indicates that 'he' lacks this vital information.

Representing Objects

23.1 Physical Characteristics

In Chapter 20 we introduced a technique for the representation of an entity based on 'states'. We noted the need for a state which represented the identity of an entity which was independent of its properties. From that starting point our problem is to find good ways of representing the various properties which an entity might have. We based the representation of the properties on the perceptions which a human might have of them. Each state was provided with a unique identifier and a time-stamp. The structure which results is illustrated in Figure 23.1.

An entity has several very obvious properties. For example it has a location in space, it may consist of several sub-parts, and it may have certain functional roles to play. All of these present us with particular problems for representation, and we shall consider them in turn.

23.2 Spatial Relationships

We are concerned here with the relationships between objects such as being 'near' to one another (or to the speaker), one object being 'above' another, or

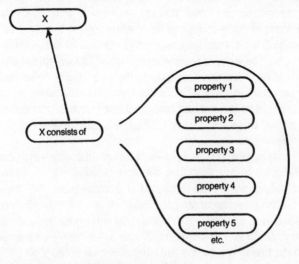

Fig. 23.1. An entity with associated properties.

'inside' another, or 'beyond' etc. We discussed in Chapter 16 the problems which can arise when we try to represent such relationships, and in Chapter 20 we introduced a method of representing 'states' based on perceptions. Specifically we introduced the notion of a 'framework' or frame of reference for a perception, which identified the sensory channel involved, the aspect of perception, the model (or coordinate system) being used, and the axis concerned.

The essence of the approach which we suggest is that a relationship such as one object being 'behind' another can be represented with reference to several frameworks at the same time. Thus 'behind' (in the sense of being 'behind a tree') is perceived visually by noting that one object is occluded from view by the other. In another framework, which uses a model with one of the objects concerned as origin, we have the notion of 'behind' meaning 'to the rear of'. In another framework, which uses the speaker as origin, 'behind' would be represented as meaning 'to the rear of the speaker' (and therefore out of sight). 'Distance' is perceived in terms of frameworks associated with texture gradients, blueness, reduced apparent size, reduced apparent sound, the possibility/impossibility of touching an object, its scent, and so on. A physical object would be endowed with a shape, size and location, whereas a fluid would have no shape, invisible gases would have no visible location, and so on. A heavy object would be associated with a significant 'heft' in the hand. A hard object would be associated with an unyielding 'feel'. These ideas could be implemented using predicates or networks of data structures, or in many other ways. The important point is that the physical properties are represented in terms of perceptual primitives rather than being represented in terms of arbitrary predicates.

Another aspect of the suggested approach is that each physical property should be represented in terms of all the associated perceptions at the same time. This will make serious demands upon storage space and is likely to produce very cumbersome representations, but it can be argued that if distance was represented in terms of the perceptions listed above (all at the same time), then it would be possible for a natural language system to detect (in a suitable context) that the sentences *'The aeroplane flew away'* and *'The aeroplane shrank and disappeared'* could be construed as meaning the same thing. When contextual information is necessary to make a choice between alternative interpretations, all interpretations should be created and sustained until further information makes it possible to choose. In such a system 'ambiguity' comes to be regarded simply as a lack of information.

In Chapter 16 we gave an example of the kind of difficulty which can arise if spatial relationships are represented in a simple-minded way: the relationship 'to-the-right-of' when people are sitting at a circular table. We have to ask ourselves what is the meaning of *'circular table'*. It is a table which has a shape such that people sitting progressively to the right end up by being on the left of the first person to sit down. *'To-the-right-of'* means *'to the right with reference to some line',* and the line in this case is the edge of the table (implied by 'sitting at the table'). The ideal way to deal with a problem like this is to develop some form of imagery representing the scene, and to read the positions of people directly from the image. We do not at present have the kind of computer power which makes this practical, but we might get some way to a solution by representing *'to-the-right-of'* in terms of the direction in which a person must turn their head to bring the next person into view.

23.3 Constituent Parts: the Anatomy of Objects

Objects usually have recognisable parts from which they are constructed. Knowledge about the anatomy of an object is necessary to understand many statements about it. For example, the statement 'She whispered in his ear' immediately informs the human reader that:

    (a) she is close to him
    (b) she is speaking quitely
    (c) few people will hear what she says
    (d) 'he' will hear what she says

This knowledge may be necessary for an adequate understanding of a narrative, and such knowledge is assumed by any storyteller. The necessary knowledge must include the knowledge that an 'ear' is part of the human anatomy, and is the part responsible for enabling hearing.

Semantic networks have frequently been used to indicate the structural relationships between objects. We could construct a tree structure such as that illustrated below:

```
human body :- (head, trunk, arms, legs)
       head :- (face, hair, neck)
      trunk :- (chest, back, waist, pelvis)
       arms :- (left arm, right arm)
        arm :- (hand, forearm, elbow)
       legs :- (left leg, right leg)
```

We could go on to break down 'hand' into fingers and thumbs. The face would break down into eyes, ears, nose, mouth and so on. Structural information would then be needed to indicate the relative positions and roles of these constituent parts — support(legs,trunk), attached(arms,trunk), attached-(head,trunk), support(trunk,head), and so on. The approach seems plausible at first sight, but it is fraught with difficulties.

The problem is — where do we stop? Every time an entity is represented and that entity is human, do we really want to create a structure like this – expanded in detail right down to fingernails, cuticle, nostril hairs, pores, blackheads, and many other parts which we will leave the reader to imagine? This seems an excessive amount of representational junk to carry around on the remote chance that it may be needed. Even if we do so there is the chance that the understanding of a statement will require knowledge of internal anatomy. We often refer to 'stomach', 'appendix', 'kidney', 'throat', 'lungs', 'nerves' etc. If carried to its logical conclusion this approach will require a representation to rival a medical textbook on anatomy.

To avoid being overwhelmed by the sheer volume of information which appears to be required, a more economical method of representation is needed. A possible solution would represent an object by only the top level of the tree structure. For example, we might represent a human as we have done above, and resist the attempt to break the parts down any further. We might add the component 'internal-anatomy'. The structure which would result is illustrated in Figure 23.2.

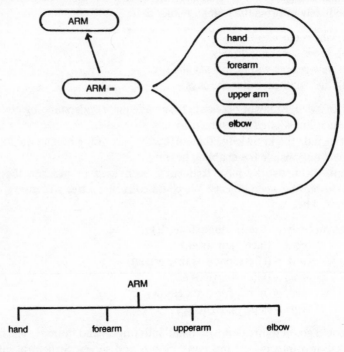

Fig. 23.2. An abbreviated tree structure.

The advantage of the additional record structure 'consists of' is that this state can be given a time-stamp of its own. We could therefore represent the situation which would arise if someone lost an arm. The arm would not cease to exist, but it would cease to be a constituent part of the person-entity. We could then have two 'consists of' states with time-stamps indicating the time at which the arm loss took place. Each component such as 'hand', 'arm' etc., would then be regarded as a 'macro', or the label for a database which could be expanded when required.

This suggestion is not a complete solution to the problem, however. There is still a difficulty in deciding when the expansion should take place. If we were dealing with the sentence *'John broke his finger'* it would be necessary to note that 'finger' was an element of human anatomy and a part of 'hand'. The word 'hand' would have as part of its definition (or one of its many possible definitions) the information that it was often used (by humans) for picking things up. The system would then be able to deduce that John's ability to pick things up had been impaired (from the definition of 'broke').

This arrangement works well, and an appropriate expansion can be triggered if the two entities concerned are sufficiently close to one another that the overlap is detectable at top level. If, however, the overlap is not obvious at top level, we have the problem of deciding whether or not it is going to be worthwhile expanding. Consider the sentence *'John broke his barometer'*. Here there is no overlap which will be detectable between the short tree structures tagged on to the definition of each entity. Both are physical objects, but there the relationship stops. The real point of connection lies in the 'role' which a barometer plays (which we will discuss in the next section).

In the tree we described above, each node represents a constituent part of the entity represented by its superior node. It is also possible to construct a tree in which each node is a 'specialisation' (or specialised example of) its superior node, and at the same time each node is a 'generalisation' of its subordinate nodes. We might call it a 'consists-of-and-is-part-of' tree. Many efforts to produce a system for the handling of semantic information have been based upon tree structures of this kind. Complications abound, however. A 'leg' is a part of a person, and it is also part of a table, a chair and so on. It appears that we need several different types of 'leg' at different points in our tree structure, and the same can be true of almost every other concept.

23.4 The Classification of Objects

In addition to a 'consists-of-and-is-part-of' tree, we can also construct an 'is-a' relationship network. We might for example classify a 'spaniel' as a 'dog' and a 'dog' as an 'animal'.

In such a tree we say that each level is a 'specialisation' of its superior node, and each is a 'generalisation' of its subordinate nodes. Furthermore, it is often not necessary to repeat all of the properties which an entity may have at each node. If all animals are physical objects and therefore have shape, size, location etc., it can be assumed that all subordinate nodes (or specialisations) of the node corresponding to 'physical object' will also have these properties. This idea is known as *inheritance* and it is an important property of semantic nets of this kind. In the previous section we noted the need for several different kinds of 'leg'. Each of these could be considered a specialisation of a general concept 'leg' which is a support for something (unspecified). Each type of 'leg' specialises the concept by specifying the thing supported. Obviously our two types of network must intersect.

But cutting across such a structure are other possible classification structures. We might classify objects into 'edible' and 'inedible' objects, or as 'solids', 'liquids' and 'gases'. There is indeed, as we noted in section 17.6, some evidence that humans do in fact classify objects according to properties such as 'edible' and 'inedible'.

For all types of classification structure we have the same dominant problem. We have potentially a very large data structure to store, almost all of which will be redundant in any given set of circumstances, and some way must be found to minimise the amount of information brought to bear on a given problem. At the same time enough information must be provided to enable the decision to be made about whether or not it would be worthwhile to expand the structure to include more information. The top level of information tagged to each entity explicitly should be regarded as 'heuristic signposts', which indicate whether or not a search through the semantic structure is likely to be fruitful.

This remains a very significant problem.

23.5 The Functional Roles of Entities

What is the meaning of the phrase 'tennis ball'? One type of definition would stress its shape, its size, its bounciness, its being made of rubber with a felted surface, its hollowness, the curiously curved pattern of lines on its surface, and so on. On learning this definition a person would presumably be able to recognise a tennis ball. We could give a tennis ball to the same person and they would be able to store a much more accurate set of information about its characteristics based on its appearance, weight and feel. All these we might be able to represent by means of the perception-based representation. But would a person whose knowledge was confined to these facts about its physical characteristics really know what a tennis ball is?

To complete their knowledge we would have to tell them about (or better still let them see) a game of tennis. That is, we would need to inform them about the role for which a tennis ball is intended. A tennis ball can, of course, be used in a variety of ways which have nothing to do with tennis, but an understanding of its intended role is part of knowing what a tennis ball is.

It is therefore necessary to include, within the representation of an object, a representation of a scenario which describes its role. This scenario must include the representation of a number of other entities. To distinguish these from the one which is the object being represented, it is necessary to mark or otherwise indicate the 'salient' element of the scenario representation. The phrase 'tennis ball' is quite a hard one to represent, and so we will leave it until the next section where we shall deal with the representation of repetitive events. Instead we will consider the representation of the word 'fertiliser'. This is usually a brown, earth-like substance which would not easily be distinguished from many other substances if its role was not known. The representation might be something like this:

```
id =
owner =
    <S1 (a plant)>
    <S2 (soil)>
*   <S3 (fertiliser)>
    <S4 (agent)>
    <S5 S3 in S2 >
    <S6 S4->S5 >
    <S7 S1 in S4 >
    <S8 size of S1 increase>
    <S9 S5->S8 >
```

That is, there exists a plant, some soil, some fertiliser and an agent. The plant is in the soil. The agent places the fertiliser in the soil, and this causes the plant to grow.

The state marked '*' is the entity being defined (the salient).

Of course we have glossed over a lot of detail in this illustration. Each state would contain many elements, including time-stamps which would be in chronological sequence. The plant and the soil would have their physical characteristics. We might indicate that the plant would grow in any case, but that the fertiliser would make it grow faster and bigger. But these are details which do not affect the point being made.

Note that the same scenario could be used to define the verb 'to fertilise', except that in that case the state S6 would be identified as the salient (i.e. the act of causing the fertiliser to be in the soil). Note also that 'fertiliser' is a noun, while 'to fertilise' is a verb, and recall the comments made (in section 11.5) about the way case grammar mistakenly places too much emphasis on the case structure of a verb and ignores the information content which a noun carries. The causal connectivity of a scenario representation is crucial to an understanding of roles.

23.6 Representing Stuff

In Chapter 16 we gave an outline of some of the major stumbling blocks in natural language research. One of them was the representation of substances (or 'stuff').

Most current NL systems make the convenient assumption that the things which populate our world are solid, well-formed objects. Locations can be assigned to them, they have shape and size and a unique identity. Computers handle data in the form of discrete chunks or structures, and it is therefore natural that we should attempt to model things in terms of these discrete structural units. 'Water', however, is not a discrete object; it is a material or substance of which other things may be made. The same is true for 'wood', 'steel', 'air', etc. Trees are made of wood, so are tables and chairs. The atmosphere is made of air, and the Atlantic Ocean is made of water, as is the River Nile.

It is first necessary to note that it is impossible to think about a substance of any kind without thinking of something made of that substance. It may not be an identifiable object with a well-known shape and a name, but any mass of substance is an entity of a kind. Furthermore, the properties possessed by a substance are the properties which it bestows on the entities which are made of it.

We have the means to represent such entities. We can represent their appearance, their feel, their shape (or lack of it), their colour, their rigidity and so on. Fluids bestow on any entity made of them a shapelessness. Entities made of gas have no fixed size (or volume). Fluid objects try to escape, and are retained by means of a container. Gaseous objects expand and sometimes float upwards.

We can begin our representation of a stuff X by inventing an entity which is made of X. It need not have a name. It will normally be represented by an anonymous identifier.

      <S1 entity X >
  *   <S2 = S3,S4,S5,S6,...>
      <S3 ... of X >
      <S4 ... of X >
      <S5 ... of X >
      <S6 ... of X >
      etc.
  where S3, S4, S5, S6 represent properties of X

Structural state S2 would be identified as the salient in this representation (the substance itself). That is, the substance is that which provides the properties of X. By representing the properties of this entity X we are thereby representing the properties of the substance.

If we have available the computational means to process large arrays of similar elements efficiently, we could represent the object as a conjunction of a multitude of discrete elements (the state S2). Each element would have certain properties which would mimic the behaviour of the substance. Elements of water would always fall if they were not supported by either a solid object or another element of water. Thus water would always adopt the shape of its container. In a solid substance the individual elements would adhere to one another and preserve a basic shape.

In addition to these characteristics we could represent the colour, texture, etc.

Within the same representation we might describe the role of the substance. Air is breathed, water is drunk, wood is burned. These roles would be represented as scenarios in which things are consumed by fire, for example. We do not want a simple predicate 'can_burn(wood)'. We should also represent where some of these substances come from. Wood comes from trees, for example. We need, then, a scenario describing the growing of trees.

All this information is an essential part of our understanding of a statement such as 'I need air!' But the complexity of the information required, and the volume of the corresponding representational structures, are such that some means is required of ensuring that the full expansion of the structure is only carried out when necessary.

CHAPTER 24

Representing Events

24.1 Scenarios

We have already introduced the ideas to be presented here. An event is regarded as a set of states, each with a time-stamp. These time-stamps are represented by parameters t1, t2, t3, etc. and they are related by expressions such as t1 < t2, which indicates that the state with time-stamp t1 is (or was, or will be) perceived before the state with time-stamp t2. We have also discussed how the causal connectivity of such a set of states might be represented. In this chapter we shall tackle some of the outstanding problems which we have so far avoided.

24.2 Repetitive Events

We can return now to the problem of finding an appropriate representation for 'tennis ball' (see section 23.4). We noted in section 16.5 that repetitive operations are hard to represent, and that a looping mechanism is unsatisfactory because each state requires a separate time-stamp, and the re-use of states on an iterative loop would make this impossible.

How might we attempt to represent the game of tennis? The following is an illustration of a possible way to represent a single rally in the game of tennis.

```
------------------------
participants in game
their properties and
relative positions
------------------------
```

1. <player-1>
2. <player-2>
3. <tenniscourt>
4. <court-1>
5. <court-2>
6. <(4) and (5) are constituent parts of (3)>
7. <net>
8. <(7) separates (4) and (5)>
9. <tennisball>
10. <properties of (9) >
11. <racket-1>
12. <racket-2>

13. \<properties of (11) and (12) \>
14. \<location (1) within (4) \>
15. \<location (2) within (5) \>

----

    (1) plays-a-stroke

----

16. \<movement of (11) \> swing of racket-1
17. \< (1) causes (16) \> by player-1
18. \< (11) contacts (9) \> hit of ball
19. \< (16) causes (18) \> by racket-1
20. \< movement of (9) \> ball moves
21. \< location of (9) within (5) \> ball in court-2
22. \< location of (9) = (out_of_court) \> out
23. \< location of (9) = (7) \> in net
24. \< (18) causes (21) or (22) or (23) \> three outcomes
25. \< point scored by (2) \> player-2 scores
26. \< (22) or (23) causes (25) \> if out or in net

    (21) causes:

----

    (2) plays-a-stroke

----

27. \< movement of (12) \> swing of racket-2
28. \< (2) causes (27) \> by player-2
29. \< (12) contacts (9) \> hit of ball
30. \< NOT((12) contacts (9) \> miss
31. \< (27) causes (29) or (30) \> miss or strike by racket-2
32. \< point scored by (1) \> player-1 scores
33. \< (30) or (37) or (38) causes (32) \>miss or net or out -\> score
34. \< movement of (9) \> ball moves
35. \< (29) causes (34) \> hit causes movement of ball
36. \< location of (9) within (4) \> ball in court-1
37. \< location of (9) = (outofcourt) \> out
38. \< location of (9) = (7) \> net

    (36) causes :

----

    (1) plays a stroke

The reader is invited to trace this representation by writing in the names of entities against the numerical references, and then translating the representation into the graphical form in order to confirm that it is a very crude representation of a tennis rally. It omits a great deal of detail. There is no reference to the line markings, and the additional restriction placed on the server to place the ball into a smaller area of the court. There is no mention of foot faults or net-cords, and above all there is no mention of the motivation of the players for carrying out this strange ritual. It is hoped that the reader will be convinced that if we had the time and patience we could incorporate the additional rules and regulations of tennis which have been omitted.

The question we wish to address is — how do we go on? A rally in tennis is potentially infinite, although it seldom continues beyond four or five strokes. One method is to use a form of recursion in which the states 16-26 are bundled up and used to define the statement 'player-1 plays a stroke'. The states from 27-38 are also bundled up and used to define the statement 'player-2 plays a stroke'. We now append the statement 'player-2 plays a stroke' to the end of the definition of 'player-1 plays a stroke', and vice-versa. These are conditional extensions, because they depend upon the disjunction of causal connections. The extensions act like macro expansions and generate the next section of representation as required.

The idea is similar to our proposal for the representation of plural entities, which uses a generation function or structure to create more and more examples of an entity as required. The iterative operation is similarly generated repeatedly, and each repetition generates a new example of the event with new time-stamps. The process is terminated if one of the causal connection options is chosen which results in a point being scored. In many cases, however, there will be no requirement for the representation to be exploded. It will be sufficient for the recursive structure to indicate that repetition is present. The main problem with such a form of representation would be that of writing appropriate pattern-matching functions.

24.3 Occasional Events

In section 16.5 we also noted the problem of representing events which occur from time to time. We say that a person *'plays tennis,'* or *'He smokes'* meaning that he plays a game occasionally or that he smokes a cigarette occasionally. We do not mean that the person concerned does these things continuously. The tense of the verb is present tense, but not present continuous.

In the case of *'He plays tennis'*, the representation will consist of the kind of structure described in the previous section. The time-stamp of the states within that structure should remain uninstantiated (or unrelated to 'now'). The difference between this representation and that of the statement *'He is playing tennis'* is that the association between the representation of the person referred to by 'He' and that of one of the players must be given the condition value 'possible' instead of 'true'.

The implication of this (and it is an important implication) is that the association between an entity and its role must be represented by a state in its own right, and be given a time-stamp. It is then possible for us to distinguish between 'He plays tennis' and 'He used to play tennis'.

Conjunction, Disjunction and Negation

25.1 Simple Negation

In order to avoid complications we will confine this part of the discussion to the use of the word 'not', and to very simple examples of its use. We will ignore negation which can creep into sentences through the use of words beginning 'un-' or 'non-'. Even so we shall find that the topic is a difficult one.

Let us assume that we know how to construct a representation of the meaning of a sentence such as *'Jack went up the hill'*. Let us represent that representation symbolically by a box with the words *'Jack went up the hill'* inside it.

The problem of negation then resolves itself into finding the most convenient way of appending a negation flag to that representation.

It is a relatively simple matter to append a true/false flag to any structure within our representational scheme, but the very multiplicity of possible locations for such a flag is one of the main sources of difficulty. If the representational structure has internal elements or sub-units, then the negation flag could be appended to any of these, all of them, or to the complete structure. If I say *'John did not go up the hill'* then I may mean that he did nothing of the kind, or I may mean that he did not go of his own free will — he was dragged by the hair, perhaps. Then again he may have gone somewhere else, and so on.

In spoken English we often indicate the element of the sentence which we wish to negate by stressing the word concerned, e.g.:

Jack did not GO up the hill.
Jack did not go up the HILL.
JACK did not go up the hill.
Jack did not go UP the hill.

But if such emphasis is missing there is no way to tell which part (or parts) of the sentence is associated with the element(s) which are being negated. In the idiom of the 'who-done-it' we have a room full of suspects and no clear evidence as to which one is the culprit. We do know, however, that at least one is the culprit.

If we look at the structure of the sentence being negated it is usually assumed that the negation applies to everything from the word 'not' to the end of the grammatical unit in which 'not' occurs. The area over which the negation applies is called the 'scope' of the negation. The scope can extend to the end of a sentence. It never extends beyond the end of a sentence.

There is no way that a computer system can decide (without additional evidence) what elements are to be negated within the scope. Humans also have difficulty with this aspect of language. Our best policy is to ensure that our form of representation is compatible with any or all of the possible interpretations. To this end it is sensible to apply the negation flag to the representational structure as a whole (e.g. to a rep-box) and not to any of its constituent parts. The representational structure will be one which corresponds to the grammatical unit covered by the scope of the negation. That way the finger of suspicion points at all constituent parts pending further evidence. That in turn means that the structure must have an identity of its own which is distinct from the list of its constituent parts.

Our simplified representation is illustrated in Figure 25.1

Fig. 25.1. The negation of 'Jack went up the hill'.

We should note, however, that there are certain aspects of the sentence and its representation which are not subject to possible negation.

On reading the sentence '*Jack did not go up the hill*' no one is likely to suspect that '*Jack*' does not exist, or that '*the hill*' does not exist. In contrast, when reading the sentence '*Jack did not go up a hill*', we cannot be sure that '*a hill*' exists for Jack to have climbed.

One explanation for this phenomenon runs as follows. The reference implicit in the noun phrase '*the hill*' has as its target of reference some hill of which the existence is known from other evidence. That reference is therefore pointing to something which lies outside the scope of the negation, and which cannot therefore be suspect. In terms of the 'who-done-it' it has a perfect alibi. So also has the word Jack, which is an implicit reference to some person known to both writer and reader. Therefore in the sentence '*It was not Jack who went up the hill*' (in which Jack lies within the scope) the existence of Jack is not doubted. What is negated is his role in the scenario. This explanation brings into question what we mean by existence, and we may need to remind ourselves that for our purposes 'existence' implies presence in someone's mental model. It should not be associated with some so-called 'real world' existence.

In the sentence '*It was not Jack who went up the hill*' the scope of the conditional extends over, but not into, the subordinate clause beginning '*who*'. What is negated is the reference between Jack and the agent of the action described by the subordinate clause. Consider also the sentence '*I did not like the book because Jack wrote it*'. This sentence could be interpreted as meaning the same as (a) '*I did not like the book. The reason for my dislike of the book is that Jack wrote it'.* or (b) *'I liked the book. However, this is not because Jack wrote it'.* Two constituent parts lie within the scope of negation — the liking of the book and the subordinate clause in the sentence beginning *'because...'.* If the first is negated the interpretation corresponds to (a). If the second is negated then the interpretation corresponds to (b). The scope of negation does not extend *into* the subordinate clause. It would be perverse, therefore, to interpret the sentence as casting doubt on Jack's authorship of the book.

And there we shall leave our discussion of negation for the time being.

25.2 Conjunction

A conjunction is a 'thing' formed by combining two or more 'things' which are of the same kind as each other. It is usually accomplished by use of the conjunction operator 'and', but such an operator is not always required. We will represent a conjunction in rather the same way as we represented the constituent parts of an entity in Chapter 23. We shall introduce an additional 'entity' state and an additional 'consists of' state, which will refer to the entities participating in the conjunction. Figure 25.2 illustrates this arrangement for the sentence *'Jack and Jill went up the hill'.*

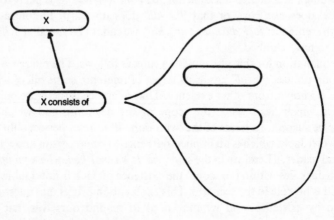

Fig. 25.2. Representing a conjunction.

When we need to compare such a structure with another, which may be a representation of the sentence *'Jack went up the hill'*, it is necessary that the matching function can detect the fact that the representation of the second sentence is embedded inside the representation of the first. Therefore the first sentence implies the second.

25.3 Conjunction and Negation

The need for a separate entity to represent a conjunction is made evident when we consider the combination of conjunction and negation. Consider the sentence *'Jack and Jill did not go up the hill'*. Here what is negated is the suggestion that *both* Jack and Jill went up the hill. Either could have gone alone. Therefore when we compare the representation of this sentence with that of the sentence *'Jack did not go up the hill'* it is important that the matching function is able to recognise that the second is not embedded in the first.

25.4 Disjunction

Disjunction is usually associated with the use of the word 'or', but other constructions are possible. We shall confine our discussion to simple 'or' sentences.

The operators 'and', 'or' and 'not' are related by the well known De Morgan's laws:

not(X and Y) $<=>$ not(X) or not(Y)
not(X or Y) $<=>$ not(X) and not(Y)

where $<=>$ means 'is equivalent to'

It follows that only one of the two operators 'and' and 'or' needs to be included in the primitive set of elements in our representational scheme. We could handle 'or' by substituting for the expression *(X or Y)* the equivalent expression *not(not(X) and not(Y))* and we could equally well define 'and' in terms of 'or' and 'not'. These rules, however, are found by most people to be counter-intuitive. Many programmers have fallen foul of conditional clauses which use a complex combination of 'and's, 'or's and 'not's and which do not mean what they think they mean. It is unlikely, therefore, that this type of substitution is normally used by humans (without prior training) as a means of dealing with the logical connectors.

We could handle the representation of disjunction in much the same way as we are proposing to deal with conjunction, that is by introducing a new, higher structure which contains the disjoined elements as its constituent parts. The difference is that in a disjunction only one of the subordinate elements is required to be true in order to satisfy the truth condition of the statement as a whole. The exact method of representation is relatively unimportant, provided the functions which match structures and work out implications do so in an appropriate way. Briefly, when we have an 'and' list, which might be denoted *and(a,b,c,d,...)* we are able to say that such a statement implies any of its individual components (a, b, c, ...). If we have an 'or' list such as *or(a,b,c,d,...)* we can only say that it implies *and(possibly(a), possibly(b), possibly(c),.....)*

This seemingly innocent step takes us into rather deep water, because we have now introduced the modal operator 'possibly'.

25.5 Modality and Negation

In modal logic a distinction is made between contingent truths and necessary truths. A statement which is necessarily true is one which must hold in all possible circumstances. A contingent truth is one which just happens to be true but could have been otherwise.

Formal modal logic makes use of the predicates 'necessarily' and 'possibly' which we shall denote 'nec' and 'pos'. Only one needs to be considered as a primitive, because it is possible to express each in terms of the other if negation is also allowed.

nec(X) <=> not(pos(not(X)))
pos(X) <=> not(nec(not(X)))

In the sentence: '*Jack MAY have gone up the hill*' the word '*may*' acts in very much the same way as the word '*not*'. It has a scope. Each element within the scope may be the culprit which is causing the entire structure to be 'possibilated' (if we can be allowed to coin such a dreadful word by analogy with the word 'negated'). The representational structure which corresponds to the part of the sentence within the scope of 'possibilation' can be given the condition value 'pos'. When two structures are being compared or matched we should use the rule $x => >$ *pos(x)*.

The combination of negation and modality produces further problems. There is a clear difference of meaning between '*possibly not X*' and '*not possibly X*'. The order of application of the two operators is therefore of great importance. We can use the rules *pos(not(x))* $=>>$ *pos(x)* and *not(pos(x))* $=>>$ *not(x)*. This rule works when applied to an expression such as *not(pos(not(x)))* because we then have *not(pos(not(x)))* $=>>$ *not(not(x))* $=>>$ *x*. We noted above that *not(pos(not(x)))* also implies *nec(x)*.

25.6 May and Must: the other Meaning

An analysis of modality involving the use of the words 'may' and 'must' always introduces an element of ambiguity, due to the fact that these words have an alternative interpretation which is concerned with 'permission' and 'requirement'. The sentence '*John may go up the hill*' could be said by someone giving permission to John. The sentence '*I must go up the hill*' usually indicates some feeling of social or psychological pressure rather than a logical conclusion. A proper interpretation of these sentences will therefore involve the representation of hidden motivation, in rather the same way as the examples shown in Chapter 21.

Quantification

26.1 Singular Nouns and Noun Phrases (again)

A singular noun is the label for a concept. A concept is associated with:
(a) a class to which entities can belong and with
(b) a set of properties which allow the class of an entity to be recognised.

A singular noun is a label for both these aspects of a concept, which in traditional semantics have been called, respectively, the 'extension' and the 'intension' of a noun. Here we shall use the terms 'concept-class' and 'concept-properties'.

In the early chapters of this book we argued that a concept can be represented by a generic structure which can be used as a template to generate any member of its associated concept-class, and we shall adopt that view here. Each noun can be associated with a procedure, and when the noun is encountered in the text being processed the procedure is activated to create the generic structure. As such it is an anonymous structure. None of its formal parameters has been instantiated, and at that stage it has no unique identity.

The processing of adjectives in association with the noun leads to modification of the generic structure by the addition, deletion or amendment of properties. At that stage it is still a generic structure and defines a new composite concept. For example, the expression 'toy dog' is represented as a concept formed by taking the generic structure belonging to 'dog' and amending its properties according to those associated with 'toy'. Where these are incompatible, those of 'toy' prevail, since these are being applied as for an adjective. What we have created is a specialisation of the two concepts 'toy' and 'dog', in the sense that we used that term in section 23.4.

The meaning of a noun phrase is represented as a specific example of the concept-class. The use of the word 'a' for example, takes the generic structure and turns it into an entity with an identity of its own by instantiating the formal parameter associated with its identifier to a specific value. The word 'the' (in the simple case) instantiates it by reference to some existing entity. What we have then is an entity in its own right, as distinct from a concept.

This analysis does have its problems. If we are dealing with a sentence such as *'If I had a car I would keep it in good condition'*, the noun phrase *'a car'* does not refer to a specific car. It lies within the scope of the modal operator *'if'*, and has therefore been 'possibilated'.

26.2 Plurals

A plural noun can form a noun phrase on its own, without the need for determiners such as 'a' or 'the'. The meaning of a plural noun is therefore not to be represented as a concept, but as a group of entities.

A single entity is represented by a single structural unit which has its own properties and its own unique identifier. At first sight there appears to be no difficulty about extending this method of representation to several entities. Two entities could be represented by two structural units, three by three structural units, and so on.

The problem which is associated with the representation of plural nouns appears when there is no definite number of entities involved, or where the number involved is so great that we are unable to consider the use of structural units on a strict one-to-one association. It is tempting to try to represent a plural entity by a single structure which has a 'number' attribute. This could be an integer or a formal parameter if the number is unknown. This approach is unsatisfactory, however, because we could be faced with a sentence in which there is a need to identify specific units within a collection of indeterminate number. Consider, for example, the following passage: *'A group of men were smashing down the door. One had a sledge hammer and another had an axe.'* What is required is a representation which is a single structural unit (for the whole group) and which can be expanded as required by generating exemplars.

A possible solution makes use of the same kind of structure which we used in our analysis of conjunction, with one additional feature. This is illustrated in Figure 26.1.

What we have here is a conjunction of two entities (X and Y) and an indefinite number of other entities which have no explicit representation. These are

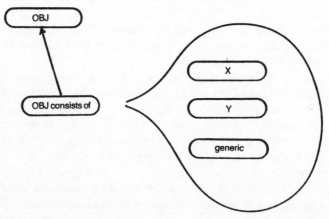

Fig. 26.1. The representation of a plural object.

represented symbolically by the generic structure which is used to generate further examples as required.

The representation is analogous to the dynamic list structure which is a feature of POP11 and is described in the appendix. If a specific number of entities is required, an additional attribute of the conjunction can hold this value.

The representation proposed seems suitable for providing us with a representation of such phrases as *'five men'*, *'the first man'*, *'the third man'*, *'lots of men'*.

There does appear to be a problem in dealing with *'the millionth man'* but this could be handled by partitioning the conjunction into a conjunction of two such groups. The first of these would provide a symbolic representation of one million (minus one) men and the second would be of indefinite length. *'The millionth man'* would be identified as the first man of the second group.

For very small numbers, such as one, two or three, it is probably appropriate to expand the definition to produce the actual number of explicit representations. For larger numbers, symbolic representation without expansion (unless required) would be preferable. The watershed number is probably round about seven, which appears to be the limit for the instantaneous perception of number in humans.

26.3 Some, Any and All

The representation of groups of indefinite size requires us to find an appropriate interpretation for the words *'some'*, *'any'* and *'all'*, and many others. We shall take these three words as a representative sample.

The dynamic list idea described in section 26.2 seems to deal adequately with 'some'. The two sentences *'A group of men was smashing down the door'* and *'Some men were smashing down the door'* mean the same thing. The syntactical structure is different, however, because the phrase 'group-of-men' is singular whereas 'men' is plural. It might be possible to make a subtle distinction between *'a group of'* and *'some'*. We could, for example, represent the word 'group' by a single structure which carries a reference pointer to the conjunctive dynamic list structure we described above.

Of more significance is the problem of dealing with an expression such as: *'Some of the men...'* Here we have a particular group of men identified *('the men')* and we are referring to an indefinite number of men selected from that group. Presumably the representation of the group to which *'the men'* refers already exists.

One method of representing the expression 'some X' is to create a dynamic list structure using the generic procedure for X. If X corresponds to the concept 'man', then we use the generic procedure for 'man'. If X corresponds to 'big men', then we must activate the generic procedures for 'big' and for 'man' and combine these to form a generic structure which will serve as a template for the generation of the derived concept *'big man'*.

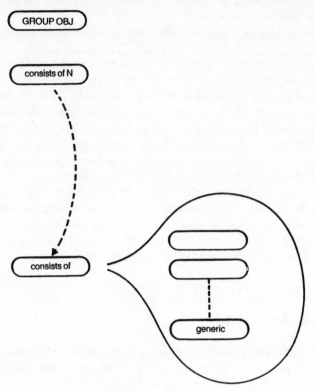

Fig. 26.2. The representation of 'some X'.

To be consistent we should do the same for *'some of the men'* where X corresponds to 'the men'. What we require, therefore, is not the generic for 'man' but the generic procedure or generic structure for that particular set of men. Figure 26.3 illustrates the suggested arrangement.

If the group referenced by *'the men'* has a definite size then the derived group *'some of the men'* will have an indefinite size which is greater than one and less than or equal to the size of the original group. It could be argued that it should be subject to a limit which is smaller than the size of the original group. In normal conversation the use of the expression 'some X' is often interpreted as meaning 'some but not all X'. This is not the case in formal logic.

The expression 'all X' can be represented in the same way as 'some X', with the group size set at 'maximum'.

The expression 'any X' introduces much more complicated issues. 'Any X' is in effect a selection of one item, at random, from the set of all Xs. One way to represent this is to generate one example of X without providing it with a unique identifier or instantiating any of the formal parameters. It is in fact a copy of the generic structure itself. Such a structure has all the properties of a member of the class of entities involved and has no properties peculiar to itself.

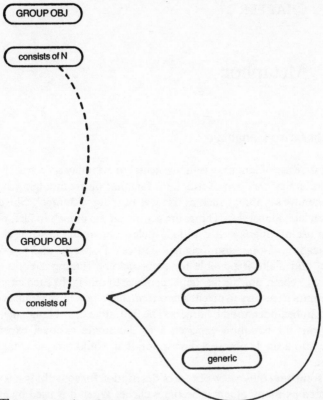

Fig. 26.3. The representation of 'some of the X'.

Anything which can be said to be true about 'any X' must (potentially) be true about any other X. It follows that the properties described must be a feature of the generic procedure or generic structure, and not of one particular example. This is why a statement such as 'any triangle has three sides' is thought of as though it meant the same thing as 'all triangles have three sides'. If, however, we say 'any triangle *can* have a right angle' we mean that it is possible that a selection made at random from the set of all triangles can be found to have a right angle. That is, the generic procedure or structure does not exclude the possibility of 'right angledness'. The correctness of the statement can be proved if manipulation of the formal parameters can produce such a triangle.

This is why the word 'any' sometimes appears to mean the same as 'all', and sometimes the same as 'one'. Consider, for example, the sentences:

S1 'Any student could answer that question'
S2 'Can any student answer that question?'

S1 appears to be synonymous with '*All students can answer that question*' and S2 appears to be synonymous with '*Can even one student answer that question?*'

Metaphor

27.1 Figurative Language

The figurative use of language is fundamental to everyday speech and writing. It is so common that we often overlook the fact that we are indulging in figurative speech when we say things such as 'He was burning with rage', 'She dropped a hint', 'I am late, I must fly', 'Things are getting on top of me'. In fact, without the figurative use of language it is a dull, lifeless and much less useful means of communication. Good and original figures of speech make writing into literature, and make it possible for someone confronting a completely new experience to communicate his/her experience to others. In such circumstances it is sometimes necessary to invent a new term, but a new term requires definition before it can be understood by others. The figurative use of language, however, draws upon our common experience to illuminate a novel experience, or condense into a single phrase a description that would otherwise take a whole paragraph.

When someone coins a new phrase or description for something it is art. When it is adopted by many others it becomes cliche. When it is used by everyone it becomes part of the standard usage and the words concerned have adopted new standard meanings. That is how language grows and adapts to circumstances, as it must.

The ease with which humans deal with figurative phrases which have never been heard or read before suggests that the mechanism of understanding is well adapted for the task. It is not a question of calling up some seldom-used procedure to deal with a statement which has defied conventional interpretation. The process of understanding proceeds smoothly, as though the mechanism for dealing with figurative speech is the normal way of dealing with any form of speech.

We conclude that any mechanism which deals with ordinary usage but cannot deal with figurative speech cannot be handling language in the way humans do it.

27.2 Metaphor

In section 25.3 we suggested how the role of an object might be represented as part of its meaning. In this representation many entities appeared, and the object itself (which is the subject or target of the definition) was identified by a special marker ("*"). We called this 'the salient feature' of the representation. The salient feature need not in fact be an object, but could be an action, a movement, or a causal connection.

The representational scheme is only a suggestion, one of many possible schemes. We would argue, however, that the notion of a definition containing representations of far more than the subject of definition itself is very important, and would be a feature common to any successful representational scheme.

Therefore if one uses a word in a statement, it brings with it a great deal of information which is built into the representation of the complete statement. We might consider them to be 'supporting cast' by analogy with a stage play, while the salient features are the 'star performers'. Now if I have just seen a new play, and I wish to describe it to someone who has not seen it, I may, to save a lot of talk, describe it in terms of other plays which we have both seen. If the new play is concerned with a boardroom struggle for power in a commercial company I might describe one character as 'a Hamlet character' and another as 'a Macbeth character', meaning that the first dithered and dithered until opportunities had passed, while the second rushed impetuously into action on the advice of his wife. The new play, however, has no princes or kings and no murders. In using this means of description I am making use of the listener's knowledge of the two plays *Hamlet* and *Macbeth*. I know that the listener knows that there are no princes or kings or murders in the new play, and so he can assume that the comparison must make reference to some other feature of the plays. *We* are referring to the *non-salient* features of the representations.

The representation of the word 'sea' must have the substance 'water' as its salient feature. In the phrase 'a sea of troubles', however, we do not imply that someone is suffering from burst pipes. The reference is being made to the non-salient aspect of 'sea', which is its extensiveness. In the phrase 'dropped a hint' we are making reference to the aspects of the representation of 'dropped' which relate to the way 'dropping' something will leave it to become the possession of someone else if they are sufficiently observant. 'I must fly' makes reference to the speed of flying as a means of travel.

We conclude that metaphor is the use of language which makes reference to non-salient features of the semantic representations of words and ignores the salient features.

Since, in any given representation, all features are present, it would not then be surprising that human understanding of metaphor should proceed smoothly, since it would involve only an extension of the pattern-matching procedures used in normal circumstances. When we encounter a phrase such as 'a stone man' the word 'man' provides a generic representation of the concept 'man'. The word 'stone' provides a generic representation of something (unspecified) which is made of stone (see section 25.6). The properties of this unspecified object are that it is rigid, heavy, unyielding and not alive. The unspecified something is then unified with the entity specified in the representation of 'man', and the additional properties provided by 'stone' are forced upon those of 'man'. Where there is a contradiction (alive/not alive) those of 'stone' will prevail.

We have therefore made use of the meaning of 'man' but have deleted one of the most important aspects of that representation. A man can scarcely be thought of as a man if he is not alive, and yet here we are with a non-alive man defined easily and conveniently by use of the phrase 'stone man'.

'Stone man' is not usually considered to be a metaphorical use of language. The argument is that it makes use of exactly the same mechanism we have suggested for dealing with metaphor, and if this is accepted we have successfully brought the processing of metaphor into the normal interpretation of language.

CHAPTER 28

Combining Representations

28.1 The Problem of Complexity

We have developed a tentative method for representing objects and events which makes use of explicit causal links, represents motivation in terms of goal and anti-goal states, roles, the classification of objects (with inheritance) and properties represented in terms of perceptions. Now it is deceptively easy to invent representational structures which seem to capture aspects of meaning, but it is difficult to define such structures in a consistent way that is amenable to manipulation by functions which can show that one structure is semantically equivalent to another, or implies another. This is one of the main reasons why formal logics are often used for semantic representation — they provide a ready-made set of consistent structures and operations which can be applied to them. It is even more difficult, however, to devise representational structures which not only meet these requirements but are such that we can seriously think of constructing them for use in a practical system (i.e. with a large and varied vocabulary) in a realistic time scale. The representational structures we have proposed here are no exception, and are likely to be extremely complex. No one would lightly embark upon writing the explicit representation of the meaning of the corpus of words required for a practical system, in all but a very limited context.

This is probably an inherent difficulty which cannot be avoided by changing the method of representation. In this chapter we wish to describe in outline one possible approach to the problem.

28.2 The 'combine' Operator

In Chapter 8 we described a parsing algorithm which was based on ATNs. At each node of an ATN the next section of input text was subjected to a three-part condition test, e.g. for node zero of an ATN called 'parse' we might have:

if node_id=0 then

    if (noun_phrase(text,0)->rem1->out1)
            and
      (parse(rem1,1)->rem2->out2)
            and

```
(combine(out1 ,out2)->out3)

then
        true; out3; rem2;
    endif;
endif;
```

Here we begin by establishing that we are dealing with the parse ATN at node zero. We then apply three tests. The first processes the input text list ('text') and checks for a noun phrase. If it is successful it leaves three results *true; semantic_output_structure; remainder.* Only two of these are removed from the stack and assigned to the variables 'rem1' and 'out1'. The truth value remains on the stack and is included in the composite (conjoined) condition test. The *remainder* is the remainder of the input text after the leading 'noun phrase' has been bitten off. The *semantic_output_structure* is some structure created to represent the meaning of the section of text which has been processed. In Chapter 8 we did not analyse the content of this semantic_output_structure in detail because we were concerned with the structure of the algorithm and with syntax. Here we want to consider the nature of this semantic structure.

The second test is a recursive application of the parse function with the node parameter set at '1'. This represents the continuation of the ATN after the first arc has been traced. It also leaves three results of the same type, including a semantic_output_structure *(out2)* which represents the meaning of the remainder of the text list.

The third test is an attempt to combine these two semantic structures to produce a third, *out3*. It leaves two results, the truth value indicating success or failure, and the semantic structure which it has formed from *out1* and *out2*.

Only if all three tests succeed has the ATN been successfully traced. The first two tests at each node are concerned with syntactical structure. The third test at each node is concerned with the semantic compatibility of the two structures stored in *out1* and *out2*.

In Chapter 20 we introduced the idea of storing a set of states, causal links, etc. inside a structure which we called a 'rep-box'. Such a structure can be generalised to be any collection of structures which together represent some unit of meaning. Such a structure could be stored in a dictionary and associated with each of the words in the vocabulary of the system. Since each word is considered to be the label for a concept, which is in turn considered to be a generic structure, it follows that each rep-box in the dictionary represents a generic structure. When a sentence is read, each word in the sentence will be looked up in the dictionary and the appropriate rep-box extracted and tagged on to the word stored in the input text list. Figure 28.1 illustrates this, and what happens to these structures.

The key to the process lies in the way the 'combine' function processes two rep-boxes to produce a third. The properties of each must be tested, and then the new rep-box must be created from the existing properties of the other two. Where properties clash, there must be a rule for selecting which of the existing

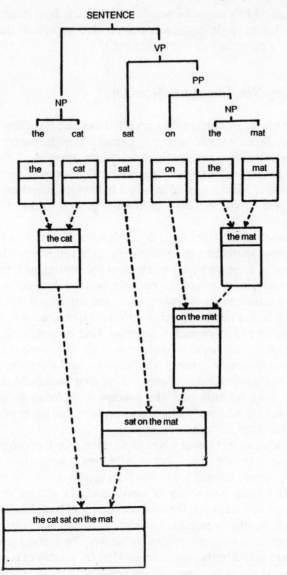

Fig. 28.1. The combining of rep-boxes as an ATN is traversed.

properties will be favoured, and where they are mutually contradictory the combination process should fail. Where there is no clash the new rep-box will have the properties of both of the other two.

The crucial point is that the new rep-box is indistinguishable in type and quality from the others, and the combination process can be applied to it as to any other. It should therefore be possible to combine these structures in pairs progressively, until a single structure is created which represents the meaning of a sentence (or a paragraph or a complete text).

28.3 Defining New Structures from Old

When two structures are combined we note that there are two different processes which can take place. We can combine properties to produce a more detailed and specific representation (specialisation) or, where there is a clash between incompatible properties (of the same general type), both could be replaced by a third which was sufficiently general to permit both as specialisations. That is, the properties could be combined to produce a generalisation of the original concepts.

We noted in section 23.4 that we could create semantic networks in which each node represents a specialisation of its parent node and a generalisation of its descendant nodes. Here we have a mechanism for creating such tree structures from known examples. It would, for example, be possible to define the concept *animal* as a generalisation of the concepts *dog* and *cat*. Such a definition would, of course, exclude fish and birds and many other types of animal, but of course it is always possible to refine such a definition later by generalising it with the definition of *fish*, or with any other concept we wish. This seems to be very much what happens with young children who learn a concept such as *animal* from obvious and easily accessible examples such as their household pets. Later, as they become more sophisticated, the concept is extended to include other categories. It is, after all, merely a human convention that the term *animal* is not restricted to just dogs and cats.

Herein lies a possible solution to the problem of excessive complexity which we noted above. It should be possible to define new concepts by combining the definitions of concepts already learned by both specialisation and generalisation procedures. If a small vocabulary of words could be defined explicitly (and laboriously) to cover, let us say, the total vocabulary of Basic English (about 600 words), then it should be possible to define all subsequent words in English sentences constructed from words already known. The concept to be tagged on to the new word would be the rep-box created by the process of combination we have described above as the sentence is processed.

Conclusion

My own interest in natural language processing is generated by the belief that a successful NL system would provide real insight into the mechanism of the mind. Computers are fascinating devices, but the human mind is many orders of magnitude more complex, and therefore more fascinating than any present-day computer. I believe that computers will one day rival the brain in the performance of most tasks requiring intelligence; as they do in certain specific tasks already. But confident predictions of the arrival of that day have been made frequently and just as often have been shown to be over-optimistic. As each layer of complexity has been penetrated, hidden depths have been revealed. I hope that this book will have communicated some of my own fascination in the subject.

The early part of the book is intended as an undergraduate study text, and for that reason is punctuated with suggested exercises. To a large extent it is concerned with syntax, and the development of algorithms to meet the demands of a parser which takes into account some aspects of the semantics. Some of the semantic problems were also explored in the context of a very concrete application.

The second part of the book discusses some of the outstanding problems of semantic interpretation and representation, and then describes some approaches to these problems. Some of the methods might provide a vehicle for a group project, but they are not suitable for an individual student exercise. To produce a non-trivial system in this field is a major undertaking. The volume of information which must be supplied to make a system function should not be underestimated.

The third part ventures into areas where there are few guidelines in the public domain. At some points I have been reduced to speculative suggestions, having been unable to find any descriptions of systems which tackle these problems. Most of the published work in these areas is confined to comment on the difficulties, without suggesting solutions.

Within these speculations the reader will perhaps have been able to detect a consistent view which I have about NL processing. It is not an original view, because many others have proposed similar schemes. It is not comprehensive as yet, but it might be summarised as follows:

Language is a vehicle for communication (Chapter 18).

Each word in a language is a label for a collection of stored information, which is pieced together to form an overall representation of the meaning of a statement (section 18.3).

A representation consists of a set of 'states', each with its time-stamp, and representing an elementary snapshot of the world. (Chapter 4, section 19.2, Chapters 21, 24, 25).

Each state is represented in terms of a 'perception' (Chapter 17).

Causal connections play a crucial role in the formation of representations. These should be represented explicitly as states in their own right.

The representation of motivation is also crucial to a successful system.

'Truth' in the context of language interpretation is not the same thing as 'truth' in the context of formal logic (Chapter 22).

The representation of an entity must represent its properties and its role. In representing the role it must include many other aspects of the scenario in which it normally plays a part (Chapter 25).

Metaphor is an important part of language interpretation, which should not be regarded as an 'optional extra' (Chapter 26).

The reader will have his/her own view. Even if I have not persuaded the reader that my view is sound, however, I hope that I have demonstrated that the task of constructing a natural language processing system is not to be undertaken lightly, and that many currently available systems which purport to be 'natural language processing systems' are not that at all. The volume and detail of the information which needs to be defined (no matter what form of representation is used) is formidable, and no system which does not tackle the problem of representing motivation can hope to capture the meaning of a huge range of normal human speech and writing.

The first stage in the process of scientific investigation is that of hypothesis formation. The next stage is the testing of the hypothesis. In this case that means the attempt to produce a practical system based on the theoretical ideas of the hypothesis.

Have fun and good hacking!

Bibliography

As mentioned earlier, much of the literature on natural language processing is contained in research papers and monographs which are not easily accessed by those outwith the small group of research workers in academic institutions. Fortunately a number of books have emerged recently which provide access to some of the most important information. The following list of texts would provide the interested reader with good background material and more detail on specific issues for which there was no space in this text.

* Barrett R., Ramsay A. and Sloman A.
POP11: A Practical Language for Artificial Intelligence
Ellis Horowood 1985

* Brachman R.J. and Levesque H.J.
Readings in Knowledge Representation
Morgan Kaufmann 1985

A collection of research papers in a form which makes them available to the ordinary reader. Some of the papers are now quite old but they were chosen for this collection because they represent major contributions to the development of the subject. The book contains seminal articles on such topics as semantic networks and several articles discuss issues which are still very much the subject of lively debate.

* Charniak E., McDermott D.
Artificial Intelligence
Addison-Wesley 1985

This is a general text on artificial intelligence but it has a chapter on NLP. It concentrates on semantic interpretation using semantic networks of various kinds, Much of the discussion is about the analysis of motivation.

* Harris M.D.
An introduction to Natural Language Processing
Reston Pub. Co. Inc. (Prentice-Hall) 1985

This text covers most of the important American work on NLP and uses an extended form of Pascal to define the relevant algorithms. It also has an early chapter on basic linguistics.

* Johnson-Laird P.N.
Mental Models
Cambridge University Press 1983

A very influential book on the topic of cognitive psychology which is relevant to the semantic representation of language.

* Quirk R., Greenbaum, S., Leech G. and Svartvik J.
A Grammar of Contemporary English
Longman 1972

A reference text.

* Ramsey A. and Barrett R.
AI in Practice: examples in POP-11.
Ellis Horwood Series in Artificial Intelligence

Lots of good examples of POP-11 in use.

* Rayward-Smith V.J.
A First Course in Formal Language Theory
Blackwell Scientific Pub. 1983

An introduction to parsing and the use of transition networks.

* Ritchie G. and Thompson H.
'Natural Language Processing: Historical Background and Basic Issues'
in
Artificial Intelligence: Tools and Techniques
edited by O'Shea and Eisentadt
Harper-Row 1984

A readable discussion and critique of many issues, particularly the relationship between parsing and semantic analysis.

* Sager N.
Natural language Information Processing
Addison-Wesley Pub. Co. 1981

The approach is strongly oriented towards syntactic processing and the book gives a very complete grammar in a form which was used successfully in a major project of which Sager was the leading researcher. The application involved was the analysis of medical text to provide a database of facts which could then be used by medical research workers as an information retrieval resource. Anyone who wanted a basic grammar for a project could probably use a sub-set of the one provided by Sager secure in the knowledge that it could be expanded later.

* Schank R.C. and Riesbeck C.K.
Inside Computer Understanding
Lawrence Erlbaum Associates 1981

This book is concerned with the authors' own research programs and the work of those associated with them. This research team was responsible for the development of conceptual dependency theory.

* Simmons R.F.
Computations from the English
Prentice-Hall 1984

This book concentrates on semantic represetation and includes a chapter on various types of logic. It also has an interesting discussion of semantic/ psychological issues and gives a number of short and useful examples of programs. Lisp is the programming language used in illustrations.

* Winograd T.
Understanding Natural Language
Edinburgh University Press 1972

This book is included mainly for its historical importance. It describes one of the best known NLP systems. The contents are widely quoted in other texts and the diagrams of Winograd's 'blocks world' system are now a ubiquitous feature of the literature. This is a very good example of a micro-world system and clearly illustrates the strengths and weaknesses of such systems.

* Winograd T.
Language as a Cognitive Process: Syntax
Addison-Wesley Pub. Co. 1983

This book is volume 1 of what was intended as a series of volumes covering various aspects of NLP. It gives a very complete account of various parsers including ATNs and an appendix provides a useful grammar. Unfortunately the subsequent volumes are not likely to appear since the author seems to have had an agonising reappraisal of his whole approach to the subject. His recent articles suggest an approach which is more strongly oriented towards semantics.

An Introduction to POP11/POPLOG

1 Background

POP11 is a derivative of POP2, a language developed at Edinburgh University for use in the field of artificial intelligence. It was implemented for various mainframe machines but was mostly associated with the DEC10/20 systems. Later it was adapted for the PDP11 (hence POP11). Subsequently research workers at the University of Sussex implemented a system called POPLOG which contains both POP11 and Prolog with an interface between them. It also provides an excellent editor, which is integrated with both compilers and a number of other features that make it into a very comprehensive package. It is, at the latest count, available for Vax, Sun, Hewlett-Packard, Apollo and Gould machines. Interested persons should refer to the University of Sussex for up-to-date information on availability.

These notes are concerned with POP11 the language, but it is impossible to separate completely the language from the system in which it is embedded, because the language has facilities which require the presence of a memory-resident compiler.

The language has some very powerful facilities, and is directly comparable with LISP. Unlike LISP, however, POP11 has a well-defined syntax which is not dissimilar to a simplified Pascal.

2 The Structure of a Program

An example:

```
define fred(x,y);    ;;; define <progname> ( <arglist> );
vars z;              ;;; vars   <local-variables>      ;
x+y->z;              ;;; assignment statement (z:=x+y) ;
z;                   ;;; result = z                    ;
enddefine;           ;;; enddefine (end of definition) ;
```

The pattern is:

```
define ......(.....);
  vars ...... ;

     ...... ;
     ...... ;

enddefine;
```

<progname> is user-defined
<arglist> is a list of user-defined data-item names separated by commas
<local_variables> is a list of user-defined variable names without commas

The body of the program is made up of several statements. There are no format or other restrictions on the number of such statements. Note how the result of such a program is defined — it is simply stated with any operation being required (in this example it is just the statement 'z;'). To understand the mechanism of leaving results and of passing argument values see the section below on the 'stack'.

Once a program has been defined (at the keyboard) it can be called immediately. The memory resident compiler compiles the source code as it is typed. The call would be (for the example above):

    fred(2,3);

which would leave the result 5 on the stack. The contents of the stack can be made visible with the 'print arrow':

    =>

so that the call

    fred(2,3)=>

will calculate and print the value 5.

It is not normal to type program source directly at the keyboard, although it is sometimes done for convenience if the program code is of no lasting importance. It is more usual to create a file of source code (using any editor or the embedded POPLOG editor) and to compile that file later with the statement:

    compile(<filename>);

<filename> is a string (in single quotes).

3 The Stack

POP11 has an implicit stack which is used for passing arguments and leaving results. The statement:

    1;

means 'place the numeric value "1" on the stack'. The statement:

    x;

means 'place the value of the variable "x" on the stack'.

The statement:

```
-> x;
```

means 'take the value on top of the stack and assign it to the variable x'. The assignment arrow is made up of the two characters '-' and '>'.

Therefore the statement:

```
1 -> x;
```

means 'assign the value 1 to x (via the stack)'.

The stack is a 'lifo' (last in first out) structure and so the statement:

```
x;y->x->y;
```

swaps the values of x and y.

When a program call, such as fred(2,3) is typed, the values of the arguments are calculated and placed on the stack (in left-to-right sequence), and the function 'fred' picks them up from there and assigns them to local variables with the names defined in the argument list.

It follows that the arguments can be any expression which leaves on the stack a value of the correct type (numeric in the example above). Therefore the call:

```
fred(fred(2,3),fred(3,4));
```

will leave the value 12 on the stack.

4 Arithmetic Statements

POP11 has all the conventional arithmetic operators and use of brackets familiar to users of Pascal or C. The operations are:

* multiplication
/ division
+ addition
- subtraction
** exponentiation
// integer division (leaves two results, the quotient and the remainder) (find out for yourself in which sequence the results are left on the stack).

5 Input and Output

POP11 uses character repeaters (similar to C) to build up a range of I/O facilities. It also provides a set of standard functions which can be extended by the user.

Input Functions

charin()->x;   reads one character from the terminal
and assigns it to x;

itemread()->x;   reads one item and assigns it to x;
an item is one element of data such as a
word or variable name or syntactical symbol
which is separated from other elements by a
standard separator (such as a space or a
comma).

Output Functions

charout(x);   prints the value of x (as a character)
if x is an integer in the range 0-127

pr(x);   prints the value of x (a number or string, say)
=>   the print arrow. It prints everything on the
stack from the bottom upwards (and clears it).

There are other more fancy methods of printing data, but the reader is referred
to standard texts for these.

File Input-Output (Character Repeaters):

To use a file one must first create a character repeater for that file. This is the
operation which is equivalent to 'opening' a file. To read a file one creates an
input character repeater, and to write a file one creates an output character
repeater (or character 'consumer').

To create an input repeater called 'in_ch' for the file 'data.txt' we write:

discin('data.txt') -> in_ch;

'Discin' is therefore a function which takes a filename (in single quotes) as its
argument, and yields as its result the starting address of another function (which
we have assigned to the variable 'in_ch'). We can now call that function (which
is the required character repeater) by the statement:

in_ch() -> x;

which not only calls the function but assigns its result (one character from the file
'data.txt') to the variable 'x'. A subsequent call of in_ch() will get the next
character from 'data.txt' and so on until the end of file is encountered. At the end
of file, the function 'in_ch' will yield as its result a special character (called

'termin'). To detect the end of file, therefore, we can use the command sequence:

```
in_ch()->x;
if x=termin then ...... endif;
```

(see conditional clauses notes below)

An output character repeater is created in the same way by the function 'discout', thus:

```
discout('data.txt') -> out_ch;
```

Subsequent calls of:

```
out_ch(x);
```

will output the character which is the value of 'x' to the file 'data.txt'.

```
out_ch(termin);
```

will close the file.

6 Item Repeaters

Handling I/O entirely with character repeaters is a powerful but clumsy technique. It is usually more congenial to handle I/O in the form of 'items'. That is, the character stream is chopped up into chunks which correspond to words and symbols rather than individual characters.

POP11 provides standard functions which construct item repeaters from character repeaters. The first task is therefore to create a suitable set of character repeaters, and then use them to construct the required item repeaters. Thus:

```
incharitem(in_ch) -> in_item;
outcharitem(out_ch) -> out_item;
```

The standard functions 'incharitem' and 'outcharitem' do this trick as shown above.

7 Redirection of I/O

In addition, all standard I/O functions such as 'itemread' and 'pr', make use of standard functions 'cucharin' and 'cucharout' (current character input repeater and current output character repeater). By default the standard repeaters 'charin' and 'charout' are assigned to these, so that all standard I/O (by default) handles I/O with the user's terminal. If, however, the user defines another character repeater and assigns that to one of the current character repeaters (e.g. myrep -> cucharout;) then the standard functions which use that current character repeater will then be directed to the appropriate device or file.

8 Conditionals

The conditional clause has several possible structures:

(a) if <condition> then <statement> else <statement> endif;

(b) if <condition> then <statement> endif;

(c) if   <condition> then <statement>
     elseif <condition> then <statement>
     elseif <condition> then <statement>
     elseif ....
     elseif ....
     else   <statement>
     endif;

Note that there should be no semi-colon between the <condition> and 'then'. The <condition> can be any boolean expression including a function call which leaves a truth value on the stack.

9 Until-loops

Loop control is achieved by means of an 'until-loop' thus:

     until <condition> do
          ....
          ....
          .... enduntil;

10 Return

The return statement is a way of exiting from a function at some point other than its normal default termination. A function corresponding to the skeletal definition below would exit in two ways, leaving 'x' on the stack in one set of circumstances and 'y' in another.

     define fred(x,y);
     ....
     ....
     if <condition> then x; return; endif;
     ....
     ....
     y;
     enddefine;

11 Lists

One of the most agreeable features of POP11 is its list handling. A list-link or 'pair' is a record structure with two elements:

head	tail

A list-link is formed by the double-colon operator '::'. The statement

    x::y;

forms a list-link with x as its head and y as its tail, and places the complete structure (or rather its address) on the stack. The list-links are formed dynamically. If in due course it becomes de-referenced by the user's program (for example by assigning its address to a variable and then assigning some other value to the same variable later) the list-link becomes inaccessible to the user and therefore to all intents and purposes destroyed. In fact the system garbage collector will eventually retrieve it and return it to the free store for later use in some other way.

The system has a standard entity 'nil' which is the terminator mark for all lists. To begin the construction of a list we can use the statement:

    x::nil -> l;

The variable 'l' now holds the address of our list which has 'x' as its head and 'nil' as its tail. To form a null list we would simply write:

    nil->l;

To place another element in the list in front of 'x' we write:

    y::l -> l;

Since the construction of lists is a common occurrence in POP11 programs, a shorthand method is provided for initialising lists at the keyboard. We can write:

    [a b c d e f] -> l;

which is identical in effect to writing:

    a::(b::(c::(d::(e::(f::nil))))) -> l;

POP11 provides two functions which select and update the elements of a list. These are 'hd' (meaning 'head') and 'tl' (meaning 'tail'). Therefore if we write:

    hd(l) -> q;

we will cause the first element in the list 'l' to be assigned to the variable 'q', and the statement:

    tl(l) -> r;

will assign to the variable 'r' the address of the second list-link in 'l'. Therefore:

```
[ a b c d e f g] -> l;
hd(l) -> q;
tl(l) -> r;
```

will result in the element 'a' being in q and the list [b c d e f g] being in r.

The standard 'cliche' for handling lists element by element in a loop is shown by the skeletal function below:

```
define fred(l);
    .........
    until null(l) do
        ....some process applied to hd(l)....
        tl(l)->l;
    enduntil;
    ..........some result based on the processing....
enddefine;
```

Note the boolean test 'null(l)'.

As an example, a function which sums the values in a list (of numbers) would be:

```
define sum_list(l);
    vars sum;
    0->sum;
    until null(l) do
        sum + hd(l) -> sum;
        tl(l) -> l;
    enduntil;
    sum;
enddefine;
```

The operator ◇ concatenates two lists so that the statements:

```
[a b c] -> l1;
[d e f] -> l2;
l1<>l2->l3;
```

will result in l3 being the list [abcdef].

Lists with 'decorated' Brackets

The expression [x] represents a list with the word "x" as its first (and only) element. The expression [% x %] represents a list with the *value* of the variable x as its first (and only) element. The notation [% ... %] is termed 'decorated' list brackets. With the use of such brackets the word "x" can still be included in a list, but it must be enclosed in double quotation marks, thus: [% "x" %]. If two or more elements are to be included they should be separated by commas, thus: [% "value", "of", "x", "is", x %]. Single quotes can also be used [% 'the value of x is', x %].

12 The 'dot' Notation'

A shorthand way of writing 'hd(l)' is 'l.hd' and for 'tl(l)' we can write 'l.tl' This means that instead of writing:

hd(tl(tl(tl(tl(tl(l))))))

which is rather confusing, we can write

l.tl.tl.tl.tl.hd

which is much clearer.

The manipulation of lists can make use of recursion. In this form the functions are relatively inefficient but very succinct, and once the user gets accustomed to this style of programming he/she will find it easy to write short programs in which one can have great confidence.

The handling of lists is best explained by means of examples.

```
define ismemb(x,l);    ;;; returns "true" if "x" is a member of the list "l"
  if l.null then false;
  elseif x=l.hd then true;
  else ismemb(x,l.tl);
  endif; enddefine;

define intersection(l1,l2);
  vars l3;
  nil->l3;
  until l1.null do
    if ismemb(l1.hd,l2) then l1.hd::l3->l3; endif;
    l1.tl->l1;
  enduntil;
  l3; enddefine;

define difference(l1,l2);
  vars l3;
  nil->l3;
  until l1.null do
    if not(ismemb(l1.hd,l2)) then l1.hd::l3->l3; endif;
    l1.tl->l1;
  enduntil;
  l3; enddefine;

define delete(x,l);    ;;; delete x from the list l
  if l.null then nil;
  elseif x=l.hd then l.tl;
  else l.hd::delete(x,l.tl);
  endif; enddefine;

define insert(x,y,l);   ;;; insert x before y in the list l
  if l.null then x::nil;
```

```
    elseif y=l.hd then x::l;
    else l.hd::insert(x,l.tl);
    endif; enddefine;
```

13 Dynamic Lists

A dynamic list is one which consists of a set of list-links (as in a normal list), but of which the final list-link has the value 'true' as its head and has a tail which is actually a function that can generate additional elements as required. A dynamic list can therefore be used to represent infinite sets. The user must write the generator function him/herself. As an example we will use a function 'random()' which it is intended should generate a random numeric value. The statement:

```
    pdtolist(random) -> number_list;
```

creates a dynamic list of random numbers which we can process using the loop structure shown above, taking successive values of the head and assigning the tail back to itself. Each time a new head is required, the function 'random' will be activated to generate such a value. If the function generates the value 'termin' the list will terminate.

14 Record Structures

A record structure (as distinct from a record itself) is created by a statement of the form:

```
    recordclass
            classname
            field_1
            field_2
            field_3
            .......
            field_n ;
```

The user invents the names corresponding to 'classname', 'field_1' etc. and once such a record structure has been defined the user will have available functions which construct and decompose records of this class. An example will explain:

```
    recordclass
            person
            pers_name
            pers_age
            pers_sex;
```

defines a three-field record structure with elements corresponding to name, age and sex. To construct a record of this class we have available a function called 'consperson', and we can write:

```
consperson("john",21,"male")->x;
```

The variable 'x' now has as its value an address pointer to a record which has the values 'john', '21' and 'male' stored in its three fields. Note that the class name 'person' is user-defined, and that the system took that name and appended to it the prefix 'cons' to form the constructor function. Another function 'desperson' (or 'destroy person') will not actually destroy the record but will decompose it (or place its elements on the stack) leaving the record itself unaltered. Fields can be pointer fields.

15 Strings

Strings are linear arrays of character-sized elements. These are created by the standard function 'inits' thus:

```
inits(100)-> mystring;
```

The variable 'mystring' now has as its value an address pointer to a character array of 100 elements.

These elements can be accessed and updated by means of the standard function 'subscrs' (meaning subscripted string), thus:

```
x->subscrs(k,s); or subscrs(k,s)->x;
```

where 'x' is a variable, 'k' is an integer and 's' is a string.

A shorthand method is available (as in most languages) for creating strings by means of single quotation marks:

```
'the cat sat on the mat' -> mystring;
```

creates a string of 22 characters and assigns its address to the variable 'mystring';

16 Vectors

A vector is created by the standard function 'initv' thus:

```
initv(100) -> newvect;
```

The variable 'newvect' now has as its value a pointer to a vector of 100 elements. Unlike a string, however, each element is a full word (or 32 bits in most machines), and can be used to store any type of item and not just characters. Individual elements are accessed by the standard function 'subscrv' in the same way as 'subscrs' is used for strings.

Again there is a shorthand way of setting up a vector, using curly brackets this time — just like single quotes for strings and square brackets for lists.

17 Length

There is a standard function 'length' which, when applied to a structure like a string, vector or list, will return an integer which is the number of separate elements in the structure.

18 Words

A "word" is often confused with a string. A string is a simple vector of characters. A word is a data structure which contains a string of characters as one of its elements. It is created by enclosing a string of characters in double-quotes, e.g. "cat". Another of its elements is used to store a value which is the value assigned to the variable which has as its label the name corresponding to the string. This value is accessed by the function 'valof'. To clarify things, consider the following example.

When the user types the word "cat" (in double-quotes) he/she creates the structure of the kind we are describing. If the user then types:

```
3 -> cat;
```

the integer value 3 is assigned to the variable *cat*. Now the variable cat is not the same thing as the word "cat", but they are associated in that if we type:

```
valof("cat")=>
```

the integer 3 will be printed. In effect POP11 makes available to the user the symbol table used to store variables and their values, and the entry in that symbol table which corresponds to the variable *cat*, is the word "cat".

Any item which appears in a list and is not a number or a symbol is automatically taken to be a word (double-quotes are not needed in this case). Therefore if we type:

```
[the cat sat on the mat] -> l;
```

we have automatically created the words "the", "cat", "sat", "on" and "mat" (unless these already existed), and indirectly we have declared the variables (the, cat, sat, on, mat).

If we now write 'l.hd->x;', the value of x will be the word "the". If it happens that the variable *the* has the value 3, then we can make the test:

```
if l.hd.valof=3 then ......
```

Since a variable can also have the address of a function as its value we can (if this is known to be the case) write:

```
l.hd.apply;
```

to get that function executed.

19　Other Things

This is intended to be a brief introduction. It would not be appropriate here to attempt a complete coverage of the features of POP11. We have instead confined the description to those features which would seem to be most appropriate for use in the kind of programs needed to complete the exercises in this book. For example, we have described the until-loop but not the while-loop, the repeat-loop or the for-loop. Only one of these is really needed, but readers who have a preferred type of loop will no doubt look up the appropriate control structure in the system documentation. We have ignored arrays which do not seem to be needed much in language processing. We have not dealt with some of the most powerful features in the language/system, for example the pattern matcher, process control and inter-process communication, or the interface with the Prolog facilities.

The only reservation felt about not including these features in this description is that the reader unfamiliar with POP11 might assume that a feature is absent from the language because it is not described here. That would be an unwise assumption.

The reader is refered to the standard text on the language *POP11: A Practical Language for Artificial Intelligence*, R. Barrett, A. Ramsay and A. Sloman, Ellis Horwood Series, 1985. Even this text does not describe all of the features available. The most up-to-date documentation is the very extensive on-line documentation provided with the system.

Index

'a', 6, 23ff, 58–59, 205
action or line definition, 19
action replay, 42
active/passive voice, 49–52, 106, 110, 161
actors, 113
acts in CD theory, 126
adjectival group 63–65
adjective, 11, 35, 60–62, 70, 148, 205
after, 42
agent, 63, 106, 126, 201
agreement
    best fit, 70
    subject/verb, 54–55, 65–66, 69–70, 74
altruistic behaviour, 177
ambiguity, 6, 23ff, 36, 45, 51, 62, 70, 110, 188
amoeba, (analogy) 147
anatomy (of objects), 189
anticipation, 165
anti-goal, 176
applications, 100, 115
aspect, 110, 172
assignment statement, 5, 14
association 159, (entity with role), 199
associativity, 68
ATN, 18, 23, 29, 34ff, 53, 59, 66, 71–79, 99, 213ff
    counting mechanism, 11, 18
    grammar, 91–98, 110
    jump-arcs, 8
    loops, 16
    noun phrase, 64
    verb_group, 53
    with side-effects, 74
augmented transition networks, (see ATN)
auxilliary verbs, 49, 110
axis, 173

back-tracking, 23, 26, 71–72, 81
Backus-Naur Form, (see BNF)

bad grammar, 146, 161
before, 42
behaviour, 150, 158, 159, 162, 177, 178
beliefs, 101, 184–185
BNF, 5–7

case grammar, 105–114
    criticism of, 111
    dependency, 109
    frames, 108
    semantic, 106–114
    traditional, 105–106
category, 10–11
cause and effect, 112, 122, 138, 154, 165ff
    causality as a state, 167
    cause causing a cause, 167
    ignoring causal links, 170
    multiple causes, 168
    notation for, 165–166
    representation of, 174, 185, 196–199
    time-stamps of, 166–167
    transitivity of, 166
    types of causal connection, 167–169
CD
    theory, 124, 126–138
        implementation, 132
        criticism of, 137
    forms, 139–140
channel (of perception), 172
    internal, 173
Charniak, 101
chemical bonds (analogy with case), 108, 114
chronological sequence, 122, 161, 162, 165
cliché, 148, 210
colour, 28, 60
combinatorial explosion, 71
combining representations, 213–216
complexity, 213–216

comma, 11, 12
common sense, 162
communication, 158ff
concept, 27, 32, 56, 58, 61, 154–159,
    178–182, 214
  classes of, 205
  learning concepts, 155–157, 183
  properties of, 205
conceptual dependency theory, (*see* CD
    theory)
condition test, 72
conjunction, 157, 202–204, 206
construction kit analogy, 162ff
constructional units, 152
consword (in POP11), 46–47
context, 11, 149, 151, 159, 213
continuation problem, 71
continuing (factor of a verb), 49–52
contract (social), 159
conversation, 150
coorddefn, 11
coordinate, 11
correspondence, 67

dative (case), 107
default property values, 37, 57, 59, 60–62
definite article, (*see* 'the')
demons, 110, 120, 124
de-referencing, 67
desirable conditions (in motivation), 176
destword (in POP11), 46
determiner, 5, 10, 35
dialogue, 146
dictionary, 68, 79
direction (case slot in CD theory), 126
discrimination (in perception), 173
disjunction, 203–207
DO (in CD theory), 135
dynamic-lists (in POP11), 207

edible (as a concept property), 154
embassy frame (example), 118
emotional states, 132, 154, 159, 162
entities, 56, 59, 60, 61, 111, 148, 165, 174,
    187, 205
  classification of, 154
equality, 67
evening star, 36
event, 41, 112, 115, 122, 138, 161, 165,
    166, 196–199
expectancy (state of), 8, 16
experiencer (case), 107
explanation (lack of, in causation), 165

extension (of a noun), 205

feelings, 177–178
fictitious environments, 159
figurative language, 210, (*see also*
    metaphor)
film-plot (analogy), 114
finished (factor of a verb)), 49–52
finite state diagram, (*see* FSD)
focus, 26ff, 41, 42, 45, 60, 106
formal logic, 172, 213
formal parameters, 59, 66, 81
frames, 108, 115–121
  narrative, 121
  object, 119
  thematic, 121
framework, 173
FRL, 120
front-end systems, 117
frozen values (in POP11), 69
FSD
  assignment statement, 14
  coorddefn, 11
  in general, 16–17
  ptname, 8
  ptname (with ambiguous 'a'), 24
  verb phrase, 13
  (*see also* ATN)
function, 8, 59, 61, 66, 67, 157, 158
functional descriptions, 140, 185, (*see
    also* roles)
future tense, 42

gating (in causation), 168
generalisation
  of concepts, 155
  in semantic networks, 191, 216
general knowledge, 154, 158
generic structure, 28, 56, 59, 67, 156, 205
genitive (case), 105–106
gerund, 10, 62
global register, 13, 18, 55, 59
global switch, 15
goal
  case, 107
  state, 176
GOTO, 9, 71
grammar, 5, 27, 65, 161
  cyclic definition of grammatical
    categories, 10–11
  for terrorist attack example, 117–118
  of English, 85–98
  of 'glunge', 156–157

of noun phrase, 63
gratification-seeking automita, 176

heuristic signposts, 192
history (of an object), 41ff, 174
human-like (behaviour of systems), 101
Hume, David, 165
hypothetical situations, 167

imperative statements, 163–164
implications, 122, 144, 151, 159
'in', 109–110
incarnations (of an object), 35, 41, 43, 57
indefinite article, 58–59 (*see also* 'a')
infinite number of possible sentences, 10
infinitive tense/verb form, 6, 13, 44
inheritance (in semantic networks), 119,
    120, 191
input text, 4, 132
instantiation, 30, 81, 82
instrumental case, 107, 109, 124, 126
intension (of a noun), 205
intentions, 101
internal representation, 4, 29, 31, 32, 39,
    43, 60, 67, 73, 74, 150ff
    (*see also* model)
internal sensors, 176
internal text, (*see* internal representation)
intransitive verb, 106
irregular verbs, 48
'it', 26, 33, 53

jump-arcs (in ATN), 8

knowledge, 184–186
    of things not known to us, 185
    representation languages, 37

labelling concepts, 155–157
lassoing (sections of internal text), 99
learning concepts, 155–157, 183, 216
limitations
    of FSM, 17
    of FSM and RTN, 18
locative case, 109
loop (in transition networks), 16

macro-expansion, 35, 42
marking, 50–52
matching, 30, 36, 37, 43, 60, 116, 202,
    203
    see also pattern matching

'may', 204
'me', 174
meaning, 3, 5, 59, 101, 109, 111, 126, 138,
    150ff, 158ff, 203, 214
memory, 41, 153–155
metaphor, 101, 148, 210
metric, 173
micro-graphics, 3
micro-worlds, 143
mind, ix, 217
modality, 110, 204
model, 150, 158ff, 172
    see also representation
models of models, 150ff, 162–163,
    174–175
mood, 110
morning star, 36
motivation, 102, 122, 125, 176–183
    in CD theory, 138, 144, 145, 150
motor actions, 155
'move', 46
movement, 31
multiple causes, 168
multiplicity (of an object), 35
'must', 204

naive physics, 145–146
negation, 200–204
negative gating (in causality), 169
negative transportation, 185
non-salient features or properties, 211
nonsensical sentences, 161
normal values, (*see* default values)
noun
    phrase, 35, 56–65, 205–209
    syntax, 63
nouns, 10, 35, 56–65, 112, 157, 193,
    205–209
'now', 39, 42, 43, 52
number, 54–55, 65, 207

object, 57, 126, 158, 187
    history, 41ff, 174
    multiplicity of, 35
    persistence of, 36, 41
object frame, 119
objective case, 105–106
obstacles (in a script), 124
'on', 110
optimism, 101, 143, 217
origin (of an object history), 40
orthogonal verb endings, 51

ownership, 144

palindromes, 17
parallel machines, 146
parameter values, 60, 62, (*see also* default values)
partial meaning, 151–152, 161
passive voice, (*see* active/passive voice)
pattern matching, 54, 66–84, 99, 198 (*see also* match)
perception, 42, 152–153, 158, 172, 187
permission, 204
persistence (of an object), 36, 41
person, 54–55
pessimism, 143
physical characteristics (of objects), 187
physical time, 39
picture producers (in CD theory), 126, 131
plans, 124–125
plurality, 65, 205–209
poison, 112–113
POP11, 7, 8, 9, 14, 25, 66, appendix
'possibilation', 205
possibility, 204, (*see also* modality)
pre-condition (of a script), 124
predicate, 144, 149, 156, 167, 188
prediction, 150ff, 165, 166, 177
preposition, 157
prepositional phrases, 109–110
present continuous, 44
present tense, 13 (*see also* tense)
prime minister (example), 36
primitive acts (in CD theory), 126–131
primitive operations, 123
primitives, 178
privacy, ix
program
    action_defn, 21–22
    agree_all, 69
    agree_prop, 69
    assignment statement, 14
    coorddefn, 12
    corresp, 67
    equal, 67
    f_match, 82
    f_release, 82
    has_properties, 68
    instant, 82
    is_gram, 69
    ismemb, 9
    isname, 8

list_match, 82–83
parse, 71–84
parse_np, 76
parse_pp, 77–78
parse_sent, 79
parse_vg, 77
parse_vp, 78
ptname, 9
ptname with ambiguous 'a', 25–26
stem-end, 47
strict_match, 83
unify, 81
went (in CD theory), 134
Prolog, 20, 25, 66
pronominal reference, 26, 53
proper noun, 57
properties, 205 (*see also* default values)
pseudo-present time, 42, 45, 52
psychological experiments, 152, 165
push_down stack, 27

quantification, 205–209
questions, 163–164

reasonableness, 161
recursion (in sentences), 18, 71, 99
Recursive Transition Networks, (*see* RTN)
register, 18, 73, 75
reference
    of a state, 173
    pronominal, 26, 32, 36, 99
    reference-arc, 35
    referential opacity, 35–36
reflexivity, 68
relative time, 39, 52
rep-box, 174, 214
representation
    combination of, 213–216
    internal, 99
    of 'ability', 182
    of 'accepts', 179
    of 'all', 207ff
    of 'any', 207ff
    of 'behind', 188
    of causal links, 174, 185, 196–199
    of 'controls', 179
    of 'deceives', 181
    of 'during', 45
    of 'duty', 181
    of events, 196–199
    of 'fertiliser', 112, 192–193

of 'flattery', 182
of fluids, 145–146, 194
of 'killed', 112
of 'likes', 178
of 'loves', 179
of motivation, 176–183
of objects, 187–195
of occasional events, 198–199
of 'owns', 180
of plurality, 205–209
of 'poisoned', 112ff
of proximity, 60
of 'redness'
of relative values, 173
of repetitive events, 147, 196–199
of representations, (*see* models of
    models)
of 'some', 207ff
of states, 172–175
of stuff, 145, 193–195
of things not known to us, 185
of truth, 184–186
of value, 173
of 'went' (in CD theory), 134
of 'while', 45
of 'with', 108, 110
nesting of representations, 185
uniformity of form, 152
representational junk, 189
'respectively', 19
requirement (meaning of 'must'), 204
result (case), 107
robotics (example), 176–178
role, 56, 106, 109, 111, 112, 115, 161, 191,
    201
  in CD theory, 140
RTN, 17, 18

salient, 192–193, 211
scenario, 113, 123, 124, 151, 159ff,
    192–199, 201
scope (of negation), 200
scripts, 121, 122–125, 139–140
seizure sentence (example), 117
semantic complexity, 102
semantic networks, 189
semantics, 62, 99, 105, 110
sensory experience, 158
shape, 37, 172
side-effects, 18, 59, 61, 73, 118
simultaneous actions, 45
skolem functions, 61

slots (in case), 108, 116, 119, 124, 126
social contract, 144
source (case), 107
spacial relationships, 149, 187
specialisation (in semantic networks),
    191, 216
stack, 46–47
stage directions (analogy), 56
standard values, (*see* default values)
state, 41, 126, 131, 166–167, 172–175,
    187, 196–199
structured programming, 9, 71ff
sub-goals, 177
subjective (case), 105–106
survival, 162, 176
symbol table, 33
symmetry, 68
syntax, 10, 63, 99, 105, (*see also*
    grammar)

template, 153, 205
tense, 43–44, 49–55, 110, 198
  in CD theory, 135
termination (of an object history), 41
terrorist attack (example), 115
'the', 59
thematic frames, 121
time, 39, 49–52
time-stamps, 39, 166–167, 172, 196–199
Tom and Jerry (analogy), 37
transformation, 31, 37
Transition Networks, (*see* FSD, RTN,
    ATN)
transitive verb, 105, 110, 112
transitivity, 68
triangles, 27, 30, 32, 40–43, 56, 58
triggers, 124
truth, 184–196
  contingent truth, 204
  inaccessibility of absolute truth, 184
  necessary truth, 204
Turing, (*see* Universal Turing machine)

undecidable, 42
understanding, introduction, x, 101, 122,
    125, 150–151, 161, 189, 210
ungrammatical, (*see* bad grammar)
unification, 66, 80–84
uniformity of representational form, 152
Universal Turing machine, 18

value (of property), 173

value judgements, 163
value table, 33, 34, 35, 40
verbs, 10, 11, 13, 46–55, 62, 109, 112,
    157, 161, 193
vocabulary, 4, 27, 29
voice, (*see* active/passive voice)

'went', (package in CD theory), 134
Winograd, 100, 144
word-stem, 46
world-knowledge, 139